COMPUTER SYSTEMS AND APPLICATIONS

COMPUTER SYSTEMS AND APPLICATIONS

Er. Nishit Mathur

A P H PUBLISHING CORPORATION
4435-36/7, ANSARI ROAD, DARYA GANJ
NEW DELHI-110002

Published by
S.B. Nangia
A P H Publishing Corporation
4435-36/7, Ansari Road, Darya Ganj
New Delhi-110002
Ph.: 011-23274050, 23285807 Fax: 011-23274050
Email: aphbooks@vsnl.net

2010

Typesetting at:
Creative Graphics

Printed at
Balaji Offset
Naveen Shahdara, Delhi-110032

Contents

Preface

The computer system includes not only the computer, but also any software and peripheral devices that are necessary to make the computer function. Every computer system, for example, requires an operating system.

In computer science, an application is a computer program designed to help people perform a certain type of work. Modern computers based on integrated circuits are millions to billions of times more capable than the early machines, and occupy a fraction of the space. Simple computers are small enough to fit into a wristwatch, and can be powered by a watch battery.

An application thus differs from an operating system which runs a computer, a utility which performs maintenance or general-purpose chores, and a programming language with which computer programs are created. Depending on the work for which it was designed, an application can manipulate text, numbers, graphics, or a combination of these elements.

Some application packages offer considerable computing power by focusing on a single task, such as word processor; others, called integrated software, offer somewhat less power but include several applications. Application software should be contrasted with system software, which is involved in integrating a computer's various capabilities, but typically does not directly apply them in the performance of tasks that benefit the user.

Author

Chapter 1

Computer Concepts

INTRODUCTION

Computer Concepts has been trading since 1980 - quite an old company among various software houses. During this time the company has grown from a two-man operation selling utilities for the Acorn Atom into a multi million pound company specializing in innovation and research in both hardware and software.

Computer Concepts is one of two companies in the Xara Group; visit the home page of the other company, Xara Limited, which produces graphics software for Windows, including a version of *ArtWorks* called *Xara* X.

COMPUTER HARDWARE

Computer hardware has advanced drastically since the early days when computers took up entire rooms and required teams of people to run. Modern computer systems fit in a small case and can draw power from a standard wall jack. It is important to learn about the components of your computer so that you can diagnose problems or replace equipment as it becomes outdated.

Function

Hardware is the corporeal and tangible portion of a computer system that you interact with to take advantage of computer programs. It is distinct from software in that it is built of physical material and generally does not perform logical operations or change its state frequently.

Main System

The central piece of hardware for any computer is the motherboard, which is a circuit board that contains all of the sockets, slots, and chip sets that all of the other hardware devices will be connected into. The central processing unit, which handles all of the mathematical calculations that the computer needs to perform, is attached to the main socket of the motherboard.

The two main companies that produce processors are AMD and Intel, each make a variety of different processor types that work with different motherboards. The random access memory attaches to slots in the motherboard and it controls the speed that computations occur. The hard drive is the component that actually stores all of the data in the computer such as files, music or games. All of these units are run by a power supply that plugs into a wall socket.

Input

In order to interact with your computer system, you will need some kind of input hardware. Most computer systems require one or more input devices to be connected or it will not boot up at all. The most popular input devices are a mouse for navigating the screen, a keyboard for typing text and a microphone for sending voice over the internet or activating voice command software.

Output

The fastest or most advanced computer in the world is useless without a means of displaying information to the user. Output hardware devices solve this problem by visually displaying graphics or text or playing sounds. A monitor is the most common type of output device. Older and bulkier cathode-ray tube monitors worked much like early televisions but most modern monitors are flat panel liquid crystal displays. Printers can also be considered output devices as they can print information from a software programme.

CONCEPT OF COMPUTER IMAGES

Computer generated images (known as CGI) have become very popular over the past two decades, and their importance and use will increase even further in the future because of their wide applicability in various fields. In the area of movies and films in general CGI has become an essential tool for filmmakers to bring their visions to the screen, be it by creating computer generated characters, props, sets, or just simplifying the process of image and sound editing.

Film production has been made faster and more efficient in the postproduction phase, offering an unprecedented level of freedom and quality.

The success of 3D computer animation and CGI in general started in the early 90s, when software bundles and processing power got more affordable even for smaller companies, and since then it turned into an accepted art form by itself. Over the years the technology evolved further and further, lowering the barrier between art and technology, and even allowing these two extremes to blend seamlessly.

CREATION OF 3D GRAPHICS

The creation of CGI and computer animation requires the use of specialized software products. Several bundles have established on the market, and it is mainly a question of personal preference which one to pick. After all the biggest factor in creating convincing digital worlds is the artist himself, whereas the software is merely the tool to transfer his creativity onto the screen.

As graphics software became more user-friendly and intuitive, the process of creating CGI started to resemble its real-world counterparts, like painting, sculpting, photography and filmmaking. The area of computer animation for example requires the same steps of "real world" filmmaking, with the addition of modeling sets, props and characters first. Bringing a mass of "digital clay" into shape to form a convincing character (or any other object or location to be shown, for that matter) is the initial step.

Then cameras, lights and other entities are arranged in the virtual space, and animated if necessary.

TELEVISION, FILM PRODUCTION AND COMMERCIALS

Computer animation and three-dimensional visualization is widely used in television, commercials and film production. The "small screen" has proven to be the perfect field for experimenting with newly developed technology and concepts, and many artists working in the area of television and commercials have made their way to the movie business. With software bundles getting cheaper and more accessible, independent artists and filmmakers seized the opportunity to create their own films and short films, a development, which gave the visual quality of films an enormous boost in the mid 90s. In the area of film production computer animation slowly started replacing hand-made models and puppets, and even the genre of animated films has gotten a digital counterpart.

SCIENTIFIC VISUALIZATION

Computer animation produced to present meteorological data, medical imaging,industriefilm, architecture and technology.

PRODUCT DESIGN AND ENGINEERING

Designers and engineers use special CAD (computer aided design) software for designing, developing and manufacturing consumer and industrial products. Product visualization extensively uses modern graphics technology and with the help of computers, designs can be rotated, cut and manipulated even before getting manufactured. This greatly helps engineers visualize the product that they are designing.

GENERATION OF COMPUTERS

The history of computer development is often referred to in reference to the different generations of computing devices A generation refers to the state of improvement in the development of a product. This term is also used in the different advancements of computer technology. With each new generation, the circuitry has gotten smaller and more advanced than the previous generation before it.

FIRST GENERATION - 1940-1956: VACUUM TUBES

The first computers used vacuum tubes for circuitry and magnetic drums for memory, and were often enormous, taking up entire rooms. A magnetic drum, also referred to as drum, is a metal cylinder coated with magnetic iron-oxide material on which data and programs can be stored. Magnetic drums were once used as a primary storage device but have since been implemented as auxiliary storage devices.

The tracks on a magnetic drum are assigned to channels located around the circumference of the drum, forming adjacent circular bands that wind around the drum. Single drum can have up to 200 tracks. As the drum rotates at a speed of up to 3,000 rpm, the device's read/write heads deposit magnetized spots on the drum during the write operation and sense these spots during a read operation. This action is similar to that of a magnetic tape or disk drive.

Programs written in high-level languages retranslated into assembly language or machine language by a compiler. Assembly language programs retranslated into machine language by a programme called an assembler.

Every CPU has its own unique machine language. Programs must be rewritten or recompiled, therefore, to run on different types of computers. Input was based on punched cards and paper tape, and output was displayed on printouts.

SECOND GENERATION - 1956-1963: TRANSISTORS

Transistors replaced vacuum tubes and ushered in the second generation of computers. Transistor is a device composed of semiconductor material that amplifies a signal or opens or closes a circuit. Invented in 1947at Bell Labs, transistors have become the key ingredient of all digital circuits, including computers. Today's microprocessors contains tens of millions of microscopic transistors.

Prior to the invention of transistors, digital circuits were composed of vacuum tubes, which had many disadvantages. They were much larger, required more energy, dissipated more heat, and were more prone to failures. It's safe to say that without the invention of transistors, computing, as we know it today would not be possible.

The transistor was invented in 1947 but did not see widespread use in computers until the late 50s. The transistor was far superior to the vacuum tube, allowing computers to become smaller, faster, cheaper, more energy-efficient and more reliable than their first-generation predecessors.

THIRD GENERATION - 1964-1971: INTEGRATED CIRCUITS

The development of the integrated circuit was the hallmark of the third generation of computers. Transistors were miniaturized and placed on siliconchips, called semiconductors, which drastically increased the speed and efficiency of computers.

Silicon is the basic material used to make computer chips, transistors, silicon diodes and other electronic circuits and switching devices because its atomic structure makes the element an ideal semiconductor. Silicon is commonly doped, or mixed, with other elements, such as boron, phosphorous and arsenic, to alter its conductive properties.

A chip is a small piece of semi conducting material (usually silicon) on which an integrated circuit is embedded. A typical chip is less than ¼-square inches and can contain millions of electronic components(transistors). Computers consist of many chips placed on electronic boards called printed circuit boards. There are different types of chips. For example, CPU chips (also called microprocessors) contain an entire processing unit, whereas memory chips contain blank memory.

FOURTH GENERATION - 1971-PRESENT: MICROPROCESSORS

The microprocessor brought the fourth generation of

computers, as thousands of integrated circuits were built onto a single silicon chip. A silicon chip that contains a CPU. In the world of personal computers, the terms microprocessor and CPU are used interchangeably. At the heart of all personal computers and most workstations sits a microprocessor. Microprocessors also control the logic of almost all digital devices, from clock radios to fuel-injection systems for automobiles.

Three basic characteristics differentiate microprocessors:

- *Instruction Set*: The set of instructions that the microprocessor can execute.
- *Bandwidth*: The number of bits processed in a single instruction.
- *Clock Speed*: Given in megahertz (MHz), the clock speed determines how many instructions per second the processor can execute.

In both cases, the higher the value, the more powerful the CPU. For example, a 32-bit microprocessor that runs at 50MHz is more powerful than a 16-bitmicroprocessor that runs at 25MHz.

Abbreviation of central processing unit, and pronounced as separate letters. The CPU is the brains of the computer. Sometimes referred to simply as the processor or central processor, the CPU is where most calculations take place. In terms of computing power, the CPU is the most important element of a computer system.

FIFTH GENERATION - PRESENT AND BEYOND: ARTIFICIAL INTELLIGENCE

Fifth generation computing devices, based on artificial intelligence, are still in development, though there are some applications, such as voice recognition, that are being used today.

Artificial Intelligence is the branch of computer science concerned with making computers behave like humans. Artificial intelligence includes coined the term in 1956:

- *Games Playing*: programming computers to play games such as chess and checkers

- *Expert Systems*: programming computers to make decisions in real-life situations (for example, some expert systems help doctors diagnose diseases based on symptoms)
- *Natural Language*: programming computers to understand natural human languages
- *Neural Networks*: Systems that simulate intelligence by attempting to reproduce the types of physical connections that occur in animal brains

VOICE RECOGNITION

The field of computer science that deals with designing computer systems that can recognize spoken words. Note that voice recognition implies only that the computer can take dictation, not that it understands what is being said. Comprehending human languages falls under a different field of computer science called natural language processing. A number of voice recognition systems are available on the market. The most powerful can recognize thousands of words. However, they generally require an extended training session during which the computer system becomes accustomed to a particular voice and accent. Such systems are said to be speaker dependent.

Many systems also require that the speaker speak slowly and distinctly and separate each word with a short pause. These systems are called discrete speech systems.

Most computers have just one CPU, but some models have several. There are even computers with thousands of CPUs. With single-CPU computers, it is possible to perform parallel processing by connecting the computers in a network. However, this type of parallel processing requires very sophisticated software called distributed processing software.

Chapter 2

Operating Systems

DEFINITION

An operating system or OS, is a software programme that enables the computer hardware to communicate and operate with the computer software. Without a computer operating system, a computer and software programs would be useless.

An operating system (sometimes abbreviated as "OS") is the programme that, after being initially loaded into the computer by a boot programme, manages all the other programs in a computer. The other programs are called *applications* or application programs. The application programs make use of the operating system by making requests for services through a defined application programme interface (API). In addition, users can interact directly with the operating system through a user interface such as a command language or a graphical user interface (GUI).

An operating system performs these services for applications:

- In a multitasking operating system where multiple programs can be running at the same time, the operating system determines which applications should run in what order and how much time should be allowed for each application before giving another application a turn.
- It manages the sharing of internal memory among multiple applications.

- It handles input and output to and from attached hardware devices, such as hard disks, printers, and dial-up ports.
- It sends messages to each application or interactive user (or to a system operator) about the status of operation and any errors that may have occurred.
- It can offload the management of what are called *batch* jobs (for example, printing) so that the initiating application is freed from this work.
- On computers that can provide parallel processing, an operating system can manage how to divide the programme so that it runs on more than one processor at a time.

All major computer platforms (hardware and software) require and sometimes include an operating system. Linux, Windows 2000, VMS,OS/400, AIX, and z/OS are all examples of operating systems.

FUNCTIONS OF OPERATING SYSTEM

The operating system provides several other functions which includes:

- System tools (programs) used to monitor computer performance, debug problems, or maintain parts of the system.
- A set of libraries or functions which programs may use to perform specific tasks especially relating to interfacing with computer system components.

The operating system makes these interfacing functions along with its other functions operate smoothly and these functions are mostly transparent to the user.

TYPES OF OPERATING SYSTEM

There are many types of operating systems.

Real-time Operating System

It is a multitasking operating system that aims at executing real-time applications. Real-time operating systems often use specialized scheduling algorithms so that they can achieve a deterministic nature of behaviour. The main object of real-time operating systems is their quick and predictable response to events. They either have an event-driven or a time-sharing design. An event-driven system switches between tasks based of their priorities while time-sharing operating systems switch tasks based on clock interrupts.

Multi-user and Single-user Operating Systems

The operating systems of this type allow a multiple users to access a computer system concurrently. Time-sharing system can be classified as multi-user systems as they enable a multiple user access to a computer through the sharing of time. Single-user operating systems, as opposed to a multi-user operating system, are usable by a single user at a time. Being able to have multiple accounts on a Windows operating system does not make it a multi-user system. Rather, only the network administrator is the real user. But for a Unix-like operating system, it is possible for two users to login at a time and this capability of the OS makes it a multi-user operating system.

Multi-tasking and Single-tasking Operating Systems

When a single programme is allowed to run at a time, the system is grouped under a single-tasking system, while in case the operating system allows the execution of multiple tasks at one time, it is classified as a multi-tasking operating system. Multi-tasking can be of two types namely, pre-emptive or co-operative. In pre-emptive multitasking, the operating system slices the CPU time and dedicates one slot to each of the programs. Unix-like operating systems such as Solaris and Linux support pre-emptive multitasking. Cooperative multitasking is achieved by relying on each process to give time to the other processes in a defined manner. MS Windows prior to Windows 95 used to support cooperative multitasking.

Distributed Operating System

An operating system that manages a group of

independent computers and makes them appear to be a single computer is known as a distributed operating system. The development of networked computers that could be linked and communicate with each other, gave rise to distributed computing. Distributed computations are carried out on more than one machine. When computers in a group work in cooperation, they make a distributed system.

Embedded System

The operating systems designed for being used in embedded computer systems are known as embedded operating systems. They are designed to operate on small machines like PDAs with less autonomy. They are able to operate with a limited number of resources. They are very compact and extremely efficient by design. Windows CE, FreeBSD and Minix 3 are some examples of embedded operating systems.

The most common is the Microsoft suite of operating systems. They include from most recent to the oldest:

- *Windows XP Professional Edition*: A version used by many businesses on workstations. It has the ability to become a member of a corporate domain.
- *Windows XP Home Edition*: A lower cost version of Windows XP which is for home use only and should not be used at a business.
- *Windows* 2000: A better version of the Windows NT operating system which works well both at home and as a workstation at a business. It includes technologies which allow hardware to be automatically detected and other enhancements over Windows NT.
- *Windows ME*: A upgraded version from windows 98 but it has been historically plagued with programming errors which may be frustrating for home users.
- *Windows* 98: This was produced in two main versions. The first Windows 98 version was plagued with programming errors but the Windows 98 Second

Edition which came out later was much better with many errors resolved.

- *Windows NT*: A version of Windows made specifically for businesses offering better control over workstation capabilities to help network administrators.
- *Windows* 95: The first version of Windows after the older Windows 3.x versions offering a better interface and better library functions for programs.

DESCRIPTION OF OPERATING SYSTEM

For a computer to be able to operate a computer programme (sometimes known as application or software), the machine must be able to perform a certain number of preparatory operations to ensure exchange between the processor, the memory and the physical resources (peripherals).

The operating system (sometimes referred to by its abbreviation OS), is responsible for creating the link between the material resources, the user and the applications (word processor, video game, etc.).

When a programme wants to access a material resource, it does not need to send specific information to the peripheral device but it simply sends the information to the operating system, which conveys it to the relevant peripheral via its driver. If there are no drivers, each programme has to recognise and take into account the communication with each type of peripheral!

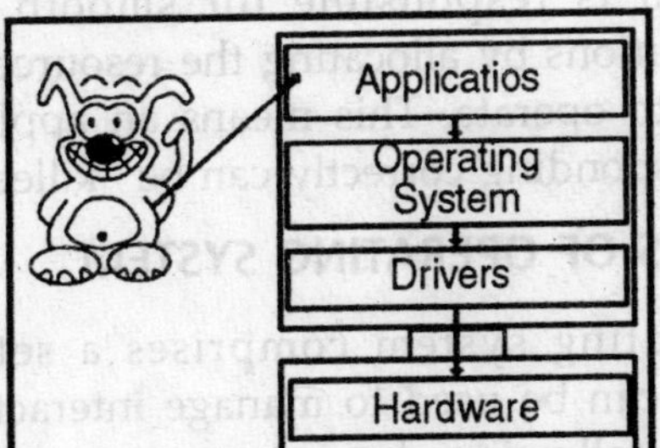

The operating system thus allows the "dissociation" of programmes and hardware, mainly to simplify resource management and offer the user a simplified Man-machine interface (MMI) to overcome the complexity of the actual machine.

ROLES OF OPERATING SYSTEM

The operating system has various roles:

- *Management of the processor*: The operating system is responsible for managing allocation of the processor between the different programmes using ascheduling algorithm. The type of scheduler is totally dependent on the operating system, according to the desired objective.
- *Management of the random access memory*: The operating system is responsible for managing the memory space allocated to each application and, where relevant, to each user. If there is insufficient physical memory, the operating system can create a memory zone on the hard drive, known as "virtual memory". The virtual memory lets you run applications requiring more memory than there is available RAM on the system. However, this memory is a great deal slower.
- *Management of input/output*: The operating system allows unification and control of access of programmes to material resources via drivers (also known as peripheral administrators or input/output administrators).
- *Management of execution of applications*: The operating system is responsible for smooth execution of applications by allocating the resources required for them to operate. This means an application that is not responding correctly can be "killed".

COMPONENTS OF OPERATING SYSTEM

The operating system comprises a set of software packages that can be used to manage interactions with the hardware. The following elements are generally included in this set of software:

- The kernel, which represents the operating system's

basic functions such as management of memory, processes, files, main inputs/outputs and communication functionalities.

- The shell, allowing communication with the operating system via a control language, letting the user control the peripherals without knowing the characteristics of the hardware used, management of physical addresses, etc.
- The file system, allowing files to be recorded in a tree structure.

OPERATING SYSTEM AS MULTI-THREADED

An operating system is known as multi-threaded when several "tasks" (also known as processes*) may be run at the same time.*

The applications consist of a sequence of instructions known as "threads". These threads will be alternately active, on standby, suspended or destroyed, according to the priority accorded to them or may be run simultaneously.

A system is known as pre-emptive when it has a scheduler (also called planner*), which, according to priority criteria, allocates the machine time between the various processes requesting it.*

The system is called a shared time system when a time quota is allocated to each process by the scheduler. This is the case of multi-user systems which allow several users to use different or similar applications on the same machine at the same time. the system is then referred to as a "transactional system". To do this, the system allocates a period of time to each user.

OPERATING SYSTEM AS MULTI-PROCESSOR SYSTEMS

Multi-processing is a technique that involves operating several processors in parallel to obtain a higher calculation power than that obtained using a high-end processor or to increase the availability of the system (in the event of processor breakdown).

The term SMP (Symmetric Multiprocessing or Symmetric Multiprocessor) refers to an architecture in which all processors access the same shared memory.

A multiprocessor system must be able to manage memory sharing between several processors but also to distribute the work load.

OPERATING SYSTEM AS EMBEDDED SYSTEMS

Embedded systems are operating systems designed to operate on small machines, such as PDAs (personal digital assistants) or autonomous electronic devices (spatial probes, robot, on-board vehicle computer, etc.) with reduced autonomy. Thus an essential feature of embedded systems is their advanced energy management and ability to operate with limited resources.

The main "general use" embedded systems for PDAs are as follows:

- Palm OS
- Windows CE / Windows Mobile / Window Smartphone

OPERATING SYSTEM AS REAL TIME SYSTEMS

Real time systems, used mainly in industry, are systems designed to operate in a time-constrained environment. A real time system must also operate reliably according to specific time constraints; in other words, it must be able to properly process information received at clearly-defined intervals (regular or otherwise).

Here are some examples of real time operating systems:

- OS-9;
- RTLinux (RealTime Linux);
- QNX;
- VxWorks.

Chapter 3

The Internet

DEFINITION

The Internet is a communication system that allows computers around the world to communicate and to exchange of the data with each other. This also allows to access their resources, such as files, services, or other people. Each of the fellowing pages explains one of the *services* that are possible thanks to the Internet. You already know and use some of them. Here's a short list.

The word internet is used to describe a network of networks which incorporate a very large and complicated set of equipment.

To understand the internet, there are three areas of discussion which are very helpful. These include the various services provided across the internet, the functions that enable the internet to work, and the various organizations that are part of the internet.

INTERNET SERVICES

The main services used on the internet include:

- *Web browsing*: Supported by the HTTP protocol, this functions allows users to view web pages using a web browser.
- *E-mail*: Allows people to send and receive electronic messages.

Other lesser used services include telnet (allows remote login to computers), FTP (Allows quick file transmission to remote computers), and gopher (An early form of text based form of reading internet documents which is rarely used today).

INTERNET FUNCTIONS

The internet provides for the following two functions which support communications. Without the communications support mentioned below, the internet could not function. These two functions are provided by internet service providers listed below under the "Internet Organizations" header.

- Physical lines that data is sent across.

Routing of data: There are special machines on the internet called routers, that determine where data needs to go to get from the sender of the data to the receiver of the data.

INTERNET ORGANIZATIONS

- *ISPs (Internet Service Providers)*: They provide the connection to the internet for users and also provide routers that direct internet traffic.
- *Corporations or Web hosting providers with mail servers and web servers*: They provide the information posted on the internet and virtual data connections to other mail servers.

There are also other organizations that regulate the internet, providing communication standards and designing new communication standards for improvements. These communication standards are also known as protocols.

ACCESSING THE INTERNET

People use an internet browser to access web pages that are available across the internet. Internet browsers include Microsoft Internet Explorer, Netscape Navigator, Mozilla, and others.

Web pages are created in a marked up form of text file called HTML (Hyper-Text Markup Language). The markup within the text indicates document structure showing where paragraphs begin and end, what items are in a list, headers, tables and other document structure.

When people are browsing of surfing the internet, they usually go from place to place by clicking on links. These links are locations for specific pages and indicate the three things:

- Protocol being used such as http or ftp
- The domain that the web page is found on. This will point to a specific organization's or company's web server.
- The location of the page on the server including the directory path and file name.

HISTORY

The Internet has become such an integral part of our lives, with such powerful capabilities, that it is easy to forget that this technological marvel was created by the long, hard, dedicated efforts of human beings — folks who had a vision of what universal networking could become and worked to make it happen. The key people, projects, and organizations that helped create the Internet are described below, first in a top-level summary and then in sections in roughly chronological order.

WORKING OF INTERNET

The Internet workings include a technical design and a management structure. The management structure consists of a generally democratic collection of loosely-coupled organizations and working groups with mostly non-overlapping responsibilities. The technical design is founded on a complex, interlocking set of hierarchical tree-like structures like Internet Protocol addresses and domain names, mixed with networked structures like packet switching and routing protocols, all tied together with millions of lines of sophisticated software that continues to get better all the time. So far this combination of management and technical structures has worked well, providing the reliable, powerful communication platform on which the rest of the complexity of the Internet is built. The following sections provide more information.

WORLD WIDE WEB

The World Wide Web is a system of Internet servers that supports hypertext to access several Internet protocols on a single interface. The World Wide Web is often abbreviated as the Web or www.

The World Wide Web was developed in 1989 by Tim Berners-Lee of the European Particle Physics Lab (CERN) in Switzerland. The initial purpose of the Web was to use networked hypertext to facilitate communication among its members, who were located in several countries. Word was soon spread beyond CERN, and a rapid growth in the number of both developers and users ensued. In addition to hypertext, the Web began to incorporate graphics, video, and sound. The use of the Web has reached global proportions and has become a defining element of human culture in an amazingly short period of time.

PROTOCOLS OF WEB

The surface simplicity of the Web comes from the fact that many individual protocols can be contained within a single Web site. Internet Protocols are sets of rules that allow for intermachine communication on the Internet. The following are a few of the protocols you can experience on the Web:

HTTP (HyperText Transfer Protocol): transmits hyptertext over networks. This is the protocol of the Web.

E-mail (Simple Mail Transport Protocol or SMTP): distributes e-mail messages and attached files to one or more electronic mailboxes.

FTP (File Transfer Protocol): transfers files between an FTP server and a computer, for example, to download software.

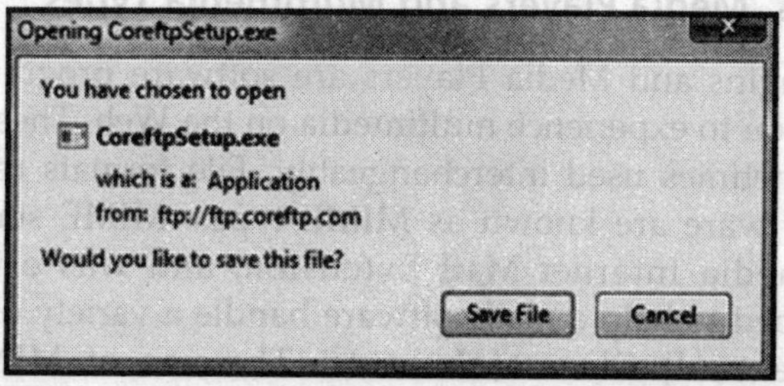

VoIP (Voice over Internet Protocol): allows delivery of voice communications over IP networks, for example, phone calls.

The Web provides a single, graphical interface for accessing these and other protocols. This creates a convenient and user-friendly environment. Once upon a time, it was necessary to know how to use protocols within separate, command-level environments.

This meant you needed to know the text commands to make things happen. The Web is much easier, since it gathers these protocols together into a unified graphical system. Because of this feature, and because of the Web's ability to work with multimedia and advanced programming languages, the Web is by far the most popular component of the Internet.

MULTIMEDIA ON WEB

Today's Web presents a diversified multimedia experience. In fact, the Web has become a broadcast medium, offering live TV and radio, pre-recorded video, photos, images, and animations. Expect to encounter multimedia just about anywhere on the Web. This tutorial presents a brief overview.

Plugins, Media Players and Multimedia Types

Plugins and Media Players are software programs that allow you to experience multimedia on the Web. These terms are sometimes used interchangeably. File formats requiring this software are known as MIME types. MIME stands for Multimedia Internet Mail Extension, and was originally developed to help e-mail software handle a variety of binary (non-textual) file attachments. The use of MIME has expanded to the Web. For example, the basic MIME type handled by Web browsers is text/html associated with the file extention .html. MIME types area also used to process multimedia on the Web. A few examples:

- *Jpeg photos*: Image/jpeg
- *Flash presentations*: Application/x-shockwave-flash
- *Quicktime movies*: Video/quicktime
- MP3s: audio/x-mpeg-3

Nowadays, many personal computers come pre-loaded with plugins and media players. This is an acknowledgement of the importance of the Web multimedia experience. If your computer doesn't have a particular piece of software, it can be easily obtained from the Web site of the company that created it. Downloading is easy and instructions are usually provided.

A common plugin used on the Web is the Adobe Reader. This software allows you to view documents created in Adobe's Portable Document Format (PDF). These documents are the MIME type "application/pdf" and are associated with the file extension .pdf. A PDF is a type of image file.

Chapter 4

C Language Fundamentals

THE C LANGUAGE

The C language is disarmingly simple, with only about 80 keywords and a dozen built-in data types, but C is highly expressive when it comes to implementing modern programming concepts. C includes all the support for structured, component-based, object-oriented programming that one expects of a modern language built on the shoulders of C++ and Java.

The C language was developed by a small team led by two distinguished Microsoft engineers, Anders Hejlsberg and Scott Wiltamuth. Hejlsberg is also known for creating Turbo Pascal, a popular language for PC programming, and for leading the team that designed Borland Delphi, one of the first successful integrated development environments for client/server programming.

At the heart of any object-oriented language is its support for defining and working with classes. Classes define new types, allowing you to extend the language to better model the problem you are trying to solve. C contains keywords for declaring new classes and their methods and properties, and for implementing encapsulation, inheritance, and polymorphism, the three pillars of object-oriented programming.

In C, everything pertaining to a class declaration is found in the decl1aration itself. C class definitions do not require separate header files or Interface Definition Language (IDL) files. Moreover, C supports a new XML style of inline documentation that simplifies the creation of online and print reference documentation for an application.

C also supports *interfaces*, a means of making a contract with a class for services that the interface stipulates. In C#, a class can inherit from only a single parent, but a class can implement multiple interfaces. When it implements an interface, a C class in effect promises to provide the functionality the interface specifies.

C also provides support for *structs*, a concept whose meaning has changed significantly from C++. In C#, a struct is a restricted, lightweight type that, when instantiated, makes fewer demands on the operating system and on memory than a conventional class does. A struct can't inherit from a class or be inherited from, but a struct can implement an interface.

NET FRAMEWORK

The goal of C is to provide a simple, safe, modern, object-oriented, Internet-centric, high-performance language for .NET development. C is a new language, but it draws on the lessons learned over the past three decades. In much the way that you can see in young children the features and personalities of their parents and grandparents, you can easily see in C the influence of Java, C++, Visual Basic (VB), and other languages.

The focus of this book is the C language and its use as a tool for programming on the .NET platform. In my primers on C++,the advocate learning the language first, without regard to Windows or Unix programming. With C that approach would be pointless.

Microsoft .NET supports not only language independence, but also language integration. This means that you can inherit from classes, catch exceptions, and take advantage of polymorphism across different languages. The .NET Framework makes this possible with a specification called the *Common Type System* (CTS) that all .NET components must obey. For example, everything in .NET is an object of a specific class that derives from the root class called System.Object. The CTS supports the general concept of classes, interfaces, delegates (which support callbacks), reference types, and value types.

NET PLATFORM

When Microsoft announced C in July 2000, its unveiling was part of a much larger event: the announcement of the .NET platform. The .NET platform is, in essence, a new development framework that provides a fresh application programming interface (API) to the services and APIs of classic Windows operating systems (especially the Windows 2000 family), while bringing together a number of disparate technologies that emerged from Microsoft during the late 1990s.

This includes COM+ component services, the ASP web development framework, a commitment to XML and object-oriented design, support for new web services protocols such as SOAP, WSDL, and UDDI, and a focus on the Internet, all integrated within the DNA architecture.

Microsoft says it is devoting 80% of its research and development budget to .NET and its associated technologies. The results of this commitment to date are impressive. For one thing, the scope of .NET is huge. The platform consists of four separate product groups:

- A set of languages, including C# and Visual Basic .NET, a set of development tools including Visual Studio .NET, a comprehensive class library for building web services and web and Windows applications, as well as the Common Language Runtime (CLR) to execute objects built within this framework.
- A set of .NET Enterprise Servers, formerly known as SQL Server 2000, Exchange 2000, BizTalk 2000, and so on, that provide specialized functionality for relational data storage, email, B2B commerce, etc.

COMPILATION AND MSIL

In .NET, programs are not compiled into executable files,

they are compiled into*Microsoft Intermediate Language* (MSIL) files, which the CLR then executes. The MSIL (often shortened to IL) files C# produces are *identical* to the IL files that other .NET languages produce; the platform is language-agnostic. A key fact about the CLR is that it is *common*: the same runtime supports development in C# as well as in VB.NET.

C code is compiled into IL when you build your project. The IL is saved in a file on disk. When you run your programme, the IL is compiled again, using the *Just In Time* (JIT) compiler (a process often called*JITing*). The result is machine code, executed by the machine's processor.

The standard JIT compiler runs *ondemand*. When a method is called, the JIT compiler analyses the IL and produces highly efficient machine code, which runs very fast.

The JIT compiler is smart enough to recognize when the code has already been compiled, so as the application runs, compilation happens only as needed. As .NET applications run, they tend to become faster and faster, as the already compiled code is reused.

CLASSES, OBJECTS AND TYPES

The essence of object-oriented programming is the creation of new types. A *type* represents a thing. Sometimes the thing is abstract, such as a data table or a thread; sometimes it is more tangible, such as a button in a window. A type defines the thing's general properties and behaviors.

If your programme uses three instances of a button type in a window say, an OK, a Cancel, and a Help button each instance will share certain properties and behaviors. Each, for example, will have a size (though it might differ from that of its companions), a position (though again, it will almost certainly differ in its position from the others), and a text label (e.g., "OK," "Cancel," and "Help").

Likewise, all three buttons will have common behaviors, such as the ability to be drawn, activated, pressed, and so forth. Thus, the details might differ among the individual buttons, but they are all of the same type.

As in many object-oriented programming languages, in C a type is defined by a *class*, while the individual instances of that class are known as *objects*. Later chapters explain that there are other types in C besides classes, including enums, structs, and delegates, but for now the focus is on classes.

METHODS

A *method* is a *function* owned by your class. In fact, member methods are sometimes called *member functions*. The member methods define what your class can do or how it behaves.

Typically, methods are given action names, such as WriteLine( ) or Add Numbers( ). In the case shown here, however, the class method has a special name, Main( ), which doesn't describe an action but does designate to the Common Language Runtime (CLR) that this is the main, or first method, for your class.

COMMENTS

A C programme can also contain comments. Take a look at the first line after the opening brace:

// Use the system console object

The text begins with two forward slash marks (//). These designate a *comment*. A comment is a note to the programmer and does not affect how the programme runs. C supports three types of comments.

The first type, just shown, indicates that all text to the right of the comment mark is to be considered a comment, until the end of that line. This is known as a C++ *stylecomment.*

C++ *programmers take note:* C does not support commenting out sections of code with #if 0...#endif.

The second type of comment, known as a *C-style comment*, begins with an open comment mark (/*) and ends with a closed comment mark (*/). This allows comments to span more than one line without having to have // characters at the beginning of each comment line, as shown in Example 2-2.

Example Illustrating multiline comments

```
class HelloWorld
{
  static void Main( )
  {
    /* Use the system console object
       as explained in the text in chapter 2
       */
  System.Console.WriteLine("Hello World");
  }
}
```

It is possible to nest C style comments within C-style comments. For this reason, it is common to use C++-style comments whenever possible, and to reserve the C-style comments for "commenting-out" blocks of code.

APPLICATIONS

"Hello World" is an example of a *console* programme. A console application has no graphical user interface (GUI); there are no list boxes, buttons, windows, and so forth. Text input and output is handled through the standard console (typically a command or DOS window on your PC). Sticking to console applications for now helps simplify the early examples in this book, and keeps the focus on the language itself. In later chapters, we'll turn our attention to Windows and web applications, and at that time we'll focus on the Visual Studio .NET GUI design tools.

All that the Main( ) method does in this simple example is write the text "Hello World" to the monitor. The monitor is managed by an object named Console. This Console object has a method called WriteLine( ) that takes a *string* (a set of characters) and writes it to the standard output. When you run this programme, a command or DOS screen will pop up on your computer monitor and display the words "Hello World."

You invoke a method with the dot operator (.). Thus,

to call the Console object's WriteLine( ) method, you write Console.WriteLine(...), filling in the string to be printed.

NAMESPACES

Console is only one of a tremendous number of useful types that are part of the .NET Framework Class Library (FCL). Each class has a name, and thus the FCL contains thousands of names, such as ArrayList, Hashtable, FileDialog, DataException,EventArgs, and so on. There are hundreds, thousands, even tens of thousands of names.

Java programmers take note: Namespaces provide many of the benefits of *packages.*

This presents a problem. No developer can possibly memorize all the names that the .NET Framework uses, and sooner or later you are likely to create an object and give it a name that has already been used.

What will happen if you develop your own Hashtable class, only to discover that it conflicts with the Hashtable class that .NET provides? Remember, each class in C# must have a unique name.

The solution to this problem is to create a *namespace.* A namespace restricts a name's scope, making it meaningful only within the defined namespace.

C programmers take note: While in C++ namespaces are delimited with the scope resolution operator (::), in C# you must use the dot (.) operator.

THE DOT OPERATOR (.)

In Example above, the dot operator (.) is used both to access a method (and data) in a class (in this case, the method WriteLine( )), and to restrict the class name to a specific namespace (in this case, to locate Console within the System namespace).

This works well because in both cases we are "drilling down" to find the exact thing we want. The top level is the System namespace (which contains all the System objects that the Framework provides); the Console type exists within that namespace, and the WriteLine( ) method is a member function of the Console type. In many cases, namespaces are divided into subspaces. For example, the System namespace contains a number of sub namespaces such as Configuration, Collections, Data, and so forth, while the Collections namespace itself is divided into multiple sub namespaces. Namespaces can help you organize and compartmentalize your types. When you write a complex C# programme, you might want to create your own namespace hierarchy, and there is no limit to how deep this hierarchy can be. The goal of namespaces is to help you divide and conquer the complexity of your object hierarchy.

CASE SENSITIVITY

C# is case-sensitive, which means that writeLine is not the same as WriteLine, which in turn is not the same as WriteLIne. Unfortunately, unlike in Visual Basic (VB), the C# development environment will not fix your case mistakes; if you write the same word twice with different cases, you might introduce a tricky-to-find bug into your programme.

To prevent such a time-wasting and energy-depleting mistake, you should develop conventions for naming your variables, functions, constants, and so forth. The convention in this book is to name variables with camel notation (e.g.,someVariableName), and to name functions, constants, and properties with Pascal notation (e.g., SomeFunction).

The only difference between camel and Pascal notation is that in Pascal notation, names begin with an uppercase letter.

STATIC KEYWORD

The Main( )method shown in Example 2-1 has one more designation. Just before the return type declaration void (which, you will remember, indicates that the method does not return a value) you'll find the keyword static:

```
static void Main( )
```

The static keyword indicates that you can invoke Main( ) without first creating an object of type Hello. This somewhat complex issue will be considered in much greater detail in subsequent chapters. One of the problems with learning a new computer language is you must use some of the advanced features before you fully understand them. For now, you can treat the declaration of the Main( ) method as tantamount to magic.

There are at least two ways to enter, compile, and run the programs in this book: use the Visual Studio .NET Integrated Development Environment (IDE), or use a text editor and a command-line compiler (along with some additional command-line tools to be introduced later).

VARIABLES AND CONSTANTS

A variable is a storage location with a type. In the preceding examples, both *x* and *y*are variables. Variables can have values assigned to them, and those values can be changed programmatically.

WRITELINE( )

The .NET Framework provides a useful method for writing output to the screen. The details of this method, System.Console.WriteLine( ), will become clearer as we progress through the book, but the fundamentals are straightforward. Call the method as shown in Example below, passing in a string that you want printed to the console (the screen) and, optionally, parameters that will be substituted. In the following example:

```
System.Console.WriteLine("After assignment,
myInt: {0}", myInt);
```

the string "After assignment, myInt:" is printed as is, followed by the value in the variable myInt.

Create a variable by declaring its type and then giving it a name. You can initialize the variable when you declare it, and you can assign a new value to that variable at any time, changing the value held in the variable. This is illustrated in Example.

Example: Initializing and Assigning Value to Variable

```
class Values
{
   static void Main( )
   {
      int myInt = 7
      System.Console.WriteLine("Initialized,
      myInt: {0}",
         myInt);
      myInt = 5;
      System.Console.WriteLine("After
   assignment, myInt: {0}",
      myInt);
   }
}
Output:
Initialized, myInt: 7
After assignment, myInt: 5
```

Here we initialize the variable myInt to the value 7, display that value, reassign the variable with the value 5, and display it again.

CONSTANTS

A *constant* is a variable whose value cannot be changed. Variables are a powerful tool, but there are times when you want to manipulate a defined value, one whose value you want to ensure remains constant. For example, you might need to work with the Fahrenheit freezing and boiling points of water in a programme simulating a chemistry experiment. Your programme will be clearer if you name the variables that store the values Freezing Point and Boiling Point, but you do not want to permit their values to be reassigned. How do you prevent reassignment? The answer is to use a constant.

Constants come in three flavors: *literals, symbolic constants,* and *enumerations*. In this assignment:

```
x = 32;
```

the value 32 is a literal constant. The value of 32 is

always 32. You can't assign a new value to 32; you can't make 32 represent the value 99 no matter how you might try.

Symbolic constants assign a name to a constant value. You declare a symbolic constant using the const keyword and the following syntax:

```
const type identifier = value;
```

A constant must be initialized when it is declared, and once initialized it cannot be altered. For example:

```
const int FreezingPoint = 32;
```

In this declaration, 32 is a literal constant and FreezingPoint is a symbolic constant of type int. Example below illustrates the use of symbolic constants.

Example: Using symbolic constants

```
class Values
{
  static void Main( )
  {
     const int FreezingPoint = 32; // degrees
     Farenheit
     const int BoilingPoint = 212;
     System.Console.WriteLine("Freezing point
     of water: {0}",
        FreezingPoint );
     System.Console.WriteLine("Boiling point
     of water: {0}",
        BoilingPoint);
     //BoilingPoint = 21;
  }
}
```

Freezing Point andBoilingPoint. As a matter of style, constant names are written in Pascal notation, but this is certainly not required by the language.

These constants serve the same purpose as always using the *literal* values 32 and 212for the freezing and boiling points of water in expressions that require them, but because these constants have names, they convey far more meaning. Also, if you decide to switch this programme to Celsius, you can reinitialize these constants at compile time, to 0 and 100, respectively; all the rest of the code ought to continue to work.

STRINGS

It is nearly impossible to write a C# programme without creating strings. A string object holds a string of characters.

You declare a string variable using the string keyword much as you would create an instance of any object:

```
string my String;
```

A string literal is created by placing double quotes around a string of letters:

"Hello World"

It is common to initialize a string variable with a string literal:

```
string my String = "Hello World";
```

Strings are covered in much greater detail in Chapter 10.

IDENTIFIERS

Identifiers are names that programmers choose for their types, methods, variables, constants, objects, and so forth. An identifier must begin with a letter or an underscore.

The Microsoft naming conventions suggest using *camel notation* (initial lowercase such as some Name) for variable names and *Pascal notation* (initial uppercase such as Some Other Name) for method names and most other identifiers.

Microsoft no longer recommends using Hungarian notation (e.g.,iSome Integer) or underscores (e.g., SOME_VALUE).

Identifiers cannot clash with keywords. Thus, you cannot create a variable named int or class. In addition, identifiers are case-sensitive, so C treats my Variable and My Variable as two different variable names.

EXPRESSIONS

Statements that evaluate to a value are called *expressions*.

You may be surprised how many statements do evaluate to a value. For example, an assignment such as:

```
myVariable = 57;
```

is an expression; it evaluates to the value assigned, which, in this case, is 57.

Note that the preceding statement assigns the value 57 to the variable myVariable. The assignment operator (=) does not test equality; rather it causes whatever is on the right side (57) to be assigned to whatever is on the left side (my Variable). All of the C# operators (including assignment and equality) are discussed later in this chapter.

Because myVariable = 57 is an expression that evaluates to 57, it can be used as part of another assignment operator, such as:

```
mySecondVariable = myVariable = 57;
```

What happens in this statement is that the literal value 57 is assigned to the variable myVariable. The value of that assignment (57) is then assigned to the second variable,mySecondVariable. Thus, the value 57 is assigned to both variables.

Chapter 5

Input-Output in C

INPUT AND OUTPUT

Input and output facilities are not part of the C language itself, so we have not emphasized them in our presentation thus far. Nonetheless, programs interact with their environment in much more complicated ways than those we have shown before. In this chapter we will describe the standard library, a set,)f functions that provide input and output, string handling, storage manage ment, mathematical routines, and a variety of other services for C programs. We will concentrate on input and output.

The ANSI standard defines these library functions precisely, so that they can exist in compatible form on any system where C exists. Programs that confine their system interactions to facilities provided by the standard library can be moved from one system to another without change.

The properties of library functions are specified in more than a dozen headers; we have already seen several of these, including <stdio.h>, <string.h>, and<ctype.h>. We will not present the entire library here, since we are more interested in writing C programs that use it.

STANDARD INPUT / OUTPUT

As we said in Chapter 1, the library implements a simple model of text input and output. A text stream consists of a sequence of lines; each line ends with a newline character. If the system doesn''t operate that way, the library does. whatever is necessary to make it appear as if it does. For instance, the library might convert carriage return and linefeed to newline on input and back again on output.

The simplest input mechanism is to read one character at a time from the *standard input,* normally the keyboard, with getchar:

```
int getchar(void)
```

getchar returns the next input character each time it is called, or EOF when it encounters end of' file. The symbolic constant EOF is defined in <stdio.h>. The value is typically -1, but tests should be written in terms of EOF so as to be independent of the specific value.

In many environments, a file may be substituted for the keyboard by using the < convention for input redirection: if a programme prog uses getchar, then the command line

```
prog <infile
```

causes prog to read characters from infile instead. The switching of the input is done in such a way that prog itself is oblivious to the change; in particular, the string "<infile" is not included in the command-line arguments in argv. Input switching is also invisible if the input comes from another programme via a pipe mechanism: on some systems, the command line

```
otherprog | prog
```

runs the two programs otherprog and prog, and pipes the standard output of otherprog into the standard input for prog. The function

```
int putchar(int)
```

is used for output: putchar (c) puts the character c on the *standard output,* which is by default the screen. putchar returns the character written, or EOF if an error occurs. Again, output can usually be directed to a file with *>filename:* if prog uses putchar,

```
prog >outfile
```

will write the standard output to outfile instead.

If pipes are supported,

```
prog | anotherprog
```

puts the. standard output of prog into the standard input of anotherprog.

Output produced by printf also finds its way to the standard output. Calls to putchar and printf may be interleaved—output appears in the order in which the calls were made.

Each source file that refers to an input/output library function must contain the line

```
#include <stdio.h>
```

before the first reference. When the name is bracketed by < and > a search is made for the header in a standard set of places (for example, on UNIX system‧. typically in the directory /usr/include).

Many programs read only one input stream and write only one output stream; for such programs, input and output with getchar, putchar, and printf may be entirely adequate, and is certainly enough to get started. This is particularly true if redirection is used to connect the output of one programme to the input of the next.

For example, consider the programme lower, which converts its input to lower case:

```
#include <stdio.h>
#include <ctype.h>
main() /* lower: convert input to lower case
*/ {
    int c;
    while ((c = getchar()) 1= EOF)
    putchar(tolower(c)); return 0;
```

The function tolower is defined in <ctype.h>; it converts an upper case letter to lower case, and returns other characters untouched. Regardless of how the<ctype.h> functions are implemented on a given machine, programs that use them are shielded from knowledge of the character set.

FORMATTED OUTPUT—PRINTF

The output function printf translates internal values to characters. We have used printf informally in previous chapters. The description here covers the typical uses but is not complete; for the full story, see Appendix B.

```
int printf( char *format, arg, , arg1, ... )
```

printf converts, formats, and prints its arguments on the standard output under control of the format. It returns the number of characters printed.

The format string contains two types of objects: ordinary characters, which are copied to the output stream, and conversion specifications, each of which can ,usconversion and printing of the next successive argument to printf. Each conversion specification begins with a % and ends with a conversion character. Between the % and the conversion character there may be, in order:

- A minus sign, which specifies left adjustment of the converted argument.
- A number that specifies the minimum field width. The converted argument will be hinted in a field at least this wide. If necessary it will be padded on the left (or right, if left adjustment is called for) to make up the field width.
- A period, which separates the field width from the precision.
- A number, the precision, that specifies the maximum number of characters to be printed from a string, or the number of digits after the decimal point of a floating-point value, or the minimum number of digits for an integer.
- An h if the integer is to be printed as a short:, or l (letter ell) if as a long
- Conversion characters are shown in Table 7-I. If the character after the % is not a conversion specification, the behaviour is undefined.

Table. Basic Printf Conversions.

Character	Argument Type;	Printed As
d.i	int;	decimal number.
o	int;	unsigned octal number (without a leading zero).

x,X	int;	unsigned hexadecimal number (without a leading 0x 0X), using abcdef or ABCDEF for 10, ..., 15.
u	int;	unsigned decimal number.
c	int; .	single character
s	char *;	print characters from the string until a '\0' or the number of characters given by the precision.
f	double;	*[-]m.dddddd*, where the number of *d's is* given by the precision (default 6).
e,E	double;	*[-]m.dddddde±xx* or *[-]m.ddddddE±xx*,where the number of *d's* is given by the precision (default 6).
g,G	double;	use %e or %E if the exponent is less than -4 or greater than or equal to the precision; otherwise use%f. Trailing zeros and a trailing decimal point are not printed.
p	void *;	pointer (implementation-dependent representation).
%	no argument isconverted;	print a %.

A width or precision may be specified as *, in which case the value is computed by converting the next argument (which must be an int). For example to print at most max characters from a string s,

```
printf("%.*s", max, s);
```

Most of the format conversions have been illustrated in earlier chapters. One exception is precision as it relates to strings. The following table shows the effect of a variety of specifications in printing "hellos, world" (12 characters). We have put colons around each field so you can see its extent.

```
:%s:          :hello, world:
:%10s:        :hello, world:
:%.10s:       :hello, wor:
:%-10s:       :hello, world:
:%.15s:       :hello, world:
:%-15s:       :hello, world ;
:%15.10s;     ; hello, wor:
:%-15.10s:    :hello, wor ;
```

A warning: printf uses its first argument to decide how many arguments follow, and what their types are; it will get confused, and give wrong answers, if there are not enough arguments, or if they are of the wrong types. You should also be aware of the difference between these two calls:

```
printf(s);           /* FAILS if s contains
                        a % */
printf("%s",s);      /* Safe */
```

FORMATTED INPUT—SCANT

The function scanf is the input analog of printf, providing many of the me conversion facilities in the opposite direction.

```
int scanf(char *format, ...)
```

scanf reads characters from the standard input, interprets them according to the specifications in format, and stores the results through the remaining arguments. The format argument is described below; the other arguments, *each of which must be a pointer,* indicate where the corresponding converted input should be stored. As withprintf, this section is a summary of the most useful features, not an exhaustive list.

scanf stops when it exhausts its format string, or when some input fails to match the control specification. It returns as its value the number of successfully matched and assigned input items. This can be used to decide how many items were found. On end of file, EOF is returned; note that this is different ' from 0, which means that the next input character does not match the first specification in the format string. The next call to scanf resumes searching immediately after the last character already converted.

There is also a function sscanf that reads from a string instead of the :standard input:

```
int sscanf (char *string, char *format, arg1,
arg2,... )
```

It scans the string according to the format in format, and stores the resulting values through arg_1, arg_2, etc. These arguments must be pointers. The format string usually contains conversion specifications, which are used to control conversion of input. The format string may contain:

- Blanks or tabs, which are ignored.
- Ordinary characters (not %), which are expected to match the next non-white space character of the input stream.
- Conversion specifications, consisting of the character %, an optional assignment suppression character *, an optional number specifying a maximum field width, an optional h, 1, or L indicating the width of the target, and a conversion character.

FILE INPUT/OUTPUT IN C

REDIRECTION

One way to get input into a programme or to display output from a programme is to use *standard input* and *standard output*, respectively. All that means is that to read in data, we use scanf() (or a few other functions) and to write out data, we use printf().

When we need to take input from a file (instead of having the user type data at the keyboard) we can use input redirection:

```
% a.out < inputfile
```

This allows us to use the same scanf() calls we use to read from the keyboard. With input redirection, the operating system causes input to come from the file (e.g., inputfile above) instead of the keyboard.

Similarly, there is *output redirection*:

```
% a.out > outputfile
```

That allows us to use printf() as before, but that causes the output of the programme to go to a file (e.g., outputfile above) instead of the screen.

Of course, the 2 types of redirection can be used at the same time...

```
% a.out < inputfile > outputfile
```

C File I/O

While redirection is very useful, it is really part of the operating system (not C). In fact, C has a general mechanism for reading and writing files, which is more flexible than redirection alone.

```
stdio.h
```

There are types and functions in the library stdio.h that are used for file I/O. Make sure you always include that header when you use files.

Type

For files you want to read or write, you need a file pointer, e.g.:

```
FILE *fp;
```

What is this type "FILE *"? Realistically, you don't need to know. Just think of it as some abstract data structure, whose details are hidden from you. In other words, the only way you can use a FILE * is via the functions that C gives you.

Note: In reality, FILE is some kind of structure that holds information about the file. We must use a FILE * because certain functions will need to change that information, i.e., we need to pass the information around *by reference*.

Functions

Reading from or writing to a file in C requires 3 basic steps:

- Open the file.

- Do all the reading or writing.
- Close the file.

Following are described the functions needed to accomplish each step.

Opening a File

In order to open a file, use the function fopen(). Use it as:

```
fp = fopen(filename, mode);
```

where:

- *Filename* is a string that holds the name of the file on disk (including a *path* like /cs/course if necessary).
- *Mode* is a string representing how you want to open the file. Most often you'll open a file for reading ("r") or writing ("w").

Note that fopen() returns a FILE * that can then be used to access the file. When the file cannot be opened (e.g., we don't have permission or it doesn't exist when opening for reading), fopen() will return NULL.

Here are Examples of Opening Files

```
FILE *ifp, *ofp;
char *mode = "r";
char outputFilename[] = "out.list";
ifp = fopen("in.list", mode);
if (ifp == NULL) {
   fprintf(stderr, "Can't open input file
   in.list!\n");
   exit(1);
}
ofp = fopen(outputFilename, "w");
if (ofp == NULL) {
   fprintf(stderr, "Can't open output file
   %s!\n",
               outputFilename);
   exit(1);
}
```

Note that the input file that we are opening for reading

("r") must already exist. In contrast, the output file we are opening for writing ("w") does not have to exist. If it doesn't, it will be created. If this output file does already exist, its previous contents will be thrown away (and will be lost).

READING FROM OR WRITING TO A FILE

Once a file has been successfully opened, you can read from it using fscanf() or write to it using fprintf(). These functions work just like scanf() and printf(), except they require an extra first parameter, a FILE * for the file to be read/written.

There are other functions in stdio.h that can be used to read or write files. Look them up in a good C reference. Continuing our example from above, suppose the input file consists of lines with a *username* and an *integer test score*, e.g.:

```
in.list
________
foo 70
bar 98
...and that each username is no more than 8
characters long.
```

We might use the files we opened above by copying each username and score from the input file to the output file. In the process, we'll increase each score by 10 points for the output file:

```
char username[9]; /* One extra for nul char.
*/
int score;
while (fscanf(ifp, "%s %d", username, &score)
!= EOF) {
fprintf(ofp, "%s %d\n", username, score+10);
}
```

The function fscanf(), like scanf(), normally returns the number of values it was able to read in. However, when it hits the end of the file, it returns the special value EOF. So, testing the return value against EOF is one way to stop the loop.

The bad thing about testing against EOF is that if the file is not in the right format (e.g., a letter is found when a number is expected):

```
in.list
foo 70
bar 98
biz A+
```

then fscanf() will not be able to read that line (since there is no integer to read) and it won't advance to the next line in the file. For this error, fscanf()will not return EOF (it's not at the end of the file)....

Errors like that will at least mess up how the rest of the file is read. In some cases, they will cause an *infinite loop.*

One solution is to test against the number of values we expect to be read by fscanf() each time. Since our format is "%s %d", we expect it to read in 2 values, so our condition could be:

```
while (fscanf(ifp, "%s %d", username, &score)
== 2) {
...
```

Now, if we get 2 values, the loop continues. If we don't get 2 values, either because we are at the end of the file or some other problem occurred (e.g., it sees a letter when it is trying to read in a number with %d), then the loop will end.

Another way to test for end of file is with the library function feof(). It just takes a file pointer and returns a true/false value based on whether we are at the end of the file.

To use it in the above example, you would do:

```
while (!feof(ifp)) {
  if (fscanf(ifp, "%s %d", username, &score)
  != 2)
    break;
  fprintf(ofp, "%s %d", username, score+10);
}
```

We see that testing != EOF, it might cause an infinite loop if the format of the input file was not as expected.

However, we can add code to make sure it reads in 2 values. When you use fscanf(...) != EOF or feof(...), they will not detect the end of the file until they try to read past it. In other words, they won't report end-of-file on the last valid read, only on the one after it.

Closing a File

When done with a file, it must be closed using the function fclose().

To finish our example, we'd want to close our input and output files:

```
fclose(ifp);
fclose(ofp);
```

Closing a file is very important, especially with output files. The reason is that output is often *buffered*. This means that when you tell C to write something out, e.g.,

```
fprintf(ofp, "Whatever!\n");
```

it doesn't necessary get written to disk right away, but may end up in a *buffer* in memory. This output buffer would hold the text temporarily:

```
Sample output buffer:
----------------------------------------------
| a | b | c | W | h | a | t | e | v | e |r|
----------------------------------------------
| ! | \n|   |   |   |   |   |   |   |   | |
----------------------------------------------
|   |   |   |   |   |   |   |   |   |   | |
----------------------------------------------
|   |   |   |   |   |   |   |   |   |   | |
----------------------------------------------
...
```

When the buffer fills up (or when the file is *closed*), the data is finally written to disk. So, if you forget to close an output file then whatever is still in the buffer may not be written out.

SPECIAL FILE POINTERS

There are 3 special FILE *'s that are always defined for a

programme. They are stdin (*standard input*), stdout (*standard output*) and stderr (*standard error*).

Standard Input

Standard input is where things come from when you use scanf(). In other words,

```
scanf("%d", &val);
```

is equivalent to the following fscanf():

```
fscanf(stdin, "%d", &val);
```

Standard Output

Similarly, *standard output* is exactly where things go when you use printf(). In other words,

```
printf("Value = %d\n", val):
```

is equivalent to the following fprintf():

```
fprintf(stdout, "Value = %d\n", val):
```

Remember that standard input is normally associated with the keyboard and standard output with the screen, unless *redirection* is used.

Standard Error

Standard error is where you should display error messages. We've already done that above:

```
fprintf(stderr, "Can't open input file in.list!\n");
```

Standard error is normally associated with the same place as standard output; however, redirecting standard output does not redirect standard error.

For example,

```
% a.out > outfile
```

Only redirects stuff going to standard output to the file outfile... anything written to standard error goes to the screen.

USING SPECIAL FILE POINTERS

We've already seen that *stderr* is useful for printing error messages, but you may be asking, "When would I ever use the special file pointers *stdin* and*stdout*?" Well, suppose you create a function that writes a bunch of data to an opened file that is specified as a parameter:

```
void WriteData(FILE *fp)
{
    fprintf(fp, "data1\n");
    fprintf(fp, "data2\n");
}
```

Certainly, you can use it to write the data to an output file (like the one above):

```
WriteData(ofp);
```

But, you can also write the data to standard output:

```
WriteData(stdout);
```

Without the special file pointer *stdout,* you'd have to write a second version of WriteData() that wrote stuff to standard output.

MANAGING INPUT/OUTPUT OPERATIONS

INTRODUCTION

One of the essential operations performed in a C language programs is to provide input values to the programme and output the data produced by the programme to a standard output device. We can assign values to variable through assignment statements such asx = 5 a = 0 ; and so on. Another method is to use the Input then scanf which can be used to read data from a key board. For outputting results we have used extensively the function printf which sends results out to a terminal. There exists several functions in 'C' language that can carry out input output operations. These functions are collectively known as standard Input/ Output Library. Each programme that uses standard input / out put function must contain the statement.

```
# include < stdio.h >
at the beginning.
```

SINGLE CHARACTER INPUT OUTPUT

The basic operation done in input output is to read a characters from the standard inputdevice such as the keyboard and to output or writing it to the output unit usually the screen. The getchar function can be used to read a character from the standard inputdevice. The scanf can also be used to achieve the function. The getchar has the following form.

```
Variable name = getchar:
```

Variable name is a valid 'C' variable, that has been declared already and that possess the type char.

Example Programme

```
# include < stdio.h > // assigns stdio-h
header file to your programme
void main ( ) // Indicates the starting
point of the programme.
{
char C, // variable declaration
printf ("Type one character:") ; // message
to user C = getchar () ; // get a character
from key board and Stores it in variable C.
Printf (" The character you typed is = %c",
C) ; // output } // Statement which displays
value of C on // Standard screen.
```

The putchar function which in analogus to getchar function can be used for writing characters one at a time to the output terminal. The general form is

```
putchar (variable name);
```

Where variable is a valid C type variable that has already been declared Ex:-

```
Putchar ( );
```

Displays the value stored in variable C to the standard screen.

Programme shows the use of getchar function in an interactive environment.

```
#include < stdio.h > // Inserts stdio.h header file into the
Pgm void main ( ) // Beginning of main function.
{
char in; // character declaration of variable in.
```

printf (" please enter one character"); // message to user
in = getchar ( ) ; // assign the keyboard input value to
in. putchar (in); // out put 'in' value to standard screen.
}

STRING INPUT AND OUTPUT

The gets function relieves the string from standard input device while put S outputs the string to the standard output device. A strong is an array or set of characters.

The function gets accepts the name of the string as a parameter, and fills the string with characters that are input from the keyboard till newline character is encountered. (That is till we press the enter key). All the end function gets appends a null terminator as must be done to any string and returns.

The puts function displays the contents stored in its parameter on the standard screen.

The standard form of the gets function is

```
gets (str)
```

Here "str" is a string variable.

Note: It is recommended NOT to make use of gets() function. It is unsafe and can even crash the C programme itself. Above description is for theoretical illustration purpose only.

The standard form for the puts character is

```
puts (str)
```

Where str is a string variable.

Example programme (Involving both gets and puts)

```
# include < stdio.h >
Void main ( )
{
char s [80];
printf ("Type a string less than 80 characters:");
gets (s);
printf ("The string types is:");
puts(s);
}
```

FORMATTED INPUT FOR SCANF

The formatted input refers to input data that has been arranged in a particular format.Input values are generally taken by using the scanf function. The scanf function has the general form.

```
Scanf ("control string", arg1, arg2, arg3
............argn);
```

The format field is specified by the control string and the arguments arg1, arg2, ...argn specifies the address of location where address is to be stored.

The control string specifies the field format which includes format specifications and optional number specifying field width and the conversion character % and also blanks, tabs and newlines.

The Blanks tabs and newlines are ignored by compiler. The conversion character % is followed by the type of data that is to be assigned to variable of the assignment. The field width specifier is optional.

The general format for reading a integer number is

```
% x d
```

Here per cent sign (%) denotes that a specifier for conversion follows and x is an integer number which specifies the width of the field of the number that is being read. The data type character d indicates that the number should be read in integer mode.

Example:

```
scanf ("%3d %4d", &sum1, &sum2);
```

If the values input are 175 and 1342 here value 175 is assigned to sum1 and 1342 to sum 2. Suppose the input data was follows 1342 and 175.

The number 134 will be assigned to sum1 and sum2 has the value 2 because of %3d the number 1342 will be cut to 134 and the remaining part is assigned to second variable sum2. If floating point numbers are assigned then the decimal or fractional part is skipped by the computer.

To read the long integer data type we can use conversion specifier % ld & % hd for short integer.

INPUT SPECIFICATIONS FOR REAL NUMBER

Field specifications are not to be use while representing a real number therefore real numbers are specified in a straight forward manner using % f specifier.

The general format of specifying a real number input is

```
Scanf (% f ", &variable);
```

Example:

```
Scanf ("%f %f % f", &a, &b, &c);
```

With the input data

321.76, 4.321, 678 The values

321.76 is assigned to a, 4.321 to b & 678 to C.

If the number input is a double data type then the format specifier should be % lf instead of %f.

INPUT SPECIFICATIONS FOR A CHARACTER

Single character or strings can be input by using the character specifiers.

The general format is

```
% xc or %xs
```

Where C and S represents character and string respectively and x represents the field width. The address operator need not be specified while we input strings.

Example:

```
Scanf ("%C %15C", &ch, nname):
```

Here suppose the input given is a, Robert then a is assigned to ch and name will be assigned to Robert.

Printing One Line:

```
printf();
```

The most simple output statement can be produced in C' Language by using printf statement. It allows you to display information required to the user and also prints the variables we can also format the output and provide text labels. The simple statement such as

```
Printf ("Enter 2 numbers");
```

Prompts the message enclosed in the quotation to be displayed.

A simple programme to illustrate the use of printf statement:-

```
#include < stdio.h >
main ( )
{
printf ("Hello!");
printf ("Welcome to the world of
Engineering!");
}
```

Output:

```
Hello! Welcome to the world of Engineering.
```

Both the messages appear in the output as if a single statement. If you wish to print the second message to the beginning of next line, a new line character must be placed inside the quotation marks.

For Example:

```
printf ("Hello!\n");
```

OR

printf ("\n Welcome to the world of Engineering");

CONVERSION STRINGS AND SPECIFIERS

The printf ( ) function is quite flexible. It allows a variable number of arguments, labels and sophisticated formatting of output. The general form of the printf ( ) function is

Syntax

```
Printf ("conversion string", variable list);
```

The conversion string includes all the text labels, escape character and conversionspecifiers required for the desired output. The variable includes all the variable to be printed in order they are to be printed. There must be a conversion specifies after each variable.

Chapter 6

C Control Statements

CONTROL STATEMENTS

A programme consists of a number of statements which are usually executed in sequence. Programs can be much more powerful if we can control the order in which statements are run.

Statements fall into three general types;

- Assignment, where values, usually the results of calculations, are stored in variables.
- Input / Output, data is read in or printed out.
- Control, the programme makes a decision about what to do next.

This chapter will discuss the use of control statements in C. We will show how they can be used to write powerful programs by;

- Repeating important sections of the programme.
- Selecting between optional sections of a programme.

THE IF ELSE STATEMENT

This is used to decide whether to do something at a special point, or to decide between two courses of action.

The following test decides whether a student has passed an exam with a pass mark of 45

```
if (result >= 45)
        printf("Pass\n");
else
        printf("Fail\n");
```

It is possible to use the if part without the else.

```
if (temperature < 0)
        print("Frozen\n");
```

Each version consists of a test, (this is the bracketed statement following the if). If the test is true then the next statement is obeyed. If is is false then the statement following the else is obeyed if present. After this, the rest of the programme continues as normal.

If we wish to have more than one statement following the if or the else, they should be grouped together between curly brackets. Such a grouping is called a compound statement or a block.

```
if (result >= 45)
{       printf("Passed\n");
        printf("Congratulations\n")
}
else
{       printf("Failed\n");
        printf("Good luck in the resits\n");
}
```

Sometimes we wish to make a multi-way decision based on several conditions. The most general way of doing this is by using the else if variant on the if statement. This works by cascading several comparisons. As soon as one of these gives a true result, the following statement or block is executed, and no further comparisons are performed. In the following example we are awarding grades depending on the exam result.

```
if (result >= 75)
        printf("Passed: Grade A\n");
else if (result >= 60)
        printf("Passed: Grade B\n");
else if (result >= 45)
        printf("Passed: Grade C\n");
else
        printf("Failed\n");
```

In this example, all comparisons test a single variable called result. In other cases, each test may involve a different variable or some combination of tests. The same pattern can be used with more or fewer else if's, and the final lone else may be left out. It is up to the programmer to devise the correct structure for each programming problem.

THE SWITCH STATEMENT

This is another form of the multi way decision. It is well structured, but can only be used in certain cases where;

- Only one variable is tested, all branches must depend on the value of that variable. The variable must be an integral type. (int, long, short or char).
- Each possible value of the variable can control a single branch. A final, catch all, default branch may optionally be used to trap all unspecified cases.

Hopefully an example will clarify things. This is a function which converts an integer into a vague description. It is useful where we are only concerned in measuring a quantity when it is quite small.

```
estimate(number)
int number;
/* Estimate a number as none, one, two,
several, many */
{  switch(number) {
   case 0: printf("None\n");
           break;
   case 1: printf("One\n");
           break;
   case 2: printf("Two\n");
           break;
   case 3:
   case 4:
   case 5: printf("Several\n");
           break;
   default: printf("Many\n");
           break;
   }
}
```

Each interesting case is listed with a corresponding action. The break statement prevents any further statements from being executed by leaving the switch. Since case 3 and case 4 have no following break, they continue on allowing the same action for several values of number.

Both if and switch constructs allow the programmer to make a selection from a number of possible actions.

The other main type of control statement is the loop. Loops allow a statement, or block of statements, to be repeated. Computers are very good at repeating simple tasks many times, the loop is C's way of achieving this.

LOOPS

C gives you a choice of three types of loop, while, do while and for.

- The while loop keeps repeating an action until an associated test returns false. This is useful where the programmer does not know in advance how many times the loop will be traversed.
- The do while loops is similar, but the test occurs after the loop body is executed. This ensures that the loop body is run at least once.
- The for loop is frequently used, usually where the loop will be traversed a fixed number of times. It is very flexible, and novice programmers should take care not to abuse the power it offers.

THE WHILE LOOP

The while loop repeats a statement until the test at the top proves false.

As an example, here is a function to return the length of a string. Remember that the string is represented as an array of characters terminated by a null character '\0'.

```
int string_length(char string[])
{  int i = 0;
   while (string[i] != '\0')
            i++;
   return(i);
}
```

The string is passed to the function as an argument.

The size of the array is not specified, the function will work for a string of any size.

The while loop is used to look at the characters in the string one at a time until the null character is found. Then the loop is exited and the index of the null is returned. While the character isn't null, the index is incremented and the test is repeated.

THE DO WHILE LOOP

This is very similar to the while loop except that the test occurs at the end of the loop body. This guarantees that the loop is executed at least once before continuing. Such a setup is frequently used where data is to be read. The test then verifies the data, and loops back to read again if it was unacceptable.

```
do
{       printf("Enter 1 for yes, 0 for no
        :");
        scanf("%d", &input_value);
} while (input_value != 1 && input_value !=
        0);
```

THE FOR LOOP

The for loop works well where the number of iterations of the loop is known before the loop is entered. The head of the loop consists of three parts separated by semicolons.

- The first is run before the loop is entered. This is usually the initialisation of the loop variable.
- The second is a test, the loop is exited when this returns false.
- The third is a statement to be run every time the loop body is completed. This is usually an increment of the loop counter.

The example is a function which calculates the average of the numbers stored in an array. The function takes the array and the number of elements as arguments.

```
float average(float array[], int count)
{ float total = 0.0;
```

```
    int i;
    for(i = 0; i < count; i++)
            total += array[i];
    return(total / count);
}
```

The for loop ensures that the correct number of array elements are added up before calculating the average.

The three statements at the head of a for loop usually do just one thing each, however any of them can be left blank. A blank first or last statement will mean no initialisation or running increment.

A blank comparison statement will always be treated as true. This will cause the loop to run indefinitely unless interrupted by some other means. This might be a return or a break statement.

It is also possible to squeeze several statements into the first or third position, separating them with commas. This allows a loop with more than one controlling variable. The example below illustrates the definition of such a loop, with variables hi and lo starting at 100 and 0 respectively and converging.

```
for (hi = 100, lo = 0; hi >= lo; hi–, lo++)
```

The for loop is extremely flexible and allows many types of programme behaviour to be specified simply and quickly.

THE BREAK STATEMENT

We have already met break in the discussion of the switch statement. It is used to exit from a loop or a switch, control passing to the first statement beyond the loop or a switch.

With loops, break can be used to force an early exit from the loop, or to implement a loop with a test to exit in the middle of the loop body. A break within a loop should always be protected within an if statement which provides the test to control the exit condition.

THE CONTINUE STATEMENT

This is similar to break but is encountered less frequently.

It only works within loops where its effect is to force an immediate jump to the loop control statement.

- In a while loop, jump to the test statement.
- In a do while loop, jump to the test statement.
- In a for loop, jump to the test, and perform the iteration.

Like a break, continue should be protected by an if statement. You are unlikely to use it very often.

THE GOTO STATEMENT

C has a goto statement which permits unstructured jumps to be made. Its use is not recommended, so we'll not teach it here. Consult your textbook for details of its use.

Chapter 7

Arrays and Functions

ARRAYS

A programmer is concerned with developing and implementing algorithms for a variety of tasks. As tasks become more complex, algorithm development is facilitated by structuring or organizing data in specialized ways. There is no best data structure for all tasks; suitable data structures must be selected for the specific task. Some data structures are provided by programming languages; others must be derived by the programmer from available data types and structures.

So far we have used integer, floating point and character data types as well as pointers to them. These data types are called base or scalar data types. Such base data types may be used to derive data structures which are organized groupings of instances of these types. The C language provides some widely used compound or derived data types together with mechanisms which allow the programmer to define variables of these types and access the data stored within them.

The first such type we will discuss is called an array. Many tasks require storing and processing a list of data items. For example, we may need to store a list of exam scores and to process it in numerous ways: find the maximum and minimum, average the scores, sort the scores in descending order, search for a specific score, etc. Data items in simple lists are usually of the same scalar type; for example a list of exam scores consists of all integer type items. We naturally think of a list as a data structure that should be referenced as a unit. C provides a derived data type that stores such a list of objects where each object is of the same data type - the array. An array name is generally equivalent to a pointer to the first element, and arrays are passed to functions as pointers. When elements in the array are modified in the function, they are also modified in the calling procedure:

```
void test(int c[])
{
   c[0] =1;
}
void main()
{
   int a[5];
   test(a);
   count << a[0];
}
```

results in '1' being written out.

The test function may be written entirely equivalently as:

```
void test(int* c)
{
   c[0] =1;
}
```

If we want a function to return an array, the pointer version is essential. The following illustrates this:

```
int* test()
{
   int* a;
   a = new int[1];
   a[0]=1; a[1]=2;
   return a;
}
void main()
{
   int* b;
   b = test();
   cout << b[0] << b[1];
}
```

In C, some variables hold values and some hold memory addresses. Both of these are binary numbers. Every variable has its own memory address.

The ones you are most familiar with hold values: int, double, float.

Pointers, arrays, and function names hold memory addresses, not ordinary numerical values. The relationship between pointers and arrays is discussed in the ABC text and below.

FUNCTIONS

hip C lingo - use parentheses after the name to show it is the name of a function: fname()

Function Declarations and Function Definitions must be consistent and we have not to depend on the compiler. Functions can be classified by what they take as inputs, and what they return as outputs.

SCALAR FUNCTIONS

```
double dV_spherical(double R, double theta)
{
   return pow(R,2)*sin(theta);
}
/* would need #include<math.h>, gcc -lm */
```

SCALAR FUNCTIONALS

Functionals take function names as arguments: they operate on functions, not just values. A simple example is the differentiation operator:

```
double deriv(double f(double), double x,
double RTOL, double ATOL);
```

call deriv() this way to evaluate the derivative of g at y to the specified tolerances:

```
dg_dy = deriv(g,y,RTOL,ATOL);
```

Convergence is usually defined by RTOL and ATOL, typically we iterate until

|Ans(N) – Ans(N – 1)| < RTOL * Ans(N) + ATOL

Although the derivative is defined by

$f'(x) = \lim_{h\to 0} (f(x + h) - f(x))/h$

for a numerical derivative h must be nonzero: you cannot divide by zero and in fact you do not want h to be too small or your accuracy will be killed by round off error, e.g. if x>>h, the computer thinks (x + h) and x are exactly the same, and the programme will say f′(x) = 0

The same problem comes up in integration, where the normal thing to do is something like

```
h =(b-a)/N;
for (i=0,i<N,i+=1)
{
    sum += f(x);
    x += h;
}
return h*sum;
```

and to achieve high accuracy you want to use a big value of N. But this always fails if N is too large. You already have written some scalar functionals: for example, root-finding programs take a function f() as input and return a number X that satisfies f(X)=0 to some tolerance.

Integration routines typically take a function as input and return a number (the value of the integral).

SCALAR FUNCTIONS OF VECTOR ARGUMENTS

In order to represent a vector, we have to use an arrays.

/* Unless you do something special, in C the INDEX STARTS AT ZERO */

A 1-d array is V[i], a 2-d array is M[i][j], etc. By convention, i is the index of the row, and j is the index of the column, i.e. M[0][j] is the first row of the matrix.

To compute the dot product a.b:

```
#define NDIM 3
double dot(double v1, double v2, int N);
int main(void)
{
    double a[NDIM], b[NDIM], a_dot_b;
    int N;
    N=Ndim;
```

```
    a_dot_b = dot(a,b,N);
    return 0;
}
double dot (double v1[ ], double v2[ ], int
N)
{
    double dot_product=0.0;
    int i;
    for (i=0; i<N, ++i)
    {
    dot_product+=v1[i]*v2[i];
    }
    return dot_product;
}
```

VECTOR FUNCTIONS

A function can only return a single value, but the elements of arrays in the argument list can also be changed. Note that ordinary variables in the argument list cannot be changed by a function.

A common example is a programme that computes the cross-product between two 3-vectors:

in main: declare

```
double a[3],b[3],c[3];
```

and fill in the values in a[0],a[1],a[2] and b[0],b[1],b[2] then cross():

```
cross(a,b,c);
```

cross() is defined this way:

```
int cross(double v1[], double v2[], double
v3[])
{ad"
for(i=0,i<3,i++)
  {
      v3[i]=...
  }
return 0;
}
```

cross () actually fills in the values of c[0],c[1]c[2] in

main(). This works because array names are actually memory addresses:

```
int i=3;
double x=4.0;
double a[3];
```

if you ask the computer what i is, it will say i is 3.

it will say x is 4.0

it will say a is 0x43219 A MEMORY ADDRESS!

To get the numbers stored in a, you need indices: a[0], a[1], ...

Of course the computer knows the memory location of i and x as well, but they are called &i and &x. If we pass those memory addresses down, a function can stuff numbers in them too.

A good example of a function that takes a function name as input and returns a vector is the numerical gradient:

int grad(double f(double v[]), double x[], double gradf [], double ATOL, double RTOL, int Ndim); /*returns gradf [], the gradient of f at x. */

first define a function which computes the derivative along one dimension, indexed by Nspecial:

```
double derivN (double f(double v[ ]), double
x[ ], int Ndim, int Nspecial, double RTOL,
double ATOL);
int grad(double f(double v[ ]), double x[ ],
double gradf[], double ATOL, double RTOL,
int Ndim)
/* gradf [] is the output, the rest are
inputs. */
{
for(i=0;i<Ndim;++i)
{
   gradf[i]=derivN(f,x,N,i,RTOL,ATOL);
}
return 0;
}
```

It might actually call grad() from main() like this:

grad(phi,V0,grad_phi,ATOL,RTOL,3);

where phi() was declared and defined as a scalar function of a 3-vector, and

we previously declared

double V0[3],grad_phi[3],ATOL,RTOL;

We see that if we want, we can overwrite the elements of a vector and return the answer in the same memory slot, e.g.

```
int miles_to_km(double distances[ ], int N)
{
  int i;
  for(i=0;i<N;i+=1)
  {
  distances[i]=distances[i]*1.63;
  }
  return N;
}
```

EQUIVALENCE OF V[I] AND *(V+I)

The variable v holds the memory address where the array v[] begins. Since it is a memory address, we can pass it down to functions

```
int f(double V[ ], int N);
```

OR

```
int f(double *V, int N);
```

In fact, C interprets V[i] as *(V+i), i.e. move over i memory slots from memory address V. And if you want to, you can actually use expressions like

*(V+7) instead of the simpler V[7].

If we read in a string of data

```
float data[100]
```

and later find out that the first two data points are screwed up, we might

want to define

```
float *good_data;
good_data=data +2;
```

and then

good_data[j] is the jth good data point (i.e. *data[j+2]*).

Say you knew that only the 42nd, 56th, and 98th data points were good?

then you might define a pointer array that points to the good data values:

```
float *good_data_pointer[3];
good_data_pointer[0]=data+41;
good_data_pointer[1]=data+55;
good_data_pointer[2]=data+98;
```

and then

`*good_data_pointer[j]` is the jth good data point.

The C language provides a capability that enables the user to define a set of ordered data items known as an array. Suppose we had a set of grades that we wished to read into the computer and suppose we wished to perform some operations on these grades, we will quickly realise that we cannot perform such an operation until each and every grade has been entered since it would be quite a tedious task to declare each and every student grade as a variable especially since there may be a very large number.

In C we can define variable called grades, which represents not a single value of grade but a entire set of grades. Each element of the set can then be referenced by means of a number called as index number or subscript.

DECLARATION OF ARRAYS

Like any other variable arrays must be declared before they are used. The general form of declaration is:

type variable-name[50];

The type specifies the type of the elements that will be contained in the array, such as int float or char and the size indicates the maximum number of elements that can be stored inside the array for ex:

```
float height[50];
```

Declares the height to be an array containing 50 real elements. Any subscripts 0 to 49 are valid. In C the array elements index or subscript begins with number zero.

So height [0] refers to the first element of the array. (For this reason, it is easier to think of it as referring to element number zero, rather than as referring to the first element).

As individual array element can be used anywhere that a normal variable with a statement such as

G = grade [50];

The statement assigns the value stored in the 50th index of the array to the variable g.

More generally if I is declared to be an integer variable, then the statement g=grades [1];

Will take the value contained in the element number 1 of the grades array to assign it to g. so if 1 were equal to 7 when the above statement is executed, then the value of grades [7] would get assigned to g.

A value stored into an element in the array simply by specifying the array element on the left hand side of the equals sign. In the statement

```
grades [100]=95;
```

The value 95 is stored into the element number 100 of the grades array.

The ability to represent a collection of related data items by a single array enables us to develop concise and efficient programs. For example we can very easily sequence through the elements in the array by varying the value of the variable that is used as a subscript into the array. So the for loop

```
for(i=0;i < 100;++i);
sum = sum + grades [i];
```

Will sequence through the first 100 elements of the array grades (elements 0 to 99) and will add the values of each grade into sum. When the for loop is finished, the variable sum will then contain the total of first 100 values of the grades array (Assuming sum were set to zero before the loop was entered)

In addition to integer constants, integer valued expressions can also be inside the brackets to reference a particular element of the array. So if low and high were defined as integer variables, then the statement next_value=sorted_data[(low+high)/2]; would assign to the variable next_valueindexed by evaluating the expression low+high)/2. If low is equal to 1 and high were equal to 9, then the value of sorted_data[5] would be assigned to the next_valueand if low were equal to 1 and high were equal to 10 then the value of sorted_data[5]would also be referenced.

Just as variables arrays must also be declared before they are used. The declaration of an array involves the type of the element that will be contained in the array such as int, float, char as well as maximum number of elements that will be stored inside the array. The C system needs this latter information in order to determine how much memory space to reserve for the particular array.

The declaration int values[10]; would reserve enough space for an array called values that could hold up to 10 integers. Refer to the below given picture to conceptualize the reserved storage space.

```
values[0]
values[1]
values[2]
values[3]
values[4]
values[5]
values[6]
values[7]
values[8]
values[9]
```

The array values stored in the memory.

INITIALIZATION OF ARRAYS

We can initialize the elements in the array in the same way as the ordinary variables when they are declared. The general form of initialization off arrays is:

```
type array_name[size]={list of values};
```

The values in the list care separated by commas, for example the statement

```
int number[3]={0,0,0};
```

Will declare the array size as a array of size 3 and will assign zero to each element if the number of values in the list is less than the number of elements, then only that many elements are initialized. The remaining elements will be set to zero automatically.

In the declaration of an array the size may be omitted, in such cases the compiler allocates enough space for all initialized elements. For example the statement

```
int counter[]={1,1,1,1};
```

Will declare the array to contain four elements with initial values 1. this approach works fine as long as we initialize every element in the array.

The initialization of arrays in c suffers two draw backs

- There is no convenient way to initialize only selected elements.
- There is no shortcut method to initialize large number of elements.

```
/* Programme to count the no of positive and
negative numbers*/
#include< stdio.h >
void main( )
{
int a[50],n,count_neg=0,count_pos=0,I;
printf("Enter the size of the array\n");
scanf("%d",&n);
printf("Enter the elements of the array\n");
for I=0;I < n;I++)
scanf("%d",&a[I]);
for(I=0;I < n;I++)
{
if(a[I] < 0)
count_neg++;
else
count_pos++;
}
printf("There are %d negative numbers in the
array\n",count_neg);
printf("There are %d positive numbers in the
array\n",count_pos);
}
```

MULTI DIMENSIONAL ARRAYS

Often there is a need to store and manipulate two

dimensional data structure such as matrices & tables. Here the array has two subscripts. One subscript denotes the row & the other the column.

The declaration of two dimension arrays is as follows:

```
   data_type array_name[row_size][column_size];
int m[10][20]
```

Here m is declared as a matrix having 10 rows(numbered from 0 to 9) and 20 columns(numbered 0 through 19). The first element of the matrix is m[0][0] and the last row last column is m[9][19]

ELEMENTS OF MULTI DIMENSION ARRAYS

A 2 dimensional array marks [4][3] is shown below figure. The first element is given by marks [0][0] contains 35.5 & second element is marks [0][1] and contains 40.5 and so on.

marks [0][0] 35.5	Marks [0][1] 40.5	Marks [0][2] 45.5
marks [1][0] 50.5	Marks [1][1] 55.5	Marks [1][2] 60.5
marks [2][0]	Marks [2][1]	Marks [2][2]
marks [3][0]	Marks [3][1]	Marks [3][2]

INITIALIZATION OF MULTIDIMENSIONAL ARRAYS

Like the one dimension arrays, 2 dimension arrays may be initialized by following their declaration with a list of initial values enclosed in braces

Example:

```
int table[2][3]={0,0,01,1,1};
```

Initializes the elements of first row to zero and second row to 1. The initialization is done row by row. The above statement can be equivalently written as

```
int table[2][3]={{0,0,0},{1,1,1}}
```

PASSING ARRAYS TO FUNCTIONS

We have now seen two examples of the use of arrays - to hold numeric data such as test scores, and to hold character strings. We have also seen two methods for determining how many cells of an array hold useful information - storing a count in a separate variable, and marking the end of the data with a special character. In both cases, the details of array processing can easily obscure the actual logic of a programme - processing a set of scores or a character string. It is often best to treat an array as an *abstract data type* with a set of allowed operations on the array which are performed by functional modules.

Let us return to exam score example to read and store scores in an array and then print them, except that we now wish to use functions to read and print the array.

LIST1: Read an array and print a list of scores using functional modules.

The algorithm is very similar to our previous task, except that the details of reading and printing the array is hidden by functions.

The function, read_intaray(), reads scores and stores them, returning the number of scores read. The function, print_intaray(), prints the contents of the array.

The refined algorithm formain() can be written as:

```
print title, etc.
    n = read_intaray(exam_scores, MAX);
    print_intaray(exam_scores, n);
```

We see that we have passed an array, exam_scores, and a constant, MAX (specifying the maximum size of the proposed list), to read_intarray() and expect it to return the number of scores placed in the array. Similarly, when we print the array using print_intarray, we give it the array to be printed and a count of elements it contains. We see that in order for a *called* function to access objects in the *calling* function (such as to store elements in an array) we must use *indirect access*, i.e. pointers. So, read_intaray() must indirectly access the array, exam_scores, in main(). One unique feature of C is that array access is *always* indirect; thus making it particularly easy for a called function to indirectly access elements of an array and store or retrieve values. As we will see in later sections, array access by index value is interpreted as an indirect access, so we may simply use array indexing as indirect access. Arrays can be passed down to functions like other single variables. We use them by their name as arguments when we call the function. The parameter list of the function must indicate the fact that a parameter is an array by augmenting the [ ] at the end of the one dimensional arrays. In one-dimensional arrays the actual size does not have to be given. In case of two-dimensional arrays we recommend that you give the size of the array in both dimensions.

ARRAY INITIALIZERS

ANSI C allows automatic array variables to be initialized in declarations by constant initializers as we have seen we can do for scalar variables. These initializing expressions must be *constant* (known at compile time) values; expressions with identifiers or function calls may not be used in the initializers. The initializers are specified within braces and separated by commas. Here are some declarations with constant initializers:

```
int ex[10] = { 12, 23, 9, 17, 16, 49 };
  char word[10] = { 'h', 'e', 'l', 'l',
  'o', '\0' };
```

Each constant initializer in the braces is assigned, in sequence, to an element of the array starting with index 0. If there are not enough initializers for the whole array, the remaining elements of the array are initialized to zero.

Thus, ex[0] through ex[5] are assigned the values 12, 23, 9, 17, 16, and 49, while ex[6] throughex[9] are initialized to zero. Similarly, word is initialized to a string "hello". String initializers may be written as string constants instead of character constants within braces, for example:

```
char mesg[] = "This is a message";
  char name[20] = "John Doe";
```

In the case of mesg[], enough memory is allocated to accommodate the string plus a terminating NULL, and we do not need to specify the size of the array. The above string initializers are allowed as a convenience, the compiler initializes the array at compile time. Remember, initializations are *not* assignment statements; they are declarations that allocate and initialize memory. As with other arrays, these array names cannot be used as *Lvalues* in assignment statements.

Here is a short programme that shows the use of initializers:

```
/* File: init.c
     Programme shows use of initializers for
     arrays.
*/
   #include <stdio.h>
   #define MAX 10
   main()
   {  int i, ex[MAX] = { 12, 23, 9, 17, 16,
      49 };
      char word[MAX] = {'S', 'm', 'i', 'l',
      'e', '\0'};
      char mesg[] = "Message of the day is:
      ";
      printf("***Array Declarations with
      Initializers***\n\n");
      printf("%s%s\n", mesg, word);
      printf("Initialized Array:\n");
      for (i= 0; i < MAX; i++)
         printf("%d\n", ex[i]);
   }
```

Output:

```
  Array Declarations with Constant
Initializers
  Message of the day is: Smile
  12 23 9 17 16 49 0 0 0 0
```

The first printf() statement uses %s to print each of the two strings accessed by pointers, mesg and word. Finally, the loop prints the array, ex, one element per line.

Chapter 8

Problem Solving

LEARNING AND TEACHING TECHNOLOGY

There seems to be clear and widespread agreement among the public and educators that students need to be proficient computer users—students need to be "computer literate." However, while districts are spending a great deal of money on technology, there seems to be only a vague notion of what computer literacy really means.

- Can the student who operates a computer well enough to play "Doom" be considered computer literate?
- Will a student who has used computers in school only for running tutorials or an integrated learning system have the skills necessary to survive in our society?
- Will the ability to do basic word processing be sufficient for students entering the workplace or post-secondary education?

Clearly not. In too many schools, most teachers and students still use computers only as the equivalent of expensive flash cards or electronic worksheets. The productivity side of computer use in the general content area curriculum is neglected or grossly underdeveloped.

There are, however, some encouraging signs concerning computers and technology in education. For example, it is becoming increasingly popular for educational technologists to advocate integrating computers into the content areas. Teachers and administrators are recognizing that computer skills should not be taught in isolation, and that separate "computer classes" do not really help students learn to apply computer skills in meaningful ways. This is an important shift in approach and emphasis. And it's a shift with which library media specialists have a great deal of familiarity.

Library media specialists know that moving from isolated skills instruction to an integrated approach is an important step that takes a great deal of planning and effort. Over the past 20 years, library media professionals have worked hard to move from teaching isolated "library skills" to teaching integrated information skills. Effective integration of information skills has two requirements: (1) the skills must directly relate to the content area curriculum and to classroom assignments, and (2) the skills themselves need to be tied together in a logical and systematic information process model.

COMPUTER LITERACY

A meaningful, unified computer literacy curriculum must be more than "laundry lists" of isolated skills, such as:

- Knowing the parts of the computer.
- Writing drafts and final products with a word processor.
- Searching for information using a CD-ROM database.

While these specific skills are certainly important for students to learn, the "laundry list" approach does not provide an adequate model for students to transfer and apply skills from situation to situation.

These curricula address the "how" of computer use, but rarely the "when" or "why." Students may learn isolated skills and tools, but they will still lack an understanding of how those various skills fit together to solve problems and complete tasks. Students need to be able to use computers flexibly, creatively and purposefully. All learners should be able to recognize what they need to accomplish, determine whether a computer will help them to do so, and then be able to use the computer as part of the process of accomplishing their task.

Individual computer skills take on a new meaning when they are integrated within this type of information problem-solving process, and students develop true "computer literacy" because they have genuinely applied various computer skills as part of the learning process.

Some computer literacy "skills" competencies which do not seem to fit into this information processing model, and which may or may not be important to have stated include:

- Knowing the basic operation, terminology, and maintenance of equipment.
- Knowing how to use computer-assisted instructional programs.
- Having knowledge of the impact of technology on careers, society, and culture.
- Computer programming.
- Specialized computer applications like music composition software, computer assisted drawing and drafting programs, mathematics modeling software, etc.

Listing computer skills is only a first step in assuring all our children become proficient information and technology users. A teacher supported scope and sequence of skills, well designed projects, and effective assessments are also critical.

Many library media specialists will need to hone their own technology skills in order to remain effective information skills teachers. But such a curriculum holds tremendous opportunities for library media specialists to become vital, indispensable staff members, and for all children to master the skills they will need to thrive in an information rich future.

COMPUTER SKILLS FOR PROBLEM-SOLVING

The first step in the information problem-solving process is to recognize that an information need exists, to define the problem, and to identify the types and amount of information needed. In terms of technology, students will be able to:

A. Use e-mail, and online discussion groups on the

Internet to communicate with teachers regarding assignments, tasks, and information-problems.*

B. Use e-mail, and online discussion groups on the Internet to generate topics and problems and to facilitate cooperative activities among groups of students locally and globally.*

C. Use desktop conferencing, e-mail, and groupware software on local area networks to communicate with teachers regarding assignments, tasks, and information problems.

D. Use desktop conferencing, e-mail, and groupware software on local area networks to generate topics and problems and to facilitate cooperative activities among groups of students locally.

E. Use computer brainstorming or idea generating software to define or refine the information problem. This includes developing a research question or perspective on a topic.

INFORMATION SEEKING STRATEGIES

Once the information problem has been formulated, the student must consider all possible information sources and develop a plan for searching. Students will be able to:

A. Assess the value of various types of electronic resources for data gathering, including databases, CD-ROM resources, commercial and Internet online resources, electronic reference works, community and government information electronic resources.*

B. Identify and apply specific criteria for evaluating computerized electronic resources.

C. Assess the value of e-mail, and online discussion groups (e.g., listservs, newsgroups) on the Internet as part of a search of the current literature or in relation to the information task.

D. Use a computer to generate modifiable flow charts, Gantt charts, time lines, organizational charts, project plans and calendars which will help the student plan and organize complex or group information problem-solving tasks.

LOCATION AND ACCESS

After students determine their priorities for information seeking, they must locate information from a variety of resources and access specific information found within individual resources. Students will be able to:

A. Locate and use appropriate computer resources and technologies available within the school library media centre, including those on the library media center's local area network, (e.g., online catalogs, periodical indexes, full-text sources, multimedia computer stations, CD-ROM stations, online terminals, scanners, digital cameras).

B. Locate and use appropriate computer resources and technologies available throughout the school including those available through local area networks (e.g., full-text resources, CD-ROMs, productivity software, scanners, digital cameras).

C. Locate and use appropriate computer resources and technologies available beyond the school through the Internet (e.g., newsgroups, listservs, WWW sites via Netscape, Lynx or another browser, gopher, ftp sites, online public access library catalogs, commercial databases and online services, other community, academic, and government resources).*

D. Know the roles and computer expertise of the people working in the school library media centre and elsewhere who might provide information or assistance.

E. Use electronic reference materials (e.g., electronic encyclopedias, dictionaries, biographical reference sources, atlases, geographic databanks, thesauri, almanacs, fact books) available through local area networks, stand-alone workstations, commercial online vendors, or the Internet.

F. Use the Internet or commercial computer networks to contact experts and help and referral services.*

G. Conduct self-initiated electronic surveys conducted through e-mail, listservs or newsgroups.*

H. Use organizational systems and tools specific to electronic information sources that assist in finding specific and general information (e.g., indexes, tables of contents, user's instructions and .manuals, legends, boldface and italics, graphic clues and icons, cross-references, Boolean logic strategies, time lines, hypertext links, knowledge trees, URLs etc.) including the use of:

USE OF INFORMATION

After finding potentially useful resources, students must engage (read, view, listen) the information to determine its relevance and then extract the relevant information. Students will be able to:

A. Connect and operate the computer technology needed to access information, and read the guides and manuals associated with such tasks.
B. View, download, decompress and open documents and programs from Internet sites and archives.*
C. Cut and paste information from an electronic source into a personal document complete with proper citation.
D. Take notes and outline with a word processor or similar productivity programme.
E. Record electronic sources of information and locations of those sources to properly cite and credit in footnotes, endnotes, and bibliographies.
F. Use electronic spreadsheets, databases, and statistical software to process and analyse statistical data.
G. Analyse and filter electronic information in relation to the task, rejecting non-relevant information.

SYNTHESIS

Students must organize and communicate the results of the information problem-solving effort. Students will be able to:

A. Classify and group information using a word processor, database or spreadsheet.

B. Use word processing and desktop publishing software to create printed documents, applying keyboard skills equivalent to at least twice the rate of handwriting speed.
C. Create and use computer-generated graphics and art in various print and electronic presentations.
D. Use electronic spreadsheet software to create original spreadsheets.
E. Generate charts, tables and graphs using electronic spreadsheets and other graphing programs.
F. Use database/file management software to create original databases.
G. Use presentation software (e.g., PowerPoint, HyperStudio, Aldus Persuasion) to create electronic slide shows and to generate overheads and slides.
H. Create hypermedia and multimedia productions with digital video and audio.
I. Create World Wide Web pages and sites using hypertext markup language (HTML).*
J. Use e-mail, ftp, and other telecommunications capabilities to share information, products, and files.*
K. Use specialized computer applications as appropriate for specific tasks, e.g., music composition software, computer assisted drawing and drafting programs, mathematics modeling software.
L. Properly cite and credit electronic sources of information in footnotes, endnotes, and bibliographies.

EVALUATION

Evaluation focuses on how well the final product meets the original task (effectiveness) and the process of how well students carried out the information problem-solving process (efficiency). Students may evaluate their own work and process or be evaluated by others (i.e. classmates, teachers, library media staff, parents). Students will be able to:

A. Evaluate electronic presentations in terms of both the content and format.

B. Use spell and grammar checking capabilities of word processing and other software to edit and revise their work.

C. Apply legal principles and ethical conduct related to information technology related to copyright and plagiarism.

D. Understand and abide by telecomputing etiquette when using e-mail, newsgroups, listservs and other Internet functions.*

E. Understand and abide by acceptable use policies in relation to use of the Internet and other electronic technologies.

F. Use e-mail, and online discussion groups (e.g., listservs, newsgroups) on local area networks and the Internet to communicate with teachers and others regarding their performance on assignments, tasks, and information-problems.*

PROGRAMME

Here is a sample programme, paytab.c compiled and linked with payutil.c:

Sample Programme:

```
***Payroll Programme***
ID <zero to quit>: 8
Hours Worked: 50
Rate of Pay: 14
ID <zero to quit>: 12
Hours Worked: 45
Rate of Pay: 12.50
ID <zero to quit>: 2
Hours Worked: 20
Rate of Pay: 5
ID <zero to quit>: 5
Hours Worked: 40
Rate of Pay: 10
ID <zero to quit>: 0
***PAYROLL: FINAL REPORT***
```

Chapter – 9

Excel Basics

INTRODUCTION

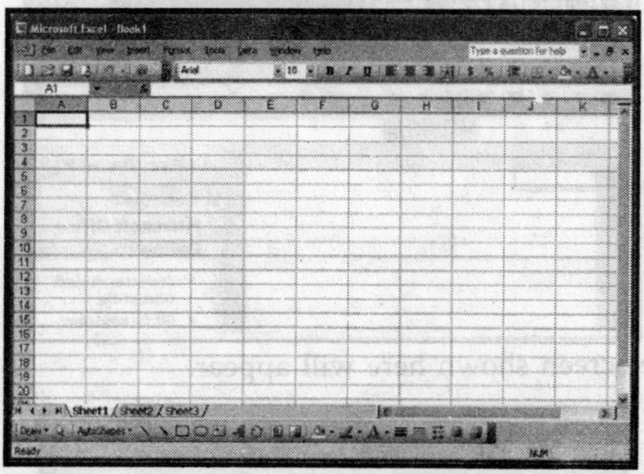

Microsoft Excel is a spreadsheet programme which allows one to enter numerical values or data into the rows or columns of a spreadsheet, and to use these numerical entries for such things as calculations, graphs, and statistical analysis.

BASIC

Microsoft Excel is an electronic spreadsheet that runs on a personal computer. You can use it to organize your data into rows and columns. You can also use it to perform mathematical calculations quickly. This tutorial teaches Microsoft Excel basics. Although knowledge of how to navigate in a Windows environment is helpful, this tutorial was created for the computer novice. This lesson will introduce you to the Excel window. You use the window to interact with Excel.

ENTERING TEXT AND NUMBERS

MICROSOFT EXCEL WINDOW

Although knowledge of how to navigate in a Windows environment is helpful, this tutorial was created for the computer novice. To begin, open Microsoft Excel. Then, if necessary, click the  in the upper right corner of the task pane to close the task pane.

The screen shown here will appear.

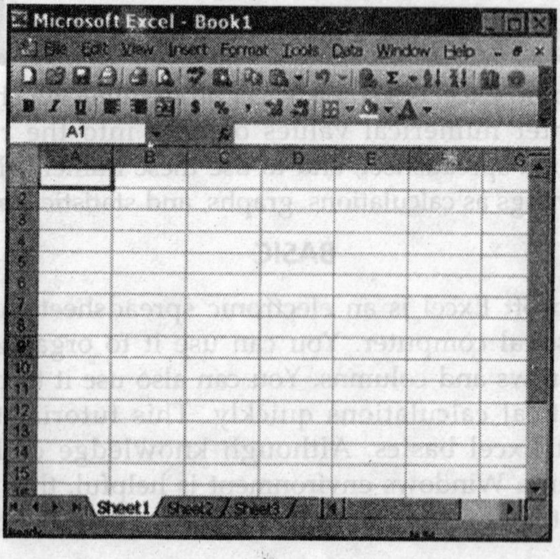

THE TITLE BAR

This chapter will familiarize you with the Microsoft Excel screen. You will start with the Title bar, which is located at the very top of the screen.

On the Title bar, Microsoft Excel displays the name of the workbook you are currently using. At the top of your screen, you should see "Microsoft Excel - Book1" or a similar name.

THE MENU BAR

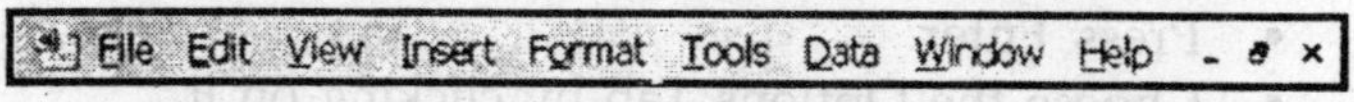

The Menu bar is directly below the Title bar. The menu begins with the word File and continues with Edit, View, Insert, Format, Tools, Data, Window, and Help. You use a menu to give instructions to the software. Point with your mouse to a menu option and click the left mouse button. A drop-down menu opens.

You can now use the left and right arrow keys on your keyboard to move left and right across the Menu bar. You can use the up and down arrow keys to move up and down the drop-down menu.

To choose an option, highlight the item on the drop-down menu and press Enter. An ellipse after a menu item signifies additional options; if you choose that option, a dialog box opens.

Do the following exercise, which demonstrates using the Microsoft Excel menu bar.

- Point to the word *File*, which is located on the Menu bar.
- Click your left mouse button.
- Press the right arrow key until Help is highlighted.
- Press the left arrow key until Format is highlighted.
- Press the down arrow key until Style is highlighted.
  Press the up arrow key until Cells is highlighted.
- Press Enter to choose the *Cells* menu option.

- Point to Cancel and click the left mouse button to close the dialog box.

When using Microsoft Excel, you can set an option to tell Microsoft Excel to always show full menus or to show only the most frequently and recently used options. All the lessons in this tutorial assume you have your menus set to Always Show Full Menus. To set your menu to display full menus:

- Point to the word Tools, which is located on the menu bar.
- Click your left mouse button.
- Press the down arrow until customise is highlighted.
- Press Enter.
- Choose the Options Tab by clicking on it.
- If Always Show Full Menus does not have a check mark in it, click in the Always Show Full Menus box.
- Click Close to close the dialog box.

TOOLBARS

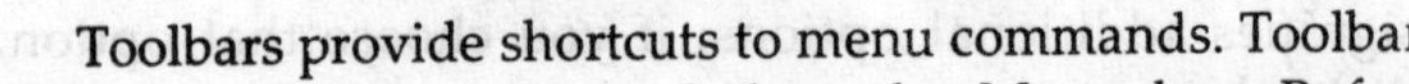

Fig. The Standard Toolbar

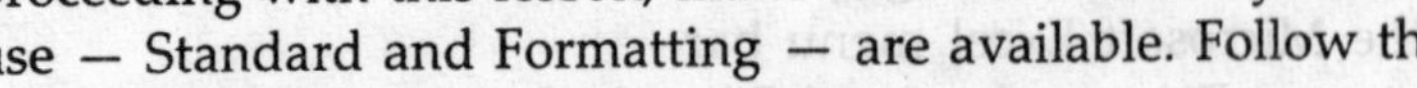

Fig. The Formatting Toolbar

Toolbars provide shortcuts to menu commands. Toolbars are generally located just below the Menu bar. Before proceeding with this lesson, make sure the toolbars you will use — Standard and Formatting — are available. Follow the steps outlined here:

- Point to *View,* which is located on the Menu bar.
- Click the left mouse button.
- Press the down arrow key until Toolbars is highlighted.
- Press the right arrow key.
- Both Standard and Formatting should have a check mark next to them. If both have a check mark next

to them, press Esc two times to close the menu. If either does not have a check mark, press the down arrow key until Customise is highlighted.

- Press Enter. The Customise dialog box opens.
- Choose the Toolbars tab.
- Point to the box or boxes next to the unchecked word or words, Standard and/or Formatting, and click the left mouse button. A check mark should appear. Note: You turn the check mark on and off by clicking the left mouse button.
- Point to Close and click the left mouse button to close the dialog box.

WORKSHEETS

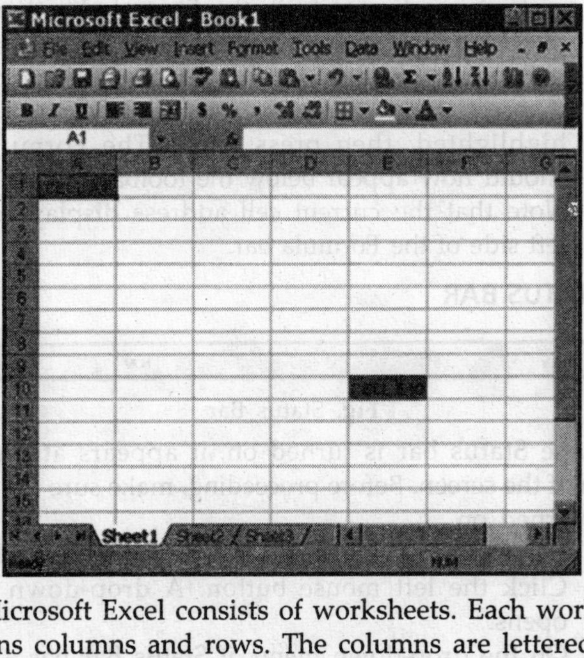

Microsoft Excel consists of worksheets. Each worksheet contains columns and rows. The columns are lettered A to IV; the rows are numbered 1 to 65536. The combination of a column coordinate and a row coordinate make up a cell address. For example, the cell located in the upper left corner of the worksheet is cell A1, meaning column A, row 1. Cell

E10 is located under column E on row 10. You enter your data into the cells on the worksheet.

The Formula Bar SH]

Fig. Formula Bar

If the Formula bar is turned on, the cell address displays in the Name box on the left side of the Formula bar. Cell entries display on the right side of the Formula bar. Before proceeding, make sure the Formula bar is turned on.

- Point to View, which is located on the Menu bar.
- Click the left mouse button. A drop-down menu opens. On the drop-down menu, if Formula Bar has a check mark next to it, the Formula bar is turned on. Press the Esc key to close the drop-down menu.
- If Formula Bar does not have a check mark next to it, press the down arrow key until Formula Bar is highlighted; then press Enter. The Formula bar should now appear below the toolbars.
- Note that the current cell address displays on the left side of the Formula bar.

THE STATUS BAR

Fig. Status Bar

If the Status bar is turned on, it appears at the very bottom of the screen. Before proceeding, make sure the Status bar is turned on.

- Point to View, which is located on the Menu bar.
- Click the left mouse button. A drop-down menu opens.
- On the drop-down menu, if Status Bar has a check mark next to it, it is turned on. Press the Esc key to close the drop-down menu.
- If Status Bar does not have a check mark next to it, press the down arrow key until Status Bar is

highlighted; then press Enter. The Status bar should now appear at the bottom of the screen.

Notice the word "Ready" on the Status bar at the lower left side of the screen. The word "Ready" tells you that Excel is in the Ready mode and awaiting your next command. Other indicators appear on the Status bar in the lower right corner of the screen.

Here are some examples:

The Num Lock key is a toggle key. Pressing it turns the numeric keypad on and off. You can use the numeric keypad to enter numbers as if you were using a calculator. The letters "NUM" on the Status bar in the lower right corner of the screen indicate that the numeric keypad is on.

- Press the Num Lock key several times and note how the indicator located on the Status bar changes.

The Caps Lock key is also a toggle key. Pressing it turns the caps function on and off. When the caps function is on, your entry appears in capital letters.

- Press the Cap Lock key several times and note how the indicator located on the Status bar changes.

Other functions that appear on the Status bar are Scroll Lock and End. Scroll Lock and End are also toggle keys. Pressing the key toggles the function between on and off. Scroll Lock causes the movement keys to move the window without moving the cell pointer. End lets you jump around the screen. Make sure the Scroll Lock and End indicators are off and complete the following exercises.

The Down Arrow Key

You can use the down arrow key to move downward one cell at a time.

- Press the down arrow key several times.
- Note that the cursor moves downward one cell at a time.

The Up Arrow Key

You can use the Up Arrow key to move upward one cell at a time.

- Press the up arrow key several times.
- Note that the cursor moves upward one cell at a time.

The Tab Key

You can use the Tab key to move across the page to the right, one cell at a time.

- Move to cell A1.
- Press the Tab key several times.
- Note that the cursor moves to the right one cell at a time.

The Shift+Tab Keys

You can hold down the Shift key and then press the Tab key to move to the left, one cell at a time.

- Hold down the Shift-key and then press Tab.
- Note that the cursor moves to the left one cell at a time.

The Right and Left Arrow Keys

You can use the right and left arrow keys to move right or left one cell at a time.

- Press the right arrow key several times.
- Note that the cursor moves to the right.
- Press the left arrow key several times.
- Note that the cursor moves to the left.

Page Up and Page Down

The Page Up and Page Down keys move the cursor up and down one page at a time.

- Press the Page Down key.
- Note that the cursor moves down one page.
- Press the Page Up key.
- Note that the cursor moves up one page.

THE END KEY

Fig. The Status Bar

The End key, used in conjunction with the arrow keys, causes the cursor to move to the far end of the spreadsheet in the direction of the arrow.

- Press the End key.
- Note that "END" appears on the Status bar in the lower right corner of the screen.
- Press the right arrow key.
- Note that the cursor moves to the farthest right area of the screen.
- Press the END key again.
- Press the down arrow key. Note that the cursor moves to the bottom of the screen.
- Press the End key again.
- Press the left arrow key. Note that the cursor moves to the farthest left area of the screen.
- Press the End key again.
- Press the up arrow key. Note that the cursor moves to the top of the screen.

You can note that If you have entered data into the worksheet, the End key moves you to the end of the data area.

THE HOME KEY

The Home key, used in conjunction with the End key, moves you to cell A1 — or to the beginning of the data area if you have entered data.

- Move the cursor to column J.
- Stay in column J and move the cursor to row 20.
- Press the End key.
- Press Home.
- You should now be in cell A1.

MOVING QUICKLY AROUND THE WORKSHEET

The following are shortcuts for moving quickly from one cell to a cell in a different part of the worksheet.

Go to — F5

The F5 function key is the "Go To" key. If you press the F5 key while in the Ready mode, you are prompted for the cell to which you wish to go. Enter the cell address, and the cursor jumps to that cell.

- Press F5. The Go To dialog box opens.
- Type J3.
- Press Enter. The cursor should move to cell J3.

Go to — Ctrl-G

You can also use Ctrl-G to go to a specific cell.

- Hold down the Ctrl key while you press "g" (Ctrl-g). The Go To dialog box opens.
- Type C4.
- Press Enter. You should now be in cell C4.

Name Box

You can also use the Name box to go to a specific cell.

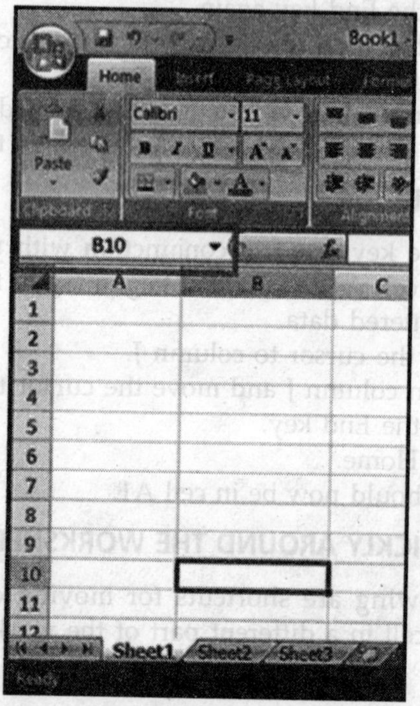

- Type B10 in the Name box
- Press Enter. Excel moves to cell D10.

SELECTING CELLS

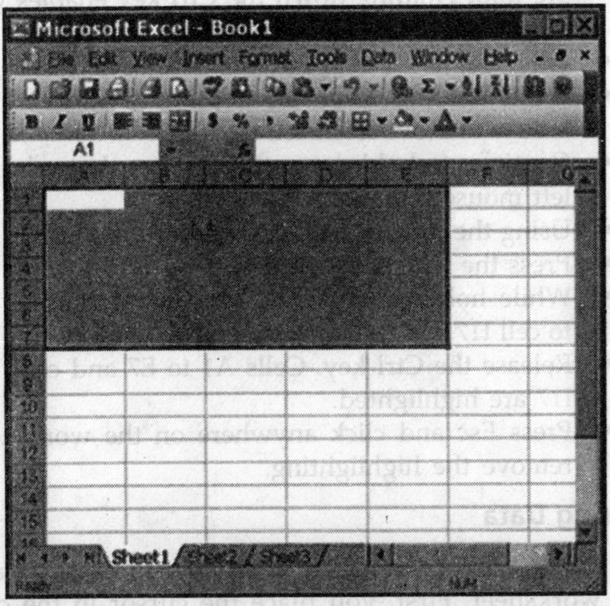

If you wish to perform a function on a group of cells, you must first select those cells by highlighting them. To highlight cells A1 to E1:

- Place the cursor in cell A1.
- Press the F8 key. This anchors the cursor.
- Note that "EXT" appears on the Status bar in the lower right corner of the screen. You are in the Extend mode.
- Click in cell E7. Cells A1 to E7 should now be highlighted.
- Press Esc and click anywhere on the worksheet to clear the highlighting.

Selecting Cells by Dragging

You can also highlight an area by holding down the left mouse button and dragging the mouse over the area. In addition, you can select noncontiguous areas of the worksheet by doing the following:

- Place the cursor in cell A1.

- Hold down the Ctrl key. Do not release it until you are told. Holding down the Ctrl key enables you to select noncontiguous areas of the worksheet.
- Press the left mouse button.
- While holding down the left mouse button, use the mouse to move from cell A1 to E7.
- Continue to hold down the Ctrl key, but release the left mouse button.
- Using the mouse, place the cursor in cell G8.
- Press the left mouse button.
- While holding down the left mouse button, move to cell I17. Release the left mouse button.
- Release the Ctrl key. Cells A1 to E7 and cells G8 to I17 are highlighted.
- Press Esc and click anywhere on the worksheet to remove the highlighting.

Entering Data

In this, you are going to learn how to enter data into your worksheet. First, you place the cursor in the cell in which you would like to enter data. Then you type the data and press Enter.

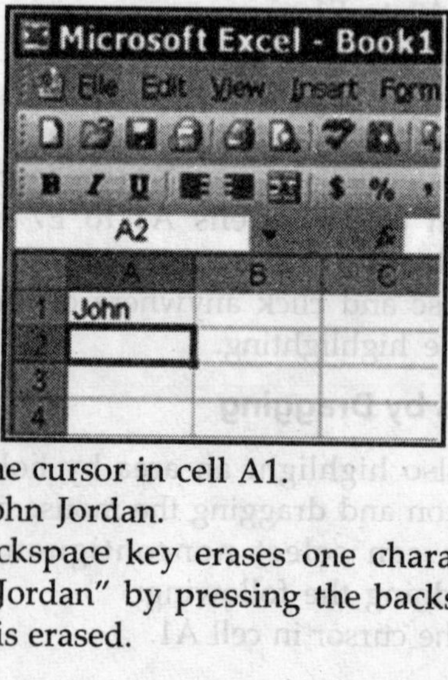

- Place the cursor in cell A1.
- Type John Jordan.
- The Backspace key erases one character at a time. Erase "Jordan" by pressing the backspace key until Jordan is erased.

- Press Enter. The name "John" should appear in cell A1.

Editing a Cell

After you enter data into a cell, you can edit it by pressing F2 while you are in the cell you wish to edit.

- Move the cursor to cell A1.
- Press F2.
- Change "John" to "Jones."
- Use the backspace key to delete the "n" and the "h."
- Type nes.
- Press Enter.

Editing a Cell by Using the Formula Bar

You can also edit the cell by using the Formula bar. You can change "Jones" to "Joker" as follows:

- Move the cursor to cell A1.

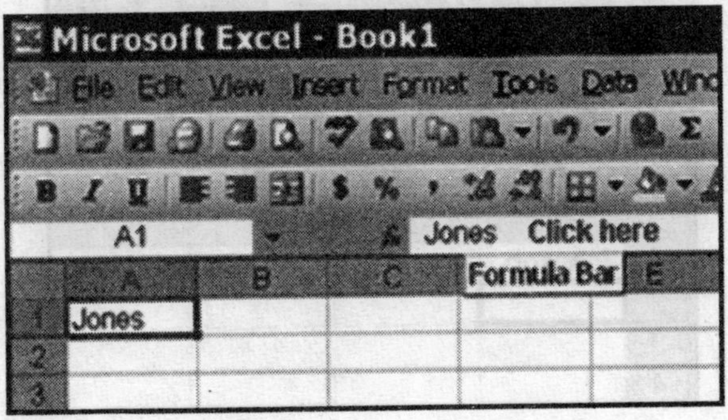

- Click in the formula area of the Formula bar.
- Use the backspace key to erase the "s," "e," and "n."
- Type ker.
- Press Enter.

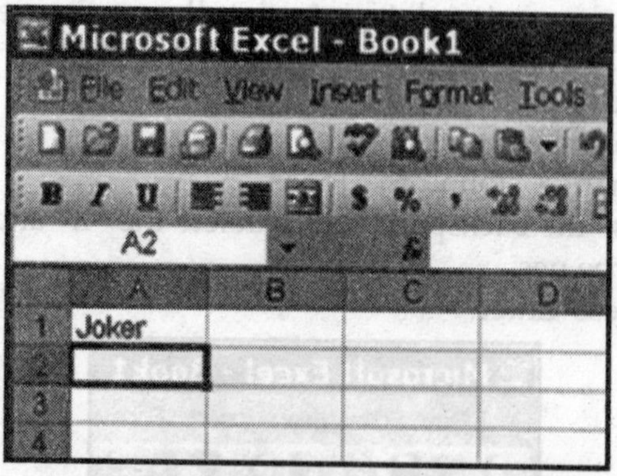

Editing a Cell by Double-Clicking in the Cell

You can change "Joker" to "Johnson" as follows:

- Move the cursor to cell A1.
- Double-click in cell A1.
- Press the End key. Your cursor is now at the end of your text.
- Use the backspace to erase "r," "e," and "k."
- Type hnson.
- Press Enter.

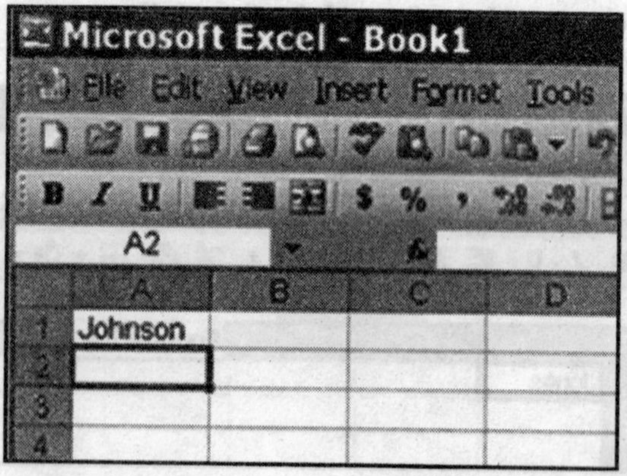

Changing a Cell Entry

Typing in a cell while you are in the Ready mode replaces the old cell entry with the new information you type.

- Move the cursor to cell A1.
- Type Cathy.
- Press Enter. The name "Cathy" should replace "Johnson."

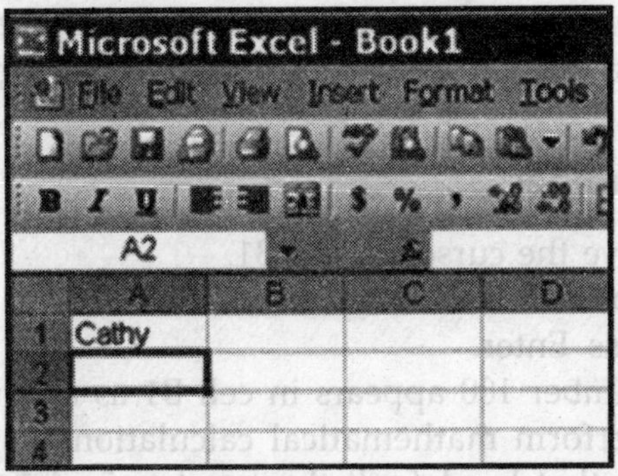

Wrapping Text

When you enter text that is too long to fit in a cell into a cell, it overlaps the next cell. If you do not want it to overlap the next cell you can wrap the text.

- Move to cell A2.
- Type Text too long to fit.
- Press Enter.
- Return to cell A2.
- Choose *Format* > *Cells* from the menu.
- Choose the Alignment tab.
- Click Wrap Text.
- Click OK. The text wraps.

Deleting a Cell Entry

To delete an entry in a cell or a group of cells, you place the cursor in the cell or highlight the group of cells and press Delete.

- Place the cursor in cell A2.
- Press the Delete key.

ENTERING NUMBERS AS LABELS OR VALUES

In Microsoft Excel, you can enter numbers as labels or as values. Labels are alphabetic, alphanumeric, or numeric text on which you do not perform mathematical calculations. Values are numeric text on which you perform mathematical calculations.

If you have a numeric entry, such as an employee number, on which you do not perform mathematical calculations, enter it as a label by typing a single quotation mark first.

Enter a Number

- Move the cursor to cell B1.
- Type 100.
- Press Enter.

The number 100 appears in cell B1 as a numeric value. You can perform mathematical calculations using this cell entry. Note that by default the number is right-aligned.

Enter a Value

- Move the cursor to cell C1.
- Type '100.
- Press Enter.

The number 100 appears in cell C1 as a label. Note that by default the cell entry is left-aligned and a green triangle appears in the upper left corner of the cell.

SMART TAGS

When you make an entry that Microsoft Excel believes you may want to change, a smart appears. Smart tags give you the opportunity to make changes easily. Cells with smart tag in them appear with a green triangle in the upper left corner.

When you place your cursor in the cell, the Trace Error icon appears. Click the Trace Error icon and options appear. When you made your entry in cell C1 in the previous section, a smart tag should have appeared.

- Move to cell C1.

- Click the Trace Error icon. An options list appears. You can convert the label to a number, obtain help, ignore the error etc.

SAVING A FILE

This is the end of Lesson1. To save your file:

- Choose *File* > *Save* from the menu.
- Go to the directory in which you want to save your file.
- Type lesson1 in the File Name field.
- Click Save.

CLOSING MICROSOFT EXCEL

Close Microsoft Excel.

- Choose *File* > *Close* from the menu.

Chapter 10

Excel Formatting and Printing

FORMATTING

You can format the numbers you enter into Microsoft Excel. You can add commas to separate thousands, specify the number of decimal places, place a dollar sign in front of the number, or display the number as a per cent in addition to several other options.

Before formatting

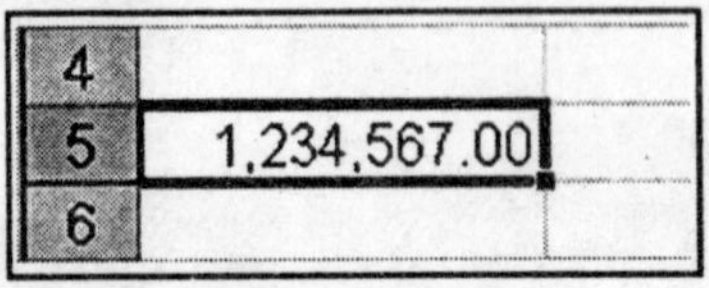

After formatting

- Move the cursor to cell A5.
- Type 1234567.
- Press Enter.
- Move the cursor back to cell A5.
- Choose *Format* > *Cells* from the menu. The Format Cells dialog box will open.
- Choose the Number tab.
- Click Number in the Category box.
- Type 2 in the Decimal Places box.
- Place a check mark in the Use 1000 Separator box.
- Click OK. The number should now display with two

decimal places. The thousands should now be separated by commas.

ADDING A SIGN TO A NUMERIC ENTRY

- Move the cursor to cell A5.
- Choose *Format* > *Cells* from the menu. The Format Cells dialog box opens.
- Choose the Number tab.
- Click Currency in the Category box.
- Make sure there is a "$" in the Symbol box.
- Click OK. The number displays with a dollar sign.

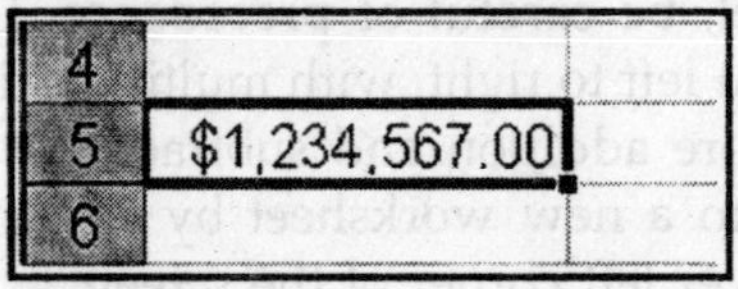

FORMATTING NUMBERS BY USING THE TOOLBAR

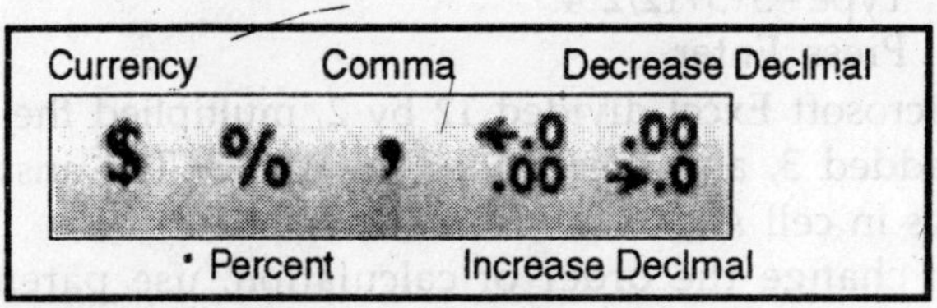

- Move the cursor to cell A6.
- Type 1234567.
- Press Enter.
- Move the cursor back to cell A6.
- Click twice on the Increase Decimal icon to change the number format to two decimal places. Clicking on the Decrease Decimal icon decreases the decimal places.
- Click once on the Comma Style icon to add commas to the number.
- To change the number to a currency format, click Currency Style format.
- Move the cursor to cell A7.
- Type .35 (note the decimal point).
- Press Enter.

- Move the cursor back to cell A7.

- Click the Per cent Style icon to turn .35 to a per cent.

ADVANCED MATHEMATICAL CALCULATIONS

When you perform mathematical calculations in Microsoft Excel, be careful of precedence. Calculations are performed from left to right, with multiplication and division performed before addition and subtraction.

- Move to a new worksheet by clicking on Sheet3 in the lower left corner of the screen.
- Go to cell A1.
- Type =3+3+12/2*4.
- Press Enter.

Microsoft Excel divided 12 by 2, multiplied the answer by 4, added 3, and then added another 3. The answer, 30, displays in cell A1.

To change the order of calculation, use parentheses. Microsoft Excel calculates the information in parentheses first.

- Double-click in cell A1.
- Edit the cell to read =(3 + 3 + 12)/2*4.
- Press Enter.

Microsoft Excel added 3 plus 3 plus 12, divided the answer by 2, and multiplied the result by 4. The answer, 36, displays in cell A1.

CELL ADDRESSING

Microsoft Excel records cell addresses in formulas in three different ways, called *absolute*, *relative*, and *mixed*. The way a formula is recorded is important when you copy it.

With relative cell addressing, when you copy a formula from one area of the worksheet to another, Microsoft Excel records the position of the cell relative to the cell that originally contained the formula. The following exercises demonstrate:

- Go to cell A7.
- Type 1. Press Enter.
- Type 1. Press Enter.
- Type 1. Press Enter.
- Go to cell B7.
- Type 2. Press Enter.
- Type 2. Press Enter.
- Type 2. Press Enter.
- Go to cell A10.

In addition to typing a formula, as you did in Lesson 1, you can also enter formulas by using Point mode. When you are in Point mode, you can enter a formula either by clicking on a cell with your mouse or by using the arrow keys.

- You should be in cell A10.
- Type =.
- Use the up arrow key to move to cell A7.
- Type +.
- Use the up arrow key to move to cell A8.
- Type +.
- Use the up arrow key to move to cell A9.
- Press Enter.
- Look at the Formula bar while in cell A10. Note that the formula you entered is recorded in cell A10.

COPYING BY USING THE MENU

You can copy entries from one cell to another cell. To copy the formula you just entered, follow these steps:

- You should be in cell A10.
- Choose *Edit > Copy* from the menu. Moving dotted lines appear around cell A10, indicating the cells to be copied.
- Press the Right Arrow key once to move to cell B10.
- Choose *Edit > Paste* from the menu. The formula in cell A10 is copied to cell B10.
- Press Esc to exit the Copy mode.

Compare the formula in cell A10 with the formula in cell B10 (while in the respective cell, look at the Formula bar). The formulas are the same except that the formula in cell A10 sums the entries in column A and the formula in cell B10 sums the entries in column B. The formula was copied in a *relative* fashion.

Before proceeding with the next exercise, you must copy the information in cells A7 to B9 to cells C7 to D9. This time you will copy by using the Formatting toolbar.

COPYING BY USING THE FORMATTING TOOLBAR

- Highlight cells A7 to B9. Place the cursor in cell A7. Press F8. Press the down arrow key twice. Press the right arrow key once. A7 to B9 should be highlighted.
- Click the Copy icon , which is located on the Formatting toolbar.
- Use the arrow key to move the cursor to cell C7.
- Click the Paste icon , which is located on the Formatting toolbar.
- Press Esc to exit Copy mode.

ABSOLUTE CELL ADDRESSING

An *absolute* cell address refers to the same cell, no matter where you copy the formula. You make a cell address an absolute cell address by placing a dollar sign in front of both the row and column identifiers. You can do this automatically by using the F4 key. To illustrate:

- Move the cursor to cell C10.
- Type =.
- Use the up arrow key to move to cell C7.
- Press F4. Dollar signs should appear before the C and before the 7.
- Type +.
- Use the up arrow key to move to cell C8.
- Press F4.
- Type +.

- Use the up arrow key to move to cell C9.
- Press F4.
- Press Enter. The formula is recorded in cell C10.

COPYING BY USING THE KEYBOARD SHORTCUT

Now copy the formula from C10 to D10. This time, you will copy by using the keyboard shortcut.

- Your cursor should be in cell C10.
- Hold down the Ctrl key while you press "c" (Ctrl-c). This copies the contents of cell C10.
- Press the right arrow once.
- Hold down the Ctrl key while you press "v" (Ctrl-v). This pastes the contents of cell C10 in cell D10.
- Press Esc to exit the Copy mode.

Compare the formula in cell C10 with the formula in cell D10. They are the same. The formula was copied in an *absolute* fashion. Both formulas sum column C.

MIXED CELL ADDRESSING

You use mixed cell addressing to reference a cell that is part absolute and part relative. You can use the F4 key.

- Move the cursor to cell E1.
- Type =.
- Press the up arrow key once.
- Press F4.
- Press F4 again. Note that the column is relative and the row is absolute.
- Press F4 again. Note that the column is absolute and the row is relative.
- Press Esc.

DELETING COLUMNS

You can delete columns from your spreadsheet. To delete columns C and D:

- Click on column C and drag to column D.
- Choose *Edit > Delete* from the menu. Column D is deleted.
- Click anywhere on the spreadsheet to remove your selection.

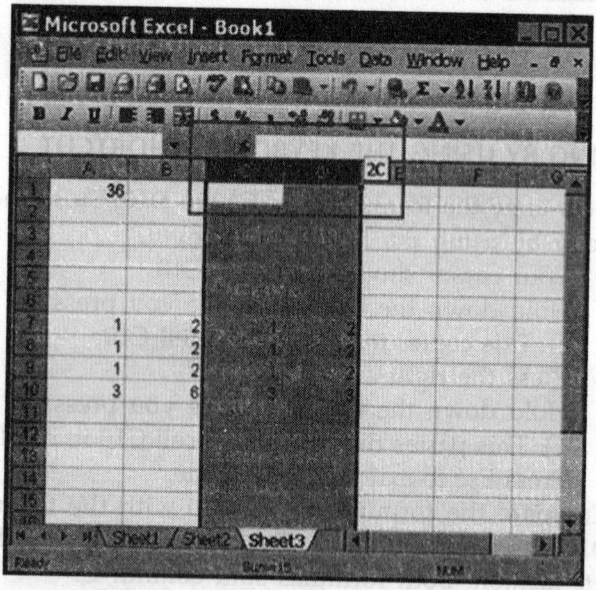

DELETING ROWS

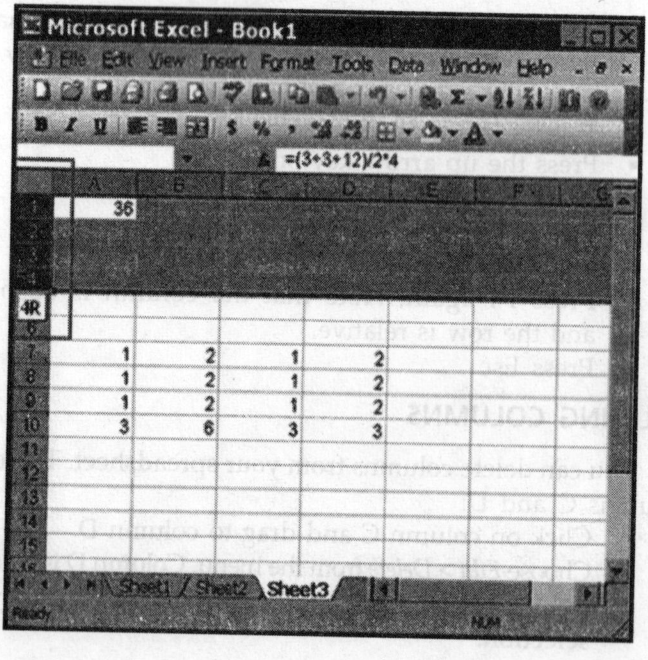

You can delete rows from your spreadsheet. To delete rows 1 through 4:

- Click the row 1 and drag to row 4.
- Choose *Edit* > *Delete* from the menu. Rows 1 through 4 are deleted.
- Click anywhere on the spreadsheet to remove your selection.

INSERTING COLUMNS

There will be times when you will need to insert a column or columns into your spreadsheet. To insert a column:

- Click on A to select column A.
- Choose *Insert* > *Columns* from the menu. A column is inserted to the right of column A.
- Click anywhere on the spreadsheet to remove your selection.

INSERTING ROWS

You can also insert rows into your spreadsheet:

- Click on 2 to select row 2.
- Choose *Insert* > *Rows* from the menu. A row is inserted above row 2.
- Click anywhere on the spreadsheet to remove your selection.

CREATING BORDERS

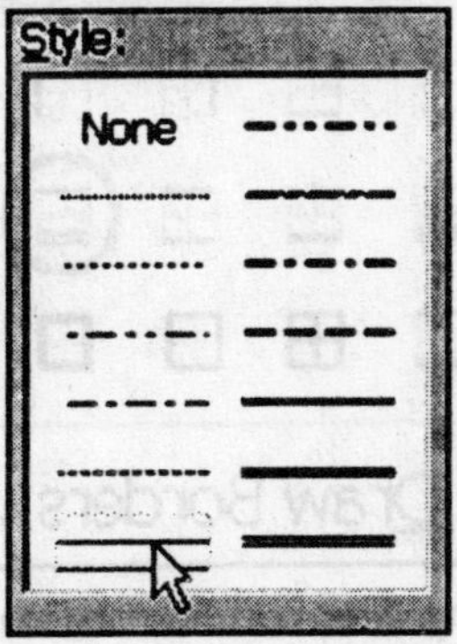

You can use borders to make entries on your spreadsheet

stand out. Accountants usually place a single underline above a final number and a double underline below. The following illustrates:

- Go to cell B7.
- Choose *Format* > *Cells* from the menu.
- Choose the Border tab.
- In the Style box, click on the single underline.

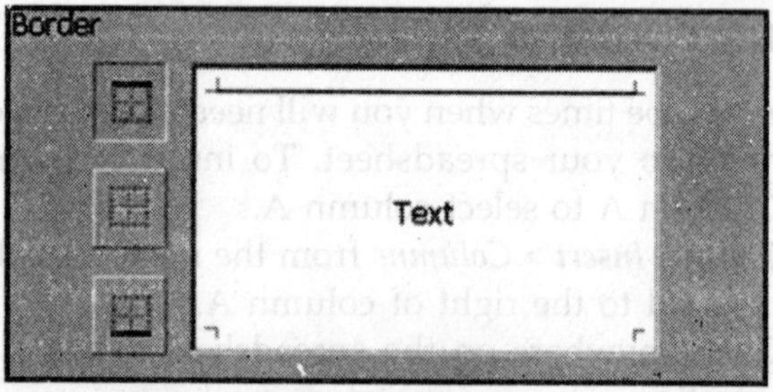

- Click the top of the Border box.
- In the Style box, click on the double underline.
- Click the bottom of the Border box.
- Click OK. Cell B7 now has a border.

CREATING BORDERS BY USING THE ICON

- Go to cell C7. Click the down arrow beside the Borders icon.

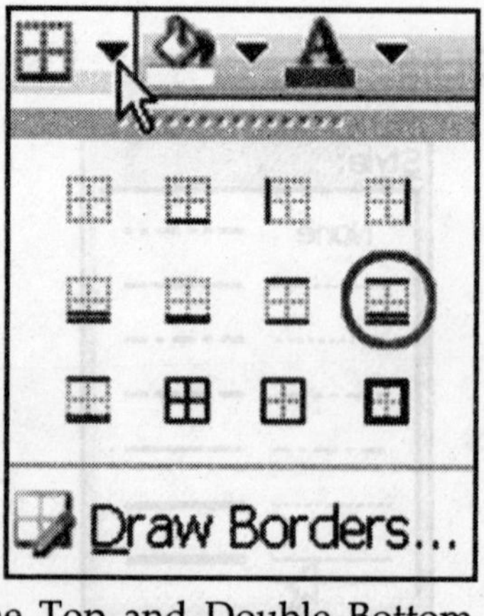

- Select the Top and Double Bottom Border. Cell C7 now has borders.

MERGE AND CENTRE

You will sometimes want to centre a piece of text over several columns. The following example shows you how.

- Go to cell B1.
- Type Sample Spreadsheet.
- Click the check mark on the Formula bar.
- Select columns B1 to D1.
- Click the Merge and Centre icon 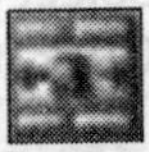 on the formatting toolbar. Cells B1, C1, and D1 are merged and centered.

ADDING BACKGROUND COLOUR

You can add background colour to a cell or group of cells:

- Go to cell B1.
- Choose *Format* > *Cells* from the menu.

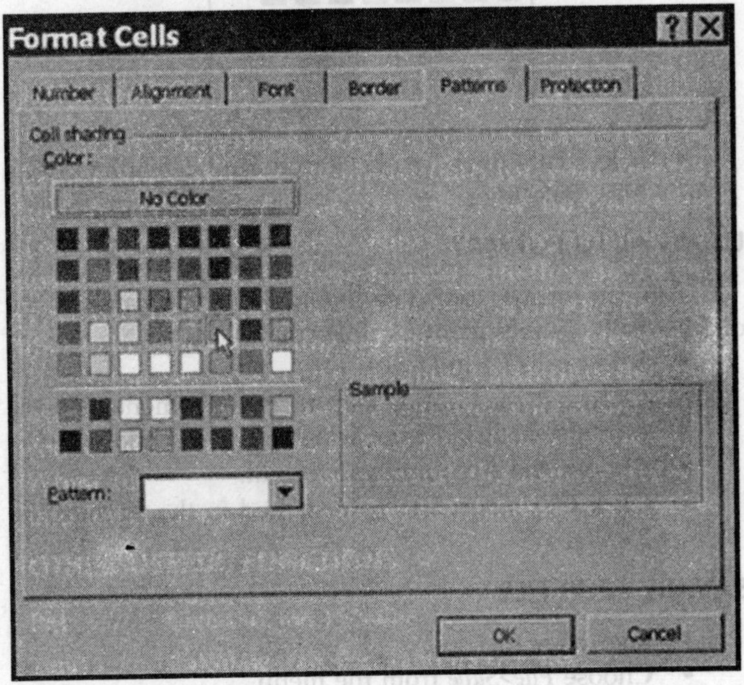

- Choose the Patterns tab.
- Choose Sky Blue.
- Click OK. The background of cell B1 is now Sky Blue.

ADDING BACKGROUND COLOUR BY USING THE ICON

- Select cells B7 to D7.
- Click the down-arrow next to the Fill Colour icon 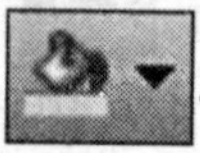.

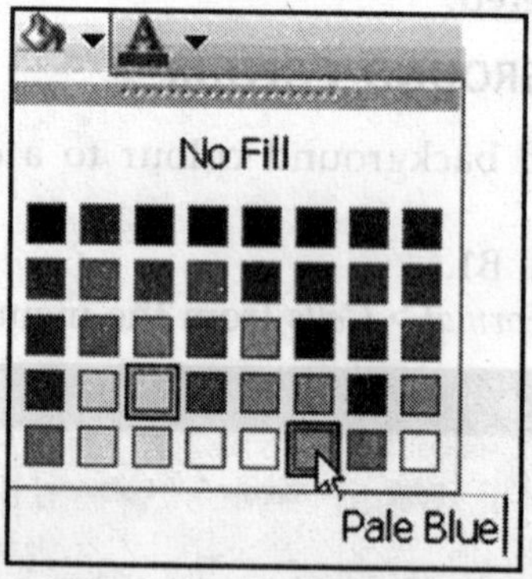

- Select Pale Blue. The background of cells B7 to D7 is now Pale Blue.

USING AUTO FORMAT

You can format your data manually or you can use one of Microsoft Excel's many AutoFormats.

- Select cells B1 to D7.
- Choose *Format > Auto Format* from the menu. Several formats are listed from which you can choose.
- Choose the Accounting 2 format.
- Click OK. Your data is formatted in the Accounting 2 style.

SAVING YOUR FILE

To save your file:

- Choose *File>Save* from the menu.

- Go to the directory in which you want to save your file.
- Type lesson2 in the File Name field.
- Click Save.

CLOSING MICROSOFT EXCEL

Now is the time to Close Microsoft Excel.

- Choose *File* > *Exit* from the menu.

PRINTING

The simplest way to print is to click the Print icon located on the Standard toolbar. Dotted lines will appear on your screen after you click the print icon. The dotted lines indicate the right, left, top, and bottom edges of your printed pages.

PRINT PREVIEW

There are many print options. You can select print options options in Page Setup or in Print Preview. In Print Preview, you can see the results of your selections onscreen. You can use print options to:

- Determine whether to print landscape or portrait. If you print portrait on an 8 1/2 by 11 sheet of paper, the length across the top of your page will be 8 1/2 inches. If you print landscape on an 8 1/2 by 11 sheet of paper, the length across the top of your page will be 11 inches.
- Scale your document. If your data is small in comparison to the page, you may want to scale upward so the data fills the entire page. If your data is too large to fit on the page, you may want to scale downward.
- Specify how many pages wide and how many pages long you want your printed document to be.
- Select the paper size and print quality.
- Set the first page number.

If you choose the Margins tab, you can:

- Set the size of your margins including your header and footer margins.

- Centre your spreadsheet horizontally and/or vertically on the page.

HEADER AND FOOTER

If you choose the Header/Footer tab, you can select headers and footers. A header is text that appears at the top of every page. A footer is text that appears at the bottom of every page. You can use headers and footers to insert page numbers, dates, and other information.

Choosing a Header

- Choose the Header/Footer tab.
- Click the down arrow next to the Header field to open the drop-down box for the header field.
- Choose a Header from the list.

Choosing a Footer

- Choose the Header/Footer tab.
- Click the down arrow next to the Footer field to open the drop-down box for the Footer field.
- Choose a Footer from the list.

Click the Custom Header or Custom Footer button to customise your headers and footers.

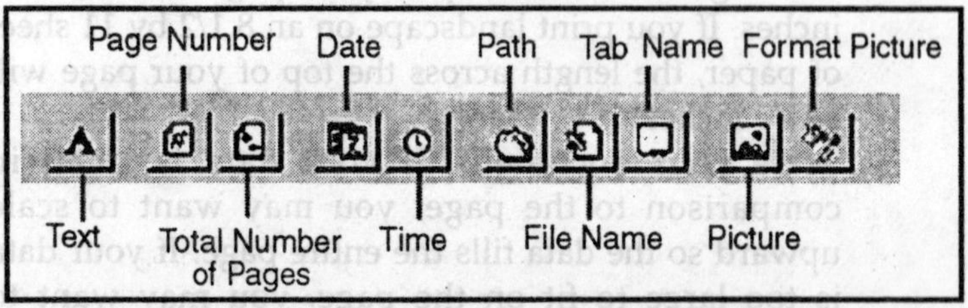

Use the Left Section to place your options on the left side of the page, the Centre Section to place your options in the centre of the page, and the Right Section to place your option 9 on the right side of the page.

The Sheet tab has options that allow you to choose which rows and columns will repeat at the left and the top of the page. It also has options that allows you to determine whether gridlines and/or row column headings print

PREVIEW AND PRINT SPREADSHEET

- Choose *File > Preview* from the menu.
- Click Setup.
- Choose the Page tab.
- Choose Portrait.
- In the Adjust To field, type 110% to set the size to 110%,.
- Choose the Margin tab.
- Check the Horizontally box in the Centre On Page frame to centre your spreadsheet horizontally.
- Click OK.
- Click Print. The Print dialog box opens.
- Click OK to print the file.

SAVING YOUR FILE

To save your file:

- Choose *File>Save* from the menu.
- Go to the directory in which you want to save your file.
- Type lesson3 in the File Name field.
- Click Save.

CLOSING MICROSOFT EXCEL

This is the time to finish and Close Microsoft Excel.

- Choose *File > Exit* from the menu.

FORMATTING TEXT AND PERFORMING MATHEMATICAL CALCULATIONS

In this chapter, you are going to learn how to format text and perform basic mathematical calculations. To start, open a blank Microsoft Excel workbook.

CHOOSING A DEFAULT FONT

Microsoft Excel enables you to choose a default font. The default font is the style of typeface that Excel will use unless you specify a different style. For the exercises in this lesson, you want your font to be set to Arial,

Regular, and Size 10. To set your font to Arial, Regular, and Size 10:

- Choose *Format* > *Cells* from the menu.
- Choose the Font tab.
- In the Font box, choose Arial.
- In the Font Style box, choose Regular.
- In the Size box, choose 10.
- If there is no check mark in the Normal Font box, click to place a check mark there. Your selections are now the default.
- Click OK.

ADJUSTING STANDARD COLUMN WIDTH

When you open Microsoft Excel, the width of each cell is set to a default width. This width is called the standard column width. You need to change the standard column width to complete your exercises. To make the change, follow these steps:

- Choose *Format* > *Column* > *Standard Width* from the menu. The Standard Width dialog box opens.
- Type 25 in the Standard Column Width field. Click OK. The width of every cell on the worksheet should now be set to 25.
- Move to cell A1.
- Type Cathy.
- Press Enter.

CELL ALIGNMENT

The name "Cathy" is aligned with the left side of the cell. You can change the cell alignment.

Centering by Using the Menu

To centre the name Cathy, follow these steps:

- Move the cursor to cell A1.

- Choose *Format* > *Cells* from the menu. The Format Cells dialog box opens.
- Choose the Alignment tab.
- Click to open the drop-down box associated with the Horizontal field. After the drop-down box is opened, click Centre.
- Click OK to close the dialog box. The name "Cathy" is centered.

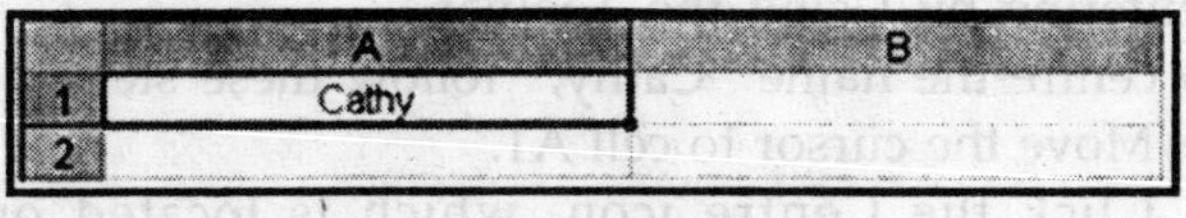

Right-Aligning by Using the Menu

To right-align the name "Cathy," follow these steps:

- Move the cursor to cell A1.
- Choose *Format* > *Cells* from the menu. The Format Cells dialog box opens.
- Choose the Alignment tab.
- Click to open the drop-down box associated with the Horizontal field. After the drop-down box opens, click Right (Indent).
- Click OK to close the dialog box. The name "Cathy" is right-aligned.

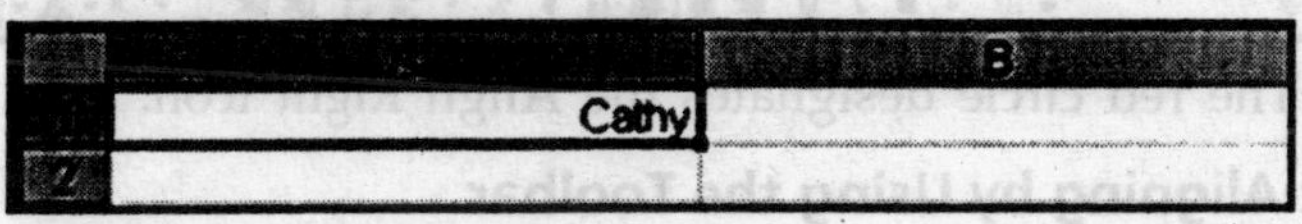

Left-Aligning by Using the Menu

To left-align the name "Cathy," follow these steps:

- Move the cursor to cell A1.
- Choose *Format* > *Cells* from the menu. The Format Cells dialog box opens.

- Choose the Alignment tab.
- Click to open the drop-down box associated with

the Horizontal field. After the drop-down box opens, click Left (Indent).

- Click OK to close the dialog box. The name "Cathy" is left-aligned.

Alignment by Using the Formatting Toolbar

Using the Formatting toolbar, you can quickly perform tasks. You can use the Formatting toolbar to change alignment.

Centering by Using the Toolbar

To centre the name "Cathy," follow these steps:

- Move the cursor to cell A1.
- Click the Centre icon, which is located on the Formatting toolbar.

The red circle designates the Align Centre icon.

Right-Aligning by Using the Toolbar

You can right-align the name "Cathy" by following these steps:

- Move the cursor to cell A1.
- Click the Align Right icon, which is located on the Formatting toolbar.

The red circle designates the Align Right icon.

Left-Aligning by Using the Toolbar

You can left-align the name "Cathy" by following these steps:

- Move the cursor to cell A1.
- Click the Align Left icon, which is located on the Formatting toolbar.

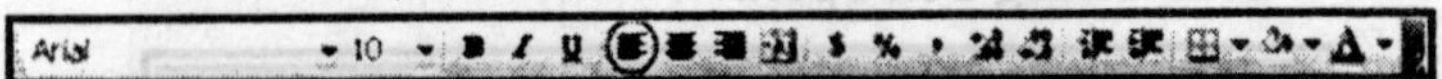

The red circle designates the Align Left icon.

ADDING BOLD, UNDERLINE, AND ITALIC

You can bold, underline, or italicize text in Microsoft

Excel. You can also combine these features – in other words, you can bold, underline, *and* italicize a single piece of text.

In the exercises that follow, you will learn three different methods for bolding, italicizing, or underlining text in Microsoft Excel. You will learn to bold, italicize, and underline by using the menu, the icons, and the shortcut keys.

Adding Bold by Using the Menu

- Type Bold in cell A2.
- Click the check mark located on the Formula bar. Clicking on the check mark is similar to pressing Enter.

- Choose *Format* > *Cells* from the menu. The Format Cells dialog box opens.
- Choose the Font tab.
- Click Bold in the Font Style box.
- Click OK. The word "Bold" should now be bolded.

Adding Italic by Using the Menu

- Type Italic in cell B2.
- Click the check mark located on the Formula bar. Clicking on the check mark is similar to pressing Enter.
- Choose *Format* > *Cells* from the menu. The Format Cells dialog box opens.
- Click Italic in the Font style box.
- Click OK. The word "Italic" is italicized.

Adding Underline by Using the Menu

Microsoft Excel provides several types on underlines. The exercise that follows illustrates some of them.

Single Underline

- Type Underline in cell C2.
- Click the check mark located on the Formula bar.

Clicking on the check mark is similar to pressing Enter.

- Choose *Format* > *Cells* from the menu. The Format Cells dialog box opens.
- Click to open the drop-down menu associated with the Underline box.
- Click Single.
- Click OK. The cell entry now has a single underline.

Double Underline

- Type Underline in cell D2.
- Click the check mark located on the Formula bar.
- Choose *Format* > *Cells* from the menu. The Format Cells dialog box opens.
- Click to open the drop-down menu associated with the Underline field.
- Click Double.
- Click OK. The cell entry now has a double underline.

Single Accounting

- Type Underline in cell E2.
- Click the check mark located on the Formula bar.
- Choose *Format* > *Cells* from the menu. The Format Cells dialog box will open.
- Click to open the drop-down menu associated with the Underline field.
- Click Single Accounting.
- Click OK. The cell entry now has a single accounting underline.

Double Accounting

- Type Underline in cell F2.
- Click the check mark located on the Formula bar.
- Choose *Format* > *Cells* from the menu. The Format Cells dialog box will open.
- Click to open the drop-down menu associated with the Underline field.
- Click Double Accounting.

- Click OK. The cell entry now has a double accounting underline.

Adding Bold, Underline, and Italic by Using the Menu

- Move the cursor to cell G3.
- Type All three.
- Click the check mark located on the Formula bar.
- Choose *Format* > *Cells* from the menu. The Format Cells dialog box opens.
- Choose the Font tab.
- Click Bold Italic in the Font Style box.
- Click to open the drop-down menu associated with the Underline field. Then click Single.
- Click OK. The words "All three" are now bolded, italicized, and underlined.

Removing Bolding and Italics by Using the Menu

- Highlight cells A2 to B2. Place your cursor in cell B2. Press the F8 key. Press the right arrow key once.
- Choose *Format* > *Cells* from the menu. The Format Cells dialog box opens.
- Click Regular in the Font style box.
- Click OK. Cell A2 is no longer be bolded. Cell B2 is no longer italized.

Removing an Underline by Using the Menu

- Move to cell C2.
- Choose *Format* > *Cells* from the menu. The Format Cells dialog box opens.
- Click to open the drop-down menu associated with the Underline field. Then click None.
- Click OK. The underdelined is removed.

Adding Bold by Using the Icon

- Type Bold in cell A3.
- Click the check mark located on the Formula bar.

- Click the Bold icon, which is on the Formatting toolbar.
- Click again on the Bold icon if you wish to remove the bolding.

Adding Italic by Using the Icon

- Type Italic in cell B3.
- Click the check mark located on the Formula bar.

- Click the Italic icon, which is on the Formatting toolbar.
- Click again on the Italic icon if you wish to remove the italics.

Adding Underline by Using the Icon

- Type Underline in cell C3.
- Click the check mark located on the Formula bar.

- Click the Underline icon, which is on the Formatting toolbar.
- Click again on the Underline icon if you wish to remove the underline.

Adding Bold, Underline, and Italic by Using Icons

- Type All Three in cell D3.
- Click the check mark located on the Formula bar.
- Click the Bold icon.
- Click the Italic icon.
- Click the Underline icon.

Alternate Method: Adding Bold by Using Shortcut Keys

- Type Bold in cell A4.
- Click the check mark located on the Formula bar.
- Hold down the Ctrl key while pressing "b" (Ctrl-b).
- Press Ctrl-b again if you wish to remove the bolding.

Adding Italic by Using Shortcut Keys

- Type Italic in cell B4.

- Click the check mark located on the Formula bar.
- Hold down the Ctrl key while pressing "i" (Ctrl-i).
- Press Ctrl-i again if you wish to remove the italic formatting.

Adding Underline by Using Shortcut Keys

- Type Underline in cell C4.
- Click the check mark located on the Formula bar.
- Hold down the Ctrl key while pressing "u" (Ctrl-u).
- Press Ctrl-u again, if you wish to remove the underline.

Adding Bold, Underline, and Italic by Using Shortcut Keys

- Type All three in cell D4.
- Click the check mark located on the Formula bar.
- Hold down the Ctrl key while pressing "b" (Ctrl-b).
- Hold down the Ctrl key while pressing "i" (Ctrl-i).
- Hold down the Ctrl key while pressing "u" (Ctrl-u).

CHANGING THE FONT, FONT SIZE, AND FONT COLOUR

You can change the Font, Font Size, and Font Colour of the data you enter.

Changing the Font

- Type Times New Roman in cell A5.
- Click the check mark located on the Formula bar.
- Choose *Format* > *Cells* from the menu. The Format Cells dialog box opens.
- Choose the Font tab. All of the Fonts listed in the Font box are available to you.
- Find and click Times New Roman in the Font box.
- Click OK. The font changes from Arial to Times New Roman.

Changing the Font Size

- Place the cursor in cell A5.

- Choose *Format* > *Cells* from the menu. The Format Cells dialog box opens.
- Choose the Font tab.
- Click 16 in the Size box.
- Click OK. The font size changes to 16.

Changing the Font Colour

- Place the cursor in cell A5.
- Choose *Format* > *Cells* from the menu. The Format Cells dialog box opens.
- Choose the Font tab.

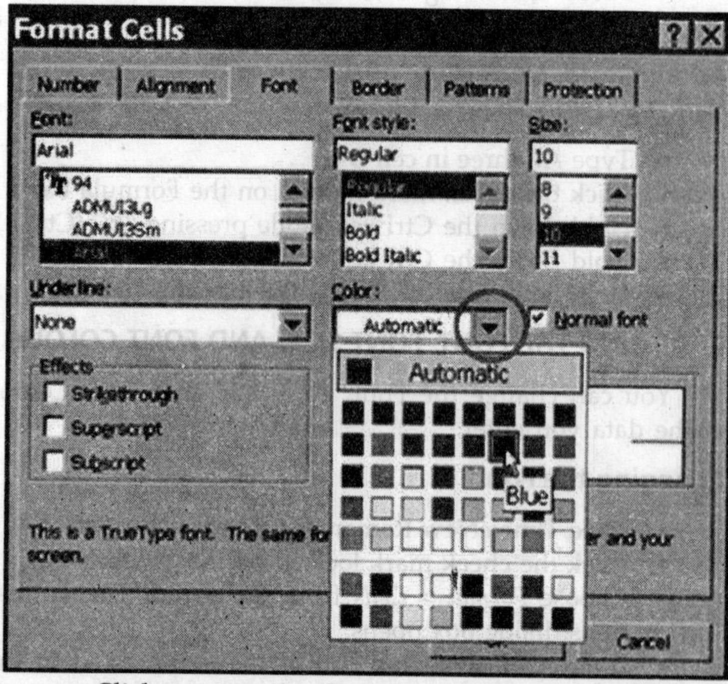

- Click to open the drop-down menu associated with the colour field.
- Click Blue.
- Click OK. The font colour changes to blue.

Changing the Font Colour by Using the Icon

- Place the cursor in cell A5.

- Click the down arrow next to the Font Colour icon.

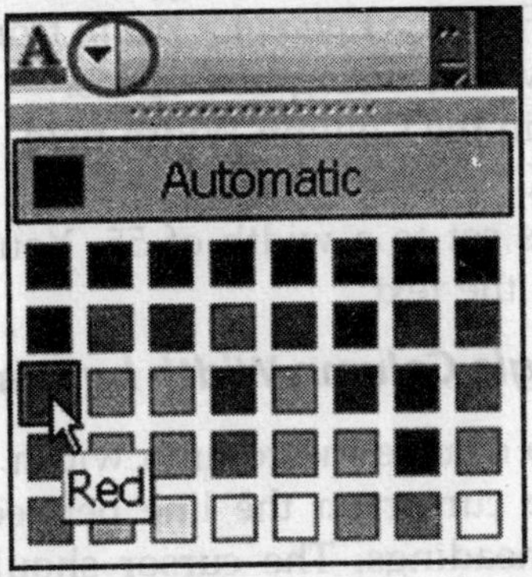

- Click on Red. Your font clolor changes to red.

WORKING WITH LONG TEXT

Whenever you type text that is too long to fit into a cell, Microsoft Excel attempts to display all the text. It left-aligns the text regardless of the alignment that has been assigned to it, and it borrows space from the blank cells to the right. However, a long text entry will never write over cells that already contain entries — instead, the cells that contain entries cuts off the long text.

- Move the cursor to cell A6.
- Type Now is the time for all good men to go to the aid of their army.
- Press Enter. Everything that does not fit into cell A6 spills over into the adjacent cell.
- Move the cursor to cell B6.
- Type TEST.
- Press Enter. The entry in cell A6 is cut off.
- Move the cursor to cell A6.
- Look at the Formula bar. The text is still in the cell.

Changing a Single Column Width

Earlier you increased the column width of every column on the worksheet. You can also increase individual column widths. If you increase the column width, you will be able to see the long text.

- Make sure the cursor is anywhere under column A.
- Choose *Format > Column > Width* from the menu. The column width dialog box opens.
- Type 55 in the Column Width field.
- Click OK.

Column A is set to a width of 55. You should now be able to see all of the text.

Changing a Single Column Width by Dragging

You can also change the column width with the cursor.

- Place the cursor on the line between the B and C column headings. The cursor should look like the one displayed here, with two arrows.

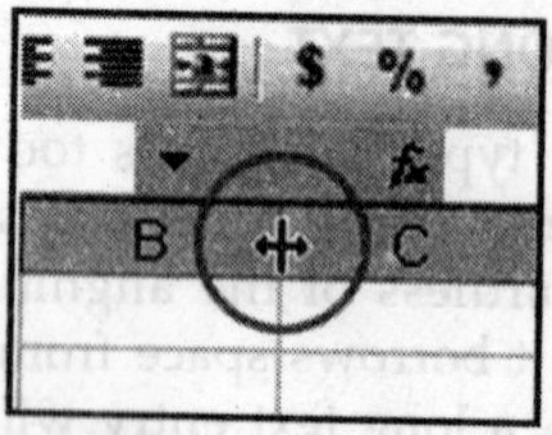

- Move your mouse to the right while holding down the left mouse button. The width indicator appears on the screen.

- Release the left mouse button when the width indicator shows approximately 40.

MOVING TO A NEW WORKSHEET

In Microsoft Excel, each workbook is made up of several

worksheets. Before moving to the next topic, move to a new worksheet.

- Click Sheet 2 in the lower left corner of the screen.

SETTING THE ENTER KEY DIRECTION

In Microsoft Excel, you can specify which direction the cursor moves when you press the Enter key. You can have the cursor move up, down, left, right, or not at all. You will now make sure the cursor is set to move down when you press the Enter key.

- Choose *Tools* > *Options* from the menu. The Options dialog box opens.
- Choose the Edit tab.
- Make sure there is a check mark in the "Move Selection after Enter" box.
- If Down is not selected, click to open the Direction drop-down box. Click Down.
- Click OK.

MAKING NUMERIC ENTRIES

In Microsoft Excel, you can enter numbers and mathematical formulas into cells. When a number is entered into a cell, you can perform mathematical calculations such as addition, subtraction, multiplication, and division. When entering a mathematical formula, precede the formula with an equal sign.

Use the following to indicate the type of calculation you wish to perform:

+ Addition
- Subtraction
* Multiplication
/ Division
^ Exponential

PERFORMING MATHEMATICAL CALCULATIONS

The following exercises demonstrate how to perform mathematical calculations.

Addition

- Move your cursor to cell A1.
- Type 1.
- Press Enter.
- Type 1 in cell A2.
- Press Enter.
- Type =A1+A2 in cell A3.
- Press Enter. Cell A1 has been added to cell A2, and the result is shown in cell A3.

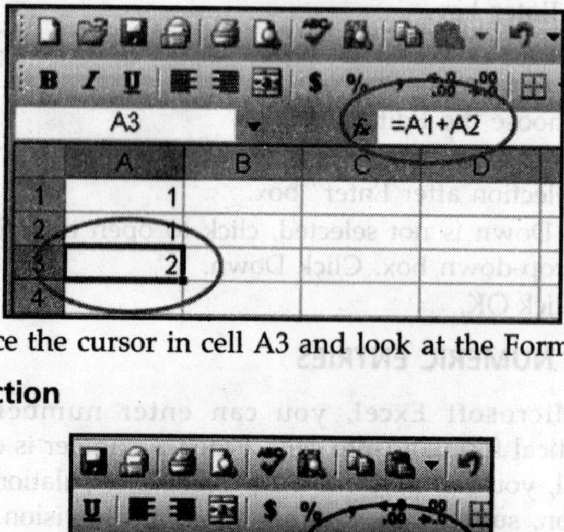

Place the cursor in cell A3 and look at the Formula bar.

Subtraction

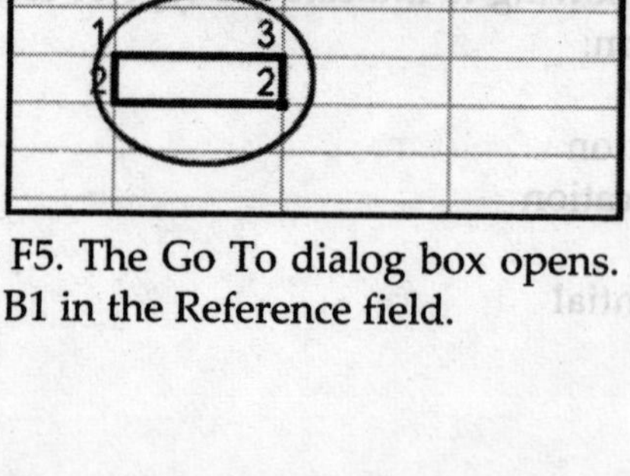

- Press F5. The Go To dialog box opens.
- Type B1 in the Reference field.

- Press Enter. The cursor should move to cell B1.
- Type 5 in cell B1.
- Press Enter.
- Type 3 in cell B2.
- Press Enter.
- Type =+B1- B2 in cell B3.
- Press Enter. Cell B1 has been subtracted from B2, and the result is shown in cell B3.

Place the cursor in cell B3 and look at the Formula bar.

Multiplication

- Hold down the Ctrl key while you press "g" (Ctrl-g). The Go To dialog box opens.
- Type C1 in the Reference field.
- Press Enter. You should now be in cell C1.
- Type 2 in cell C1.
- Press Enter.
- Type 3 in cell C2.
- Press Enter.
- Type =C1*C2 in cell C3.
- Press Enter. Cell C1 is multiplied by cell C2 and the result is displayed in cell C3.

Place the cursor in cell C3 and look at the Formula bar.

Division

- Press F5.
- Type D1 in the Reference field.
- Press Enter. You should now be in cell D1.

- Type 6 in cell D1.
- Press Enter.
- Type 3 in cell D2.
- Press Enter.
- Type =D1/D2 in cell D3.
- Press Enter. Cell D1 is divided by cell D2 and the result is displayed in cell D3.

Place the cursor in cell D3 and look at the Formula bar.

The AutoSum Icon

The AutoSum icon on the Standard toolbar automatically adds a column of numbers. The following illustrates the SUM function:

- Go to cell F1.
- Type 3. Press Enter.
- Type 3. Press Enter.
- Type 3. Press Enter.
- Click the AutoSum button, which is located on the Standard toolbar.

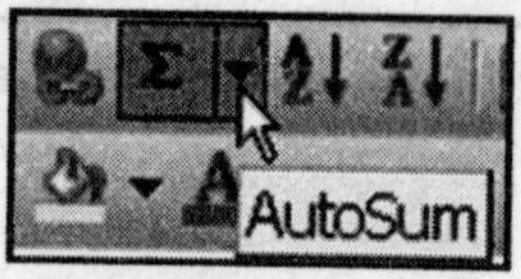

- F1 to F3 should now be highlighted.
- Press Enter. Cells F1 through F3 are added.

AUTOMATIC CALCULATION

If you have automatic calculation turned on, Microsoft Excel recalculates the worksheet as you change cell entries. You can check to make sure automatic calculation is turned on.

Setting Automatic Calculation

- Choose *Tools* > *Options* from the menu.
- Choose the Calculation tab.
- Select Automatic if it is not already selected.
- Click OK.

Trying Automatic Calculation

Make the changes outlined below and note how Microsoft Excel automatically recalculates.

- Move to cell A1.
- Type 2. Press the Enter key. The results shown in cell A3 have changed. The number in cell A1 has been added to the number in cell A2 and the results display in cell A3.
- Move to cell B1.
- Type 6.
- Press the Enter key. The results shown in cell B3 have changed. The number in cell B1 has been subtracted from the number in cell B2 and the results display in cell B3.
- Move to cell C1.
- Type 4. Press the Enter key. The results shown in cell C3 have changed. The number in cell C1 has been multiplied by the number in cell C2 and the results display in cell C3.
- Move to cell D1.
- Type 12. Press the Enter key. The results shown in cell D3 have changed. The number in cell D1 has been divided by the number in cell D2 and the results display in cell D3.

Chapter 11

Excel Functions

NUMBERS AND MATHEMATICAL CALCULATIONS

Microsoft Excel has many functions that you can use. Functions allow you to quickly and easily find an average, the highest number, the lowest number, a count of the number of items in a list, and make many other useful calculations.

REFERENCE OPERATORS

Reference operators refer to a cell or a group of cells. There are two types of reference operators, *range* and *union*.

A range reference refers to all the cells between and including the reference. A range reference consists of two cell addresses separated by a colon. The reference A1:A3 includes cells A1, A2, and A3. The reference A1:C3 includes A1, A2, A3, B1, B2, B3, C1, C2, and C3.

A union reference includes two or more references. A union reference consists of two or more cell addresses separated by a comma. The reference A7,B8,C9 refers to cells A7, B8, and C9.

FUNCTIONS

Microsoft Excel has a set of prewritten formulas called *functions*. Functions differ from regular formulas in that you supply the value but not the operators, such as +, -, *, or /. For example, you can use the SUM function to add. When using a function, remember the following:

Use an equal sign to begin a formula.

Specify the function name.

Enclose arguments within parentheses.

Use a comma to separate arguments.

Here is an example of a function:

=SUM(2,13,A1,B27)

In this function:

The equal sign begins the function.

SUM is the name of the function.

2, 13, A1, and B27 are the arguments.

Parentheses enclose the arguments.

A comma separates the arguments.

The SUM function adds the arguments together. In the exercises that follow, we will look at various functions.

TYPING A FUNCTION

- Open Microsoft Excel.
- Type 12 in cell B1.
- Press Enter.
- Type 27 in cell B2.
- Press Enter.
- Type 24 in cell B3.
- Press Enter.
- Type =SUM(B1:B3) in cell A4.
- Press Enter. Microsoft Excel sums cells B1 to B3.

Entering a Function by Using the Menu

- Type 150 in cell C1.
- Press Enter.
- Type 85 in cell C2.
- Press Enter.
- Type 65 in cell C3.
- Press Enter. Your cursor should be in cell C4.
- Choose *Insert > Function* from the menu.
- Choose Math & Trig in the Or Select A Category box.
- Click Sum in the Select A Function box.

- Click OK. The Functions Arguments dialog box opens.
- Type C1:C3 in the Number1 field, if it does not automatically appear.
- Click OK. Microsoft Excel sums cells C1 to C3.
- Move to cell A4.
- Type the word Sum.
- Press Enter.

CALCULATING AN AVERAGE

You can use the AVERAGE function to calculate the average of a series of numbers.

- Move your cursor to cell A6.
- Type Average.Press the right arrow key to move to cell B6.
- Type =AVERAGE(B1:B3).
- Press Enter. The average of cells B1 to B3, which is 21, will appear.

Calculating an Average by Using the Sum Icon

In Microsoft Excel XP, you can use the Sum icon to calculate an average.

- Move your cursor to cell C6.
- Click the drop-down arrow next to the Sum icon.
- Click Average.
- Highlight C1 to C3.
- Press Enter. The average of cells C1 to C3, which is 100, appears.

Calculating Min

You can use the MIN function to find the lowest number in a series of numbers.

- Move your cursor to cell A7.
- Type Min.
- Press the right arrow key to move to cell B7.
- Type = MIN(B1:B3).

- Press Enter. The lowest number in the series, which is 12 appears.

Calculating Max

You can use the MAX function to find the highest number in a series of numbers.

- Move your cursor to cell A8.
- Type Max.
- Press the right arrow key to move to cell B8.
- Type = MAX(B1:B3).
- Press Enter. The highest number in the series, which is 27, appears.

You can also use the drop-down menu next to the Sum icon to calculate minimums and maximums.

Calculating Count

You can use the count function to count the number of items in a series.

- Move your cursor to cell A9.
- Type Count
- Press the right arrow key to move to cell B9.
- Click the down arrow next to the Sum icon.
- Click Count.
- Highlight B1 to B3.
- Press Enter. The number of items in the series, which is 3 appears.

FILLING CELLS AUTOMATICALLY

You can use Microsoft Excel to fill cells automatically with a series. For example, you can have Excel automatically fill in times, the days of the week or months of the year, years, and other types of series.

Days of the week and months of the year fill in a similar fashion. The following demonstrates filling the days of the week:

- Move to Sheet2.
- Move to cell A1.
- Type Sun.

- Move to cell B1.
- Type Sunday.
- Highlight cells A1 to B1.
- Bold cells A1 to B1.
- Find the small black square in the lower right corner of the highlighted area. This is called the Fill Handle.
- Grab the Fill Handle and drag with your mouse to fill cell A1 to B24. Note how the days of the week fill the cells in a series. Also, note that the Auto Fill Options icon appears.

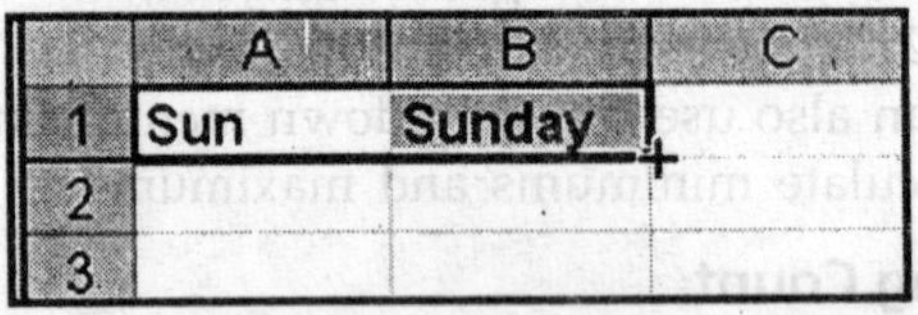

- Click the Auto Fill Options icon.
- Choose the Copy Cells radio button. The entry in cells A1 and B1 are copied to all the cells highlighted.
- Click the Auto Fill Options icon again.
- Choose the Fill Series radio button. The cells fill as a series from Sunday to Saturday again.
- Click the Auto Fill Options icon again.
- Choose the Fill Without Formatting radio button. The cells fill as a series from Sunday to Saturday, but the entries are not bolded.
- Click the Auto Fill Options icon again.
- Choose the Fill Weekdays radio button. The cells fill as a series from Monday to Friday.

Some of the entries in column B are too long to fit in the column. You can quickly adjust the column width to fit the longest entry.

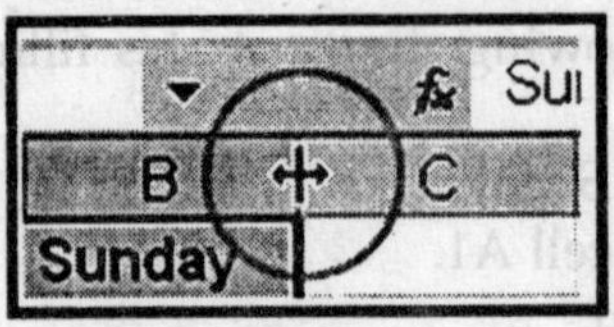

- Move your cursor over the line that separates column B and C. The Width Indicator appears.
- Double-click. The Column adjusts to fit the longest entry.

The following demonstrates filling time:

- Type 1:00 into cell C1.
- Grab the Fill Handle and drag with your mouse to highlight cells A1 to A24. Note that each cell fills using military time.
- Press Esc and then click anywhere on the worksheet to remove the highlighting.

To change the format of the time:

- Select cells C1 to C24.
- Choose *Format* > *Cells* from the menu.
- Choose the Number tab.
- In the Category box, choose Time.
- In the Type box, choose 1:30 PM.
- Click OK. The time is no longer in military time.

You can also fill numbers.

Type a 1 in cell D1.

- Grab the Fill Handle and drag with your mouse to highlight cells D1 to D24. The number 1 fills each cell.
- Click the Auto Fill Options icon.
- Choose the Fill Series radio button. The cells fill as a series starting with 1, 2, 3.

Here is another interesting fill feature.

- Go to cell E1.
- Type Lesson 1.
- Grab the Fill Handle and drag with your mouse to highlight cells E1 to E24.

CREATING CHARTS

Using Microsoft Excel, you can represent numbers in a chart. You can choose from a variety of chart types. And, as you change your data, your chart will automatically update. You can use Microsoft Excel's Chart Wizard to take you through the process step-by-step.

CREATING A COLUMN CHART

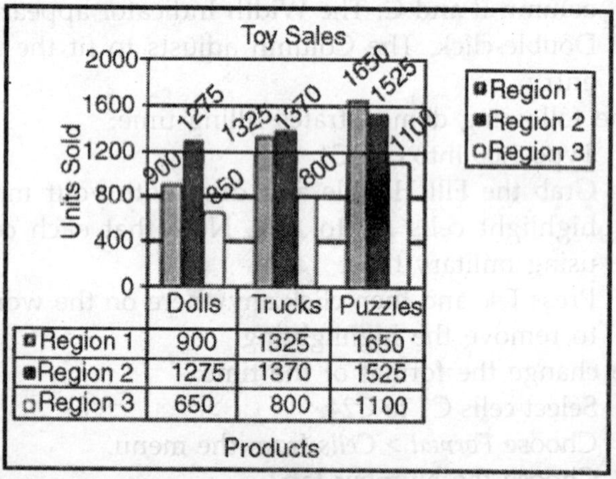

To create the column chart shown above, start by creating the spreadsheet below exactly as shown.

	A	B	C	D	E
1		Toy Sales			
2					
3	Products	Region 1	Region 2	Region 3	
4	Dolls	900	1275	650	
5	Trucks	1325	1370	800	
6	Puzzles	1650	1525	1100	
7					

After you have created the spreadsheet, you are ready to create your chart.

- Highlight cells A3 to D6. You must highlight all the cells containing the data you want in your chart. You should also include the data labels.
- Choose *Insert > Chart* from the menu.
- Click Column to select the type of chart you want to create.
- In the Chart Sub-type box, choose the Clustered Column icon to select the chart sub-type.
- Click Next.
- To place the product names on the x-axis, select the Columns radio button.
- Click Next.

- Type Toy Sales in the Chart Title field. Toy Sales will appear as the title of your chart.

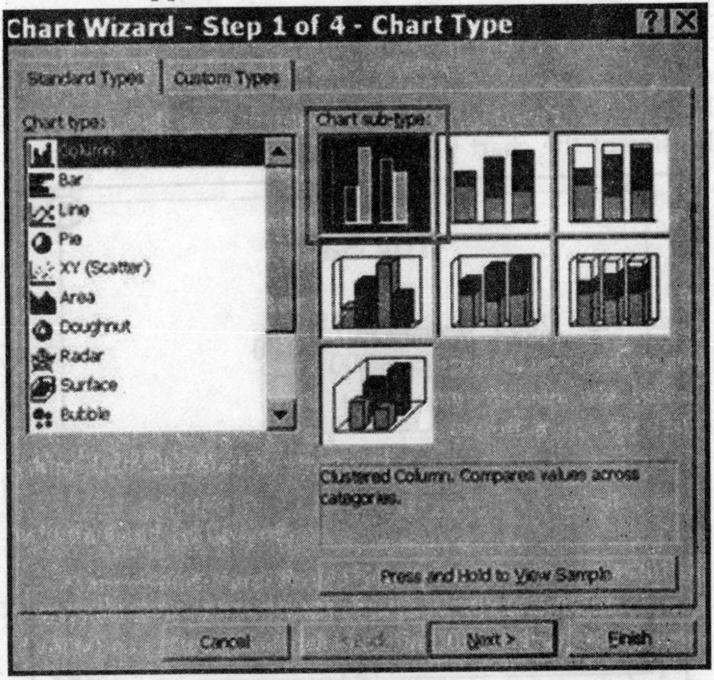

- Type Products in the Category (X) Axis field. Products will appear as your x-axis title.
- Type Units Sold in the Value (Y) Axis field. Units Sold will appear as your y-axis title.
- Choose the Data Labels tab.
- Select Value in the Labels Contain Frame to display the data labels as values.
- Choose the Data Table tab.
- Select Show Data Table. The data table will appear below your chart.
- Click Next.
- Click Finish
- Your chart will appear on the spreadsheet.

CHANGING THE SIZE AND POSITION OF A CHART

When you select a chart, handles appear on the right

and left sides, the top and bottom, and the corners of the chart. You can drag the handles on the top and bottom of the chart to increase or decrease the height of the chart. You can drag the handles on the left and right sides of the chart to increase or decrease the width of the chart. You can drag the handles on the corners of the chart to increase or decrease the size of the chart proportionally.

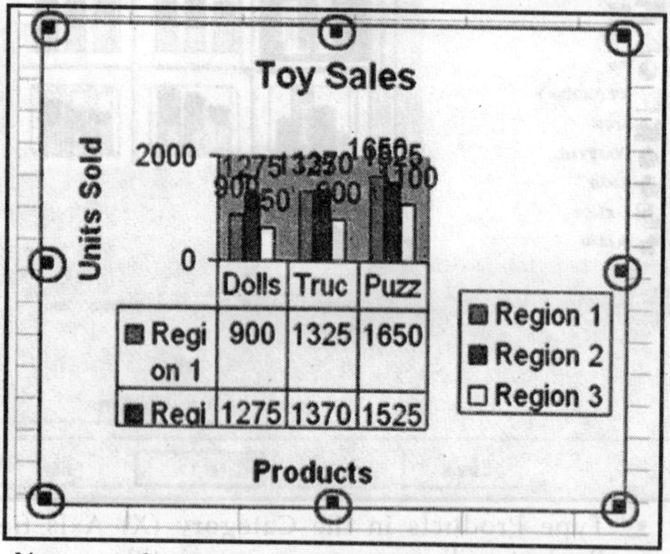

You can change the position of a chart by clicking on the chart and dragging

- Use the handles to adjust the size of your chart.
- Click the chart and drag to position the chart under the data.

MODIFYING CHART

You can modify your chart by using the Chart toolbar. If the Chart toolbar is not already available, choose View > Toolbars > Chart from the menu.

Fig. Chart Toolbar

To Change the Data Area Font Size

- Click the down arrow on the Chart toolbar. A drop-down menu opens.
- Choose Data Table from the drop-down menu.

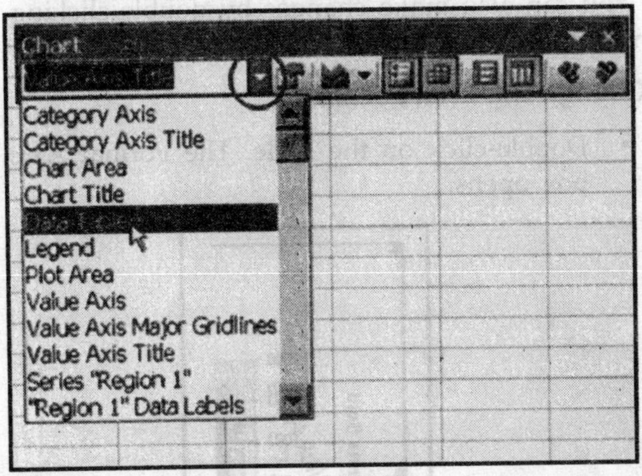

- Click the Options icon . Choose the Font tab.
- In the Size box, type 8.
- Click OK. Your font size is now 8.

To Change the Angle of the Data Labels

- Click the down arrow on the Chart toolbar. A drop-down menu opens.
- Choose "Region 1" Data Labels from the drop-down menu.
- Click the Angle Counter Clockwise icon 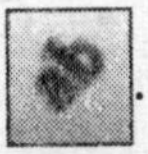. The Region 1 Data Labels are angled counter-clockwise.
- Repeat this process for Regions 2 and 3.

To Change the Font Size of the Region Data Labels

- Click the down arrow on the Chart toolbar. A drop-down menu opens.
- Choose "Region 1" Data Labels from the drop-down menu.

- Click the Options icon. Choose the Font tab.
- In the Size box, type 6.
- Click OK. Your font size is now 6.
- Repeat this process for Region 2 and 3.

You can also make changes by double-clicking on the item you want to change.

To Change the Chart Scale

- Double-click on the scale. The Format Axis dialog box opens.

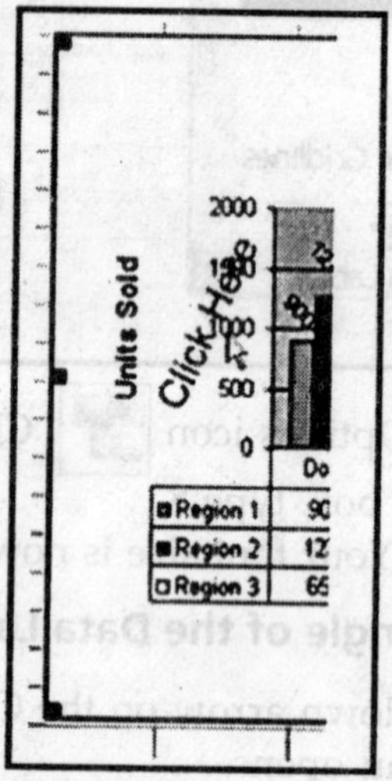

- Choose the Scale tab.
- Type 400 in the Major Unit field.
- Click OK. Your chart is now scaled in units of 400.

SAVING YOUR FILE

TO SAVE YOUR FILE

- Choose *File>Save* from the menu.
- Go to the directory in which you want to save your file.
- Type lesson4 in the File Name field.
- Click Save.

Chapter 12

Advance Excel

INTRODUCTION

This workbook has been prepared to help you create a Table report – an interactive table that automatically extracts, organizes, and summarizes your data. You can use this report to analyse the data, make comparisons, detect patterns and relationships, and discover trends. To assist your learning, a series of practical tasks are available in a separate document.

PIVOT TABLES

A Pivot Table organises and then summarises large amounts of data from any range that has labelled columns. Any number of column headings can act as category items. You can alternatively choose to create a Pivot Chart which will summarise the data in chart format rather than as a table. Details on creating a Pivot Chart are set out later in this section.

It is called a Pivot Table because the headings can be rotated around the data to view or summarise it in different ways. You can filter the data to display just the details for areas of interest.

The source data can be:

- An Excel worksheet database/list or any range that has labelled columns.
- A collection of ranges to be consolidated. The ranges must contain both labelled rows and columns.
- A database file created in an external application such as Access or Dbase.

The data in a PivotTable cannot be changed as they are the summary of other data. The data itself can be changed and the PivotTable recalculated thereafter. However, formatting changes such as bold, number formats, etc. can be made directly to the PivotTable data.

CREATING PIVOTTABLE

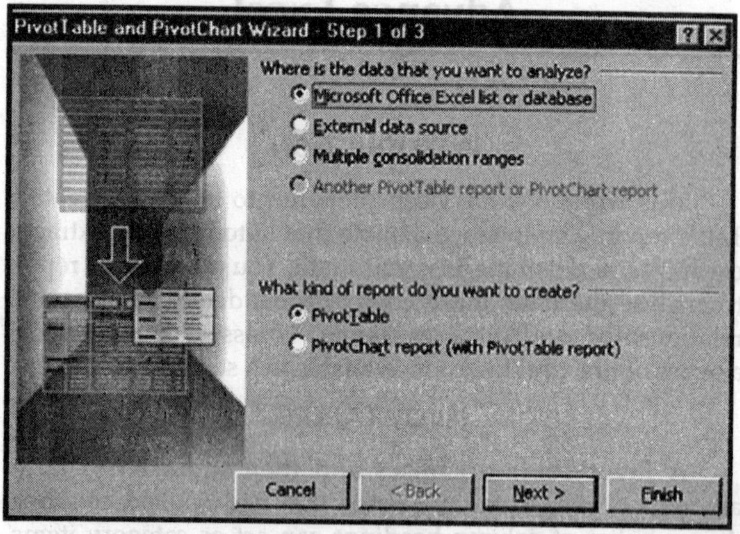

- Select a cell within your list.
- From the *Data* menu select PivotTable and PivotChart Report.
- Choose Microsoft Excel list or database.
- Choose PivotTable as the kind of report to be created.
- Click the *Next* button to go to step 2 of the wizard.
- This step verifies where your list data are. Provided the active cell was within your list when you launched the PivotTable wizard, the worksheet range will be your list.
- Click *Next*.
- Step 3 is where you need to decide whether you want to construct the PivotTable on the worksheet or as part of the wizard process. Whenever possible,

lay out the PivotTable or PivotChart directly on the worksheet so that you can easily view the data while you arrange the fields.

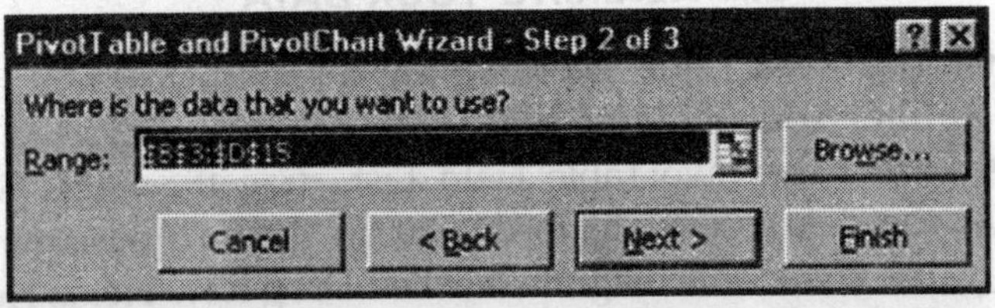

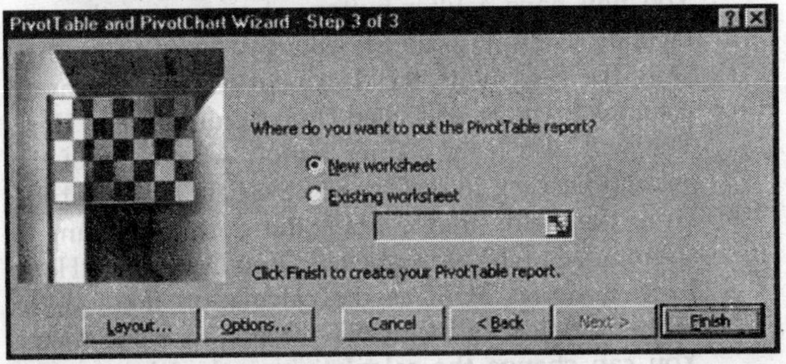

LAYOUT OF PIVOTTABLE

At Step 3 of the Wizard, select whether you want to put the PivotTable in a new worksheet or on the existing worksheet.

- If you choose to put the PivotTable into the existing worksheet, you need to make sure you tell the wizard where to place it. The easiest way to do this is to click into an area in the existing spreadsheet. The cell reference will appear in the *Cell Reference* box.
- Click on the Finish button.

- The PivotTable layout, PivotTable toolbar and PivotTable Field List will be displayed.

ARRANGING AND FILTERING YOUR DATA

- The PivotTable layout allows you to arrange and filter your data for analysis.
- From the PivotTable Field List, drag the fields with the data you want to display in rows to the area on the PivotTable diagram labelled Drop Row Fields Here. You will have a filter button ▾ as part of the row heading to display just the data you want to see.
- Drag the fields with the data you want to display in columns to the area labelled Drop Column Fields Here. You will also have a filter button ▾ as part of the column heading to display just the data you want to.
- Drag the fields that contain the data you want to summarise to the area labelled Drop Data Items Here. Excel assumes SUM as the calculation method for numeric fields and COUNT for non-numeric fields. You can change the calculation method by double-clicking the field in the DATA area.
- If you drag more than one data field, set the order by right-clicking a data field and then point to Order on the shortcut menu. Use the commands on the Order menu to move each field to the position you want.
- Drag the fields that you want to use as page fields to the area labelled Drop Page Fields Here. Page fields allow you to display one data item at a time using a drop-down list.
- To rearrange the fields at any time, simply drag them from one area to another.
- To remove a field, drag it out of the PivotTable report. Fields that you remove remain available in the field list on the PivotTable toolbar.

LAYOUT PIVOTTABLE USING THE WIZARD

- At Step 3 of the wizard, click on the Layout button.

- A list of column labels from your list will appear to the right of the dialog box.
- Drag and drop the field buttons for the ROW, COLUMN and PAGE labels. Each row, column or page can have more than one label(s). This can be omitted for that dimension provided at least one dimension has one.
- The PAGE area allows you to display one data item at a time using a drop-down list.
- Drag column labels to the DATA area for the fields to summarise. Excel assumes SUM as the calculation method for numeric fields and COUNT for non-numeric fields. You can change the calculation method by double-clicking the field in the DATA area.
- Format your summary field in the DATA area by double-clicking it and choosing the appropriate option. Click OK.
- Choose *Next* to move to the last step of the PivotTable wizard. Select a destination for your PivotTable. If you do not key in a destination cell, the result will be placed on a new Worksheet.
- Click *Finish.*
- Whichever method you have used, the PivotTable Report will be displayed.

PIVOT TABLE TOOLBAR

When you create or work with a PivotTable a PivotTable toolbar automatically displays.

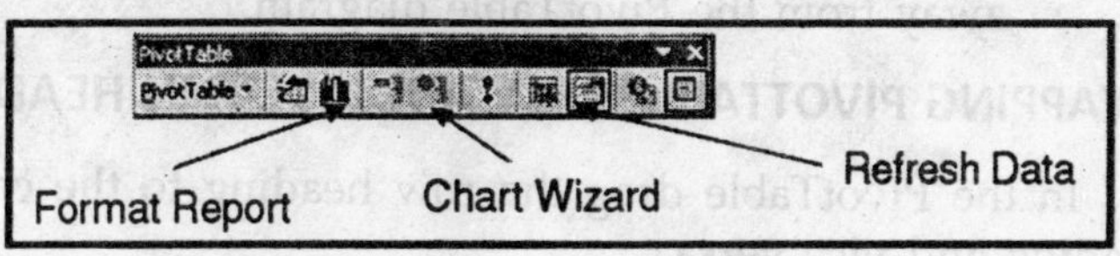

MANAGING PIVOTTABLES

When data is changed in the PivotTable source list, the PivotTable does not automatically recalculate.

Refreshing a PivotTable

- Select any cell in the PivotTable to be refreshed.
- From the *Data* menu, select Refresh Data or click the refresh button ! on the PivotTable toolbar.

Modifying a PivotTable

A PivotTable can be modified by adding or deleting fields. Fields can be added and removed from the PivotTable in the worksheet or in *Layout* view.

In the PivotTable Report in the Worksheet

- Select any cell in the PivotTable to be modified.
- To add a field simply drag the required field(s) from the PivotTable Field List into position on the PivotTable report.
- To remove a field, select the field name and drag it away from the PivotTable report.

In Layout View

- Make sure the worksheet with the PivotTable is in view.
- From the *Data* menu select PivotTable and PivotChart Report.
- Click on the Layout option in the dialog box.
- To add a field simply drag the required field(s) from the list of fields on the right into position on the diagram on the left of the screen.
- To remove a field, select the field name and drag it away from the PivotTable diagram.

SWAPPING PIVOTTABLE ROW AND COLUMN HEADINGS

In the PivotTable drag the row heading to the column heading and vice versa.

FORMATTING CELLS IN THE DATA AREA

- To format the cells in a PivotTable you need to click in the area in the PivotTable to be formatted and then on the PivotTable button on the PivotTable toolbar and select Field Settings.

- Click on the Number button.
- Select the Number format you want and click OK.
- Click OK again and your PivotTable will be re-formatted.

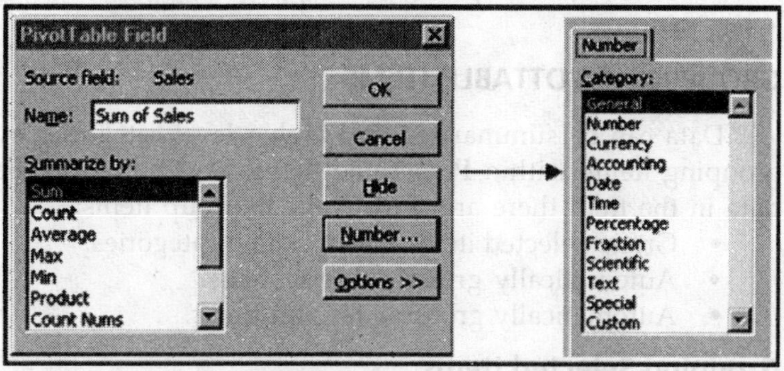

PIVOTTABLE OPTIONS

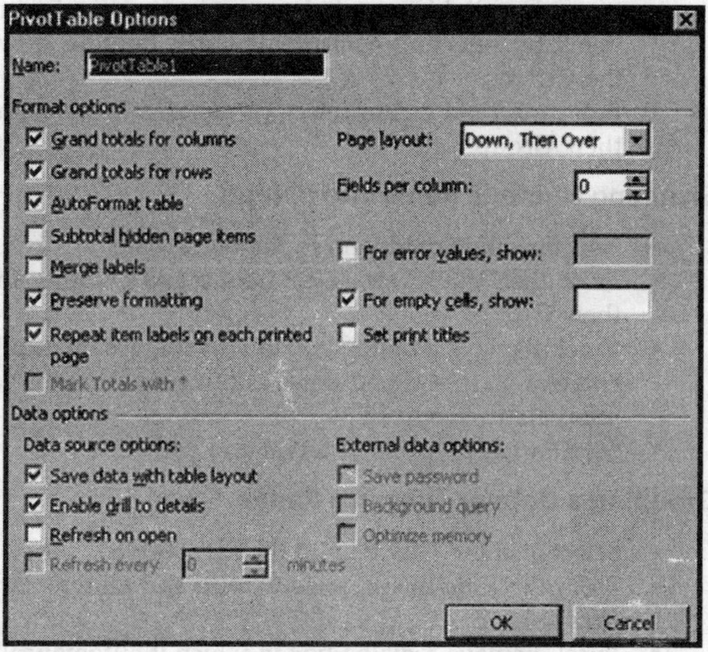

- Clicking on the Pivot Table button on the PivotTable toolbar, then selecting Table Options opens the PivotTable Options dialog box.
- You can set PivotTable print options to set page breaks and repeat rows and columns labels for PivotTable reports that appear in an indented format.

GROUPING PIVOTTABLE ITEMS

Data can be summarised into higher level categories by grouping items within PivotTable fields. Depending on the data in the field there are three ways to group items:

- Group selected items into specified categories.
- Automatically group numeric items.
- Automatically group dates and times.

Grouping Selected Items

- Select the items you wish to group. Select adjacent items by clicking and dragging, or non-adjacent items by selecting each item whilst holding down the Ctrl key.
- From the *Data* menu, select Group and Outline, and then Group.

Grouping Numeric Items into Ranges

- Select a single field item in the PivotTable.
- From the *Data* menu, select Group and Outline, and then Group.
- Excel displays a dialog box in which it automatically enters a start and end date. It also lists a number of intervals to group by.
- Select an appropriate interval and click *OK*.

Grouping a Date or Time in a Range

- Select a single field item in the PivotTable.
- From the *Data* menu, select Group and Outline, and then Group.
- Excel displays a dialog box in which it automatically

enters a start and end date. It also lists a number of intervals to group by.

- Select an appropriate interval and click *OK*.

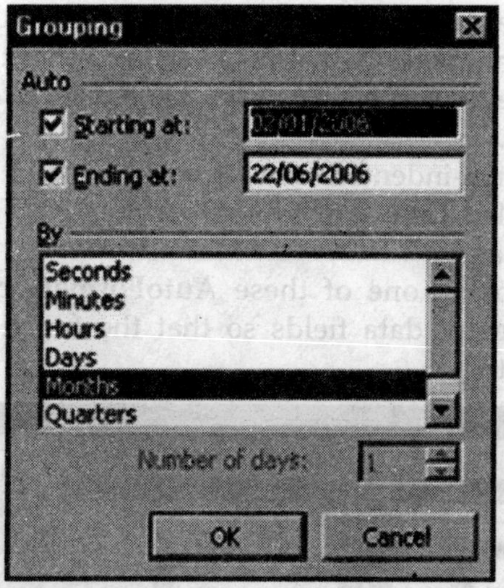

FORMATTING PIVOT TABLE REPORTS

There are two types of formatting that can be used when displaying PivotTable reports – indented formats or non-indented formats. Indented formats are similar to traditional banded or formatted database reports which make a large or complex PivotTable report easier to read.

The PivotTable wizard initially formats all PivotTable reports with a non-indented layout i.e., Table format. To change the layout:

- Click the Format report button on the PivotTable toolbar.
- For indented formats choose one of the formats labelled Report 1 to Report 10.
- Choosing one of these AutoFormats changes the report to indented format, changes the layout and applies character and cell formats.
- All column fields in the PivotTable report are moved so that they become row fields. Column fields also

move to the left of existing row fields so that the column fields become outer row fields.

- Data fields move to the right of row fields.
- If the name of the data field identifies the function for the field, the name changes so that the function name is omitted. For example *Sum of Sales* becomes *Sales*.
- For non-indented formats choose one of the formats labelled Table 1 to Table 10 or the PivotTable Classic format.
- Choosing one of these AutoFormats changes the names of data fields so that the function name is omitted.

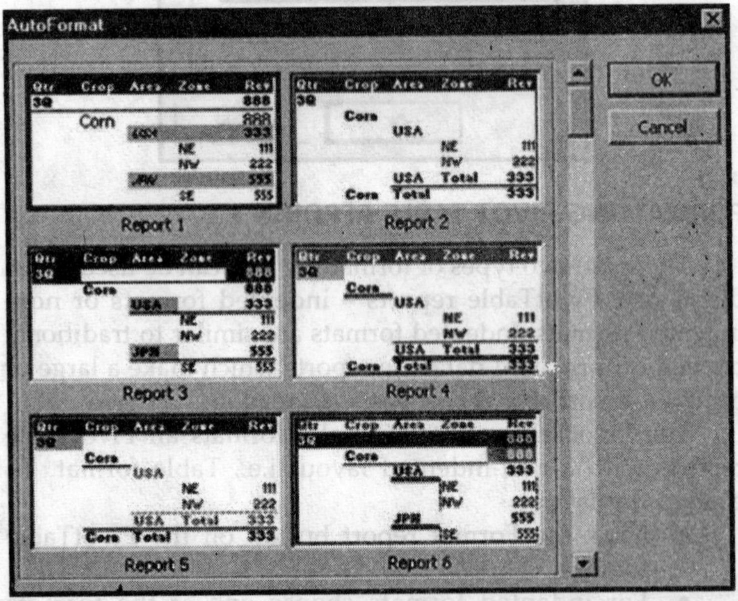

PIVOT CHART

When you create a Pivot Chart report, Excel automatically creates an associated PivotTable report. If you have an existing PivotTable report you can use it at any time to create a PivotChart Report which will reflect the view of that table.

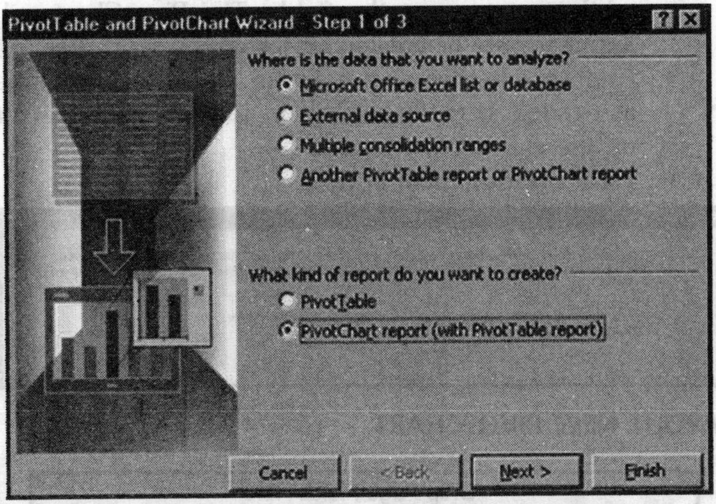

CREATING A PIVOTCHART

- Select a cell within your list. Then from the *Data* menu select PivotTable and PivotChart Report.
- Choose Microsoft Excel list or database.
- Choose PivotChart (with PivotTable) as the kind of report to be created.
- Click the *Next* button to go to step 2 of the wizard.
- This step verifies where your list data is. Provided the active cell was within your list when you launched the PivotTable wizard, the worksheet range will be your list.
- Click *Next*.
- If you have already created a PivotTable report from your current data, you will be asked if you want to base your next PivotTable report on the existing report. Click Yes if you want to save space or No if you want to create a separate PivotTable report.
- Step 3 is where you need to decide whether you want to construct the associated PivotTable on the worksheet or as part of the wizard process. Whenever possible lay out the PivotTable directly on the worksheet so that you can view the data

while you arrange the fields. The PivotChart will automatically be created on a separate worksheet.

- Choose whether you want to put the PivotTable associated with this chart on a new worksheet or on the existing worksheet.
- Click on the Finish button.

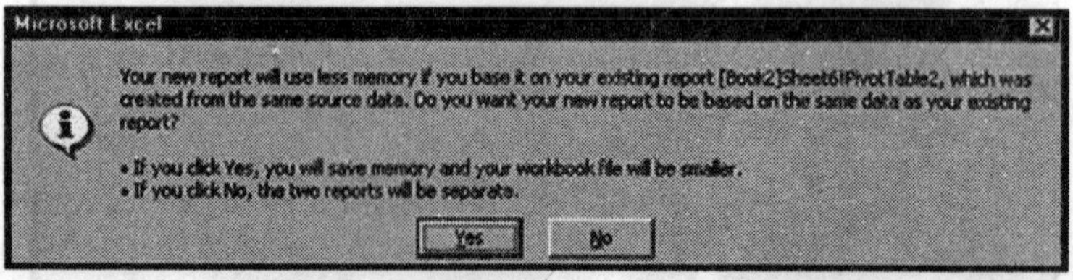

LAYOUT NEW PIVOTCHART

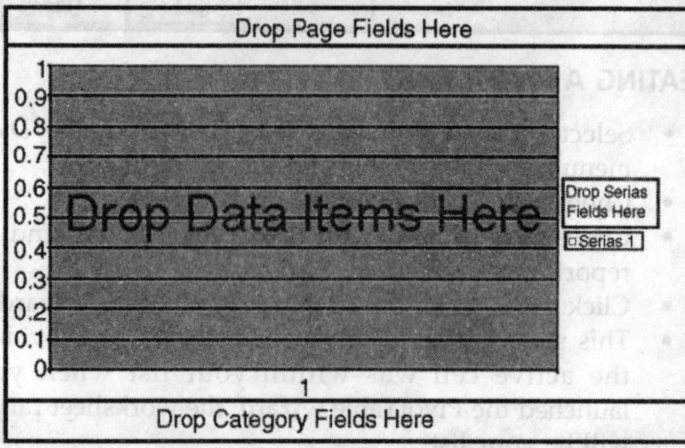

- The outline of the PivotChart as well as the PivotTable toolbar will now be displayed.
- From the group of buttons on the toolbar, drag the fields with the data you want to display in categories i.e., on the category axis to the area on the PivotChart diagram labelled Drop Category Fields Here. In the sample chart the Date field was selected.
- Drag the fields that contain the data you want to compare or measure to the area labelled Drop Data Items Here. The value axis will automatically be created and will be based on this data. In the sample

chart the Sales field was selected.

- Drag the fields that you want to use as page fields to the area labelled Drop Page Fields Here. Page fields allow you to display one data item at a time using a drop-down list. In the sample chart the Sales Rep field was selected.
- Drag the field that you want use as series fields to the area labelled Drop Series Fields here. In the sample chart the Customer field was selected.
- To rearrange the fields at any time, simply drag them from one area to another. To remove a field, drag it out of the PivotChart report. Fields that you remove remain available in the field list on the PivotTable toolbar.
- The resulting PivotChart report will then be displayed on screen and the associated PivotTable will be created in the location you specified.
- Each field on the PivotChart will have a filter button so that you can display just the data you want to see.

FORMATTING PIVOT CHART

Use the Excel Chart toolbar to format your chart as required

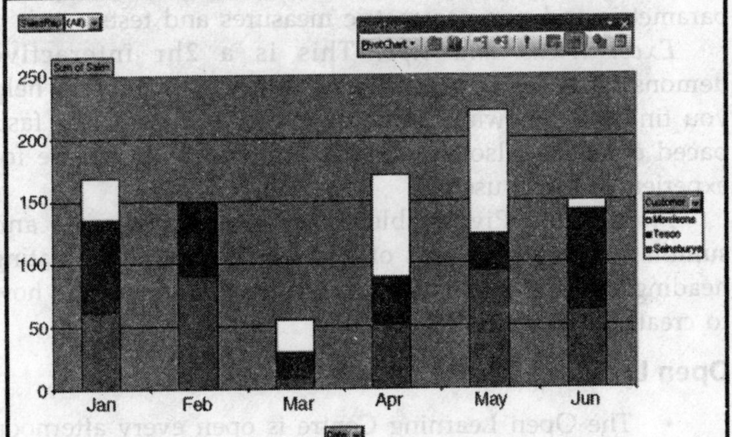

IT TRAINING

Information Systems detail as shown below:

Getting started with Excel: This 3hr course is for those who are new to spreadsheets or to Excel, and wish to explore the basic features of spreadsheet design. Note that it does not cover formulae and functions.

Getting more from Excel (no formulae or functions): This 3hr course is for users of Excel who wish to learn more about the non-mathematical features of Excel and to work more efficiently.

Using Excel to manage lists: This course is for those already familiar with Excel who would like to use some of its basic data-handling functions.

Excel formulae and functions: This 3hr course is aimed at introducing users, who are already familiar with the Excel environment, to formulae and functions.

Advanced formulae and functions: This course is aimed at competent Excel users who are already familiar with basic functions. It aims to introduce you to functions from several different categories so that you are equipped to try out other functions on your own.

Excel statistical functions: This course aims to introduce you to built-in Excel statistical functions and those in the Analysis ToolPak. The course covers major descriptive, parametric and non-parametric measures and tests.

Excel tricks and tips: This is a 2hr interactive demonstration of popular Excel shortcuts. It aims to help you find quicker ways of doing everyday tasks. This fast-paced course is also a good all-round revision course for experienced Excel users.

Pivot tables: Pivot tables allow you to organise and summarise large amounts of data by filtering and rotating headings around them. This 2hr course also shows you how to create pivot charts.

Open Learning Centre

- The Open Learning Centre is open every afternoon for members of staff who wish to obtain training on specific features in Excel on an individual or small group basis.

- If you want help with specific advanced features of Excel you will need to book a session in advance at: www.ucl.ac.uk/is/olc/bookspecial.htm
- Sessions will last for up to an hour, or possibly longer, depending on availability. Please let us know your previous levels of experience, and what areas you would like to cover, when arranging to attend.

Getting help

The following faculties have a dedicated Faculty Information Support Officer (FISO) who works with faculty staff on one-to-one help as well as group training, and general advice tailored to your subject discipline:

- Arts and Humanities
- The Bartlett
- Engineering
- Life Sciences
- Maths and Physical Sciences
- Social and Historical Sciences

Chapter – 13

Excel Charts and Macros

EXCEL CHART WIZARD

The sample data has been selected as a first step to making our chart. From here we will run the Chart Wizard. The Chart Wizard can be started by using the Chart Wizard button on the Standard command bar (left) or from the Chart... button on the Insert menu (shown below). The data can be selected prior to running the chart wizard, filled in while running the chart wizard, or added to the chart later.

The Chart Wizard runs through a series of steps that help you set up your chart.

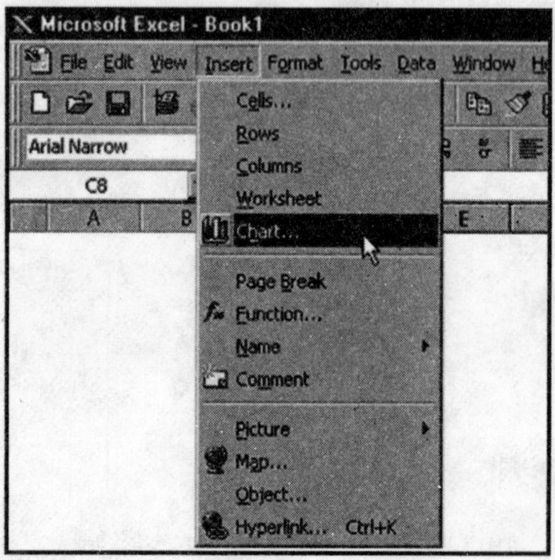

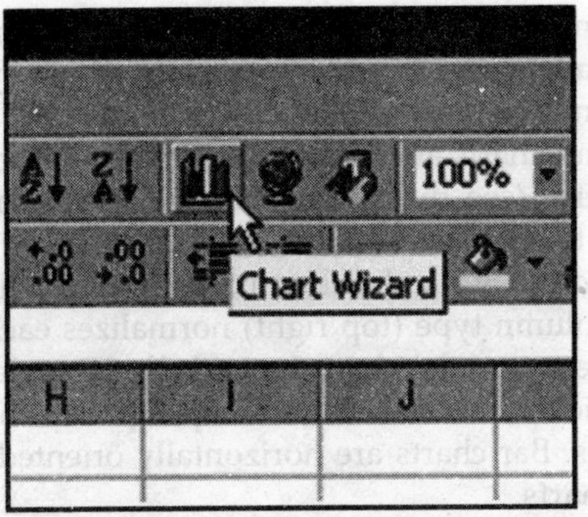

SELECT A CHART TYPE

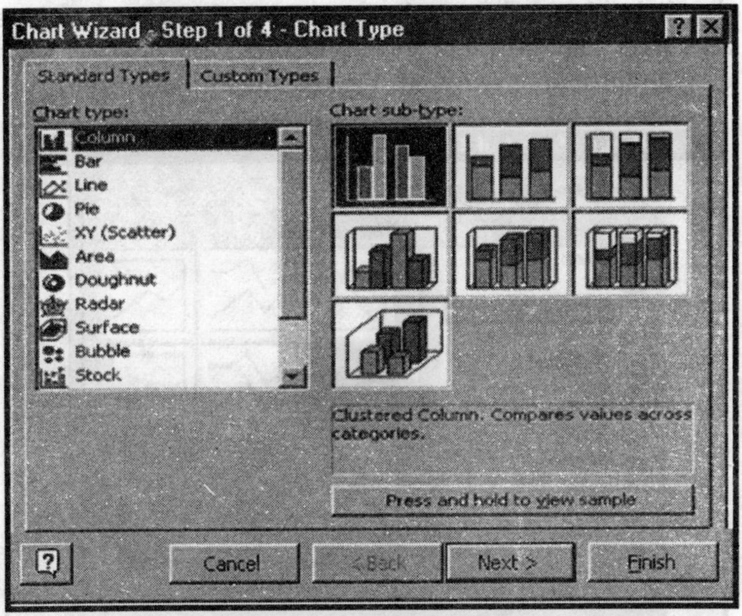

The Standard Types tab of Step 1 of the Chart Wizard shows a list of chart types on the left side, and several chart sub-types on the right. The Custom Types tab has a number of built-in custom types of charts, including several combination charts (not an exhaustive list: Roll

Your Own Combination Charts elsewhere on this site). You can add your favourite custom chart types to the User-Defined list.

Column charts are among the most common chart types you will use (see dialog box below). The two commonly used sub-types are the Clustered Column type (top left option) and the Stacked Column type (top middle); the 100% Stacked Column type (top right) normalizes each stack so it reaches the top of the chart. I avoid the 3D styles, because I find it difficult to line the column tops up with the tick marks on the axes. Bar charts are horizontally oriented versions of column charts.

Line charts are also commonly used in Excel. The default Line-With-Markers is probably most common (selected in the dialog box below); other options include Stacked Line and 100% Stacked Line, and all of these are available with or without markers. Again, I avoid the 3D Line type.

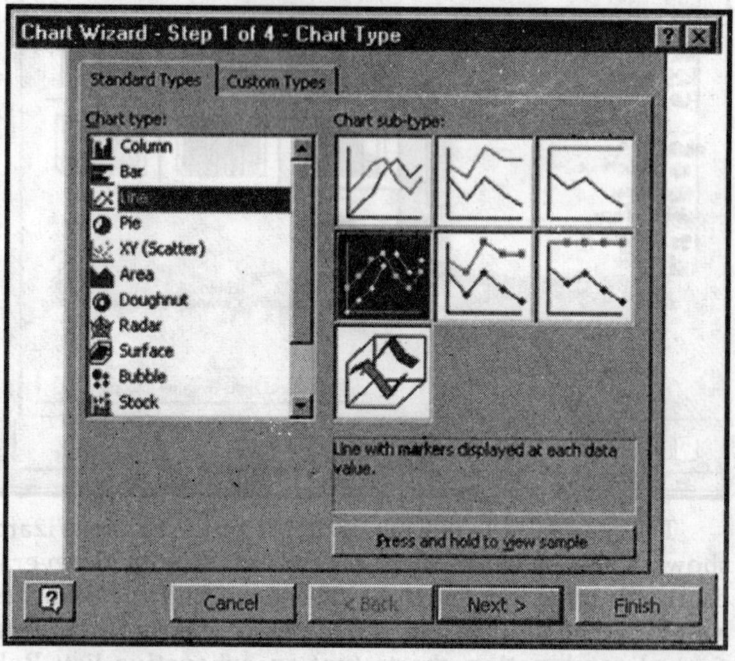

The Category (X) values in a line chart are treated as

equally-spaced non-numeric categories, unless a time-scale category axis is selected in Step 3-Chart Options, and points are plotted in order from left to right.

For a discussion of X axis types, X Axis: Category vs. Value; for a comparison of Line charts and XY Scatter charts, see my article, Scatter Chart or Line Chart?, in the Tech Traxweb magazine.

The XY (Scatter) Chart is the type I use most often. In addition to the default Markers-Only style, you can select smoothed or straight line connectors, with or without markers, as shown below. In a Scatter chart, both the X and Y values are treated as continuously variable numeric values. A logarithmic X axis can only be produced in an XY chart.

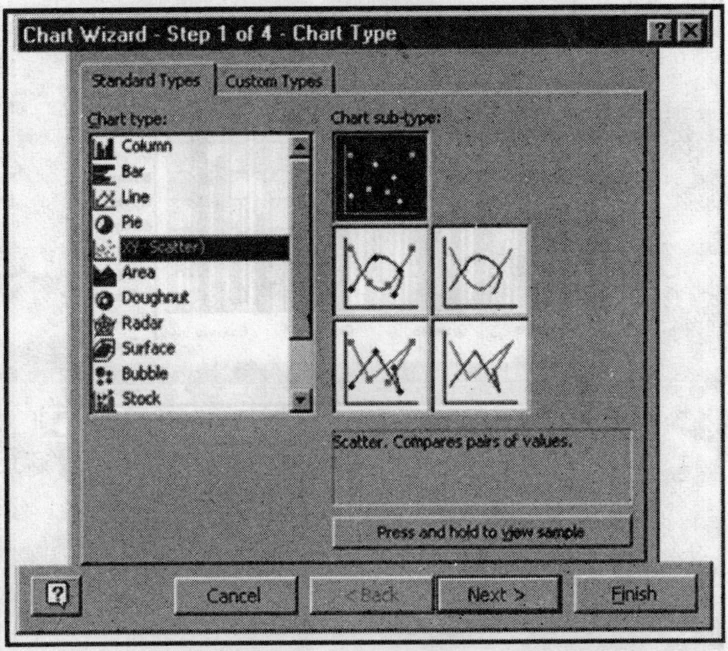

Excel offers a number of other chart types. Area charts are similar to line charts, with the areas under the lines filled in with some colour pattern. You can make several versions of Pie charts, and Doughnut charts are similar, but allow multiple series, plotted concentrically. Bubble charts allow an additional value to be plotted for each point, where the diameter of the circle representing the point is sized according to the third variable.

Stock charts let you plot high, low, and closing stock prices, with some options allowing opening prices and additional series, representing volume or a market index. Cylinder, Cone, and Pyramid charts are 3D Column charts which use other shapes instead of rectangular columns. You are encouraged to experiment with these chart types outside of this tutorial.

SOURCE DATA

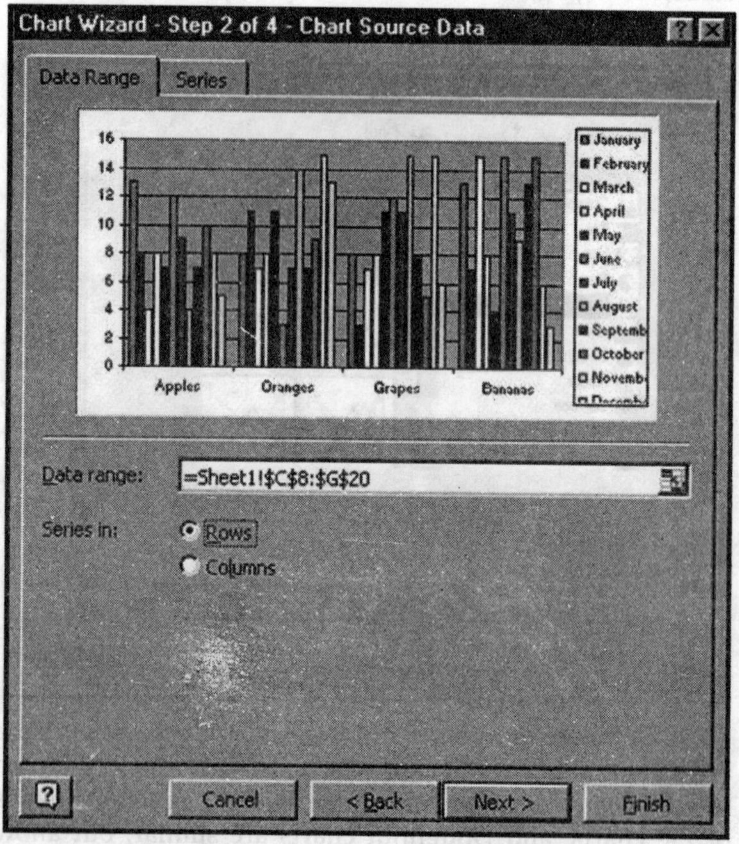

The Data Range tab gives you a preview of the chart style you selected in Step 1, indicating where the chart's source data range is, and allowing you to plot by row or by column.

The first dialog box below shows a column chart, plotted by rows. The second shows an area chart plotted by columns.

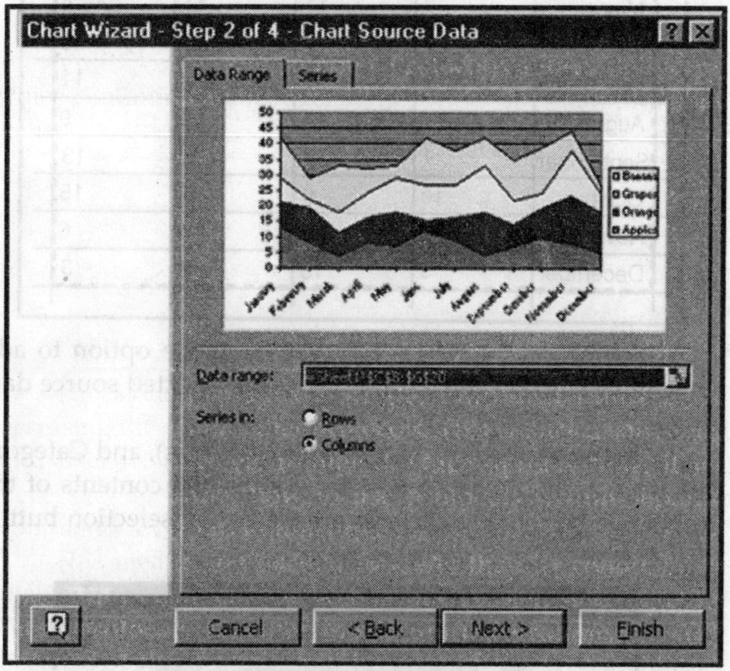

If you click in the Data range box, or click on the Range selection button, the dialog box shrinks to the size of just the data range box, obscuring less of the worksheet, so you are able to adjust this range with your mouse.

When the Source Data dialog box is activated, the source data range is highlighted by a "marching ants" border, shown in unanimated form below.

	Apples	Oranges	Grapes	Bananas
January	13	8	8	13
February	8	11	3	7
March	4	7	7	15
April	8	8	8	8
May	7	11	11	4
June	12	3	12	15
July	9	7	11	11
August	4	14	15	9
September	7	7	8	13
October	10	9	5	15
November	8	15	15	6
December	5	13	6	3

Clicking on the Series tab gives you the option to add or remove some of the data series in the selected source data range.

You can change the Name, Values (Y axis), and Category labels (X axis) of each series, by editing the contents of the respective box, or by clicking on the Range selection button , then dragging with the mouse.

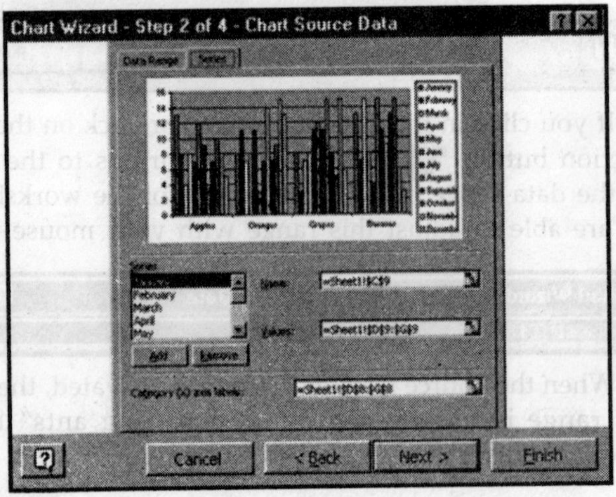

CHART OPTIONS

This step allows you to provide a title for the chart and for the chart axes, to select which and what kind of axes to put in your chart, and whether to show other options, such as gridlines, a legend, and data labels.

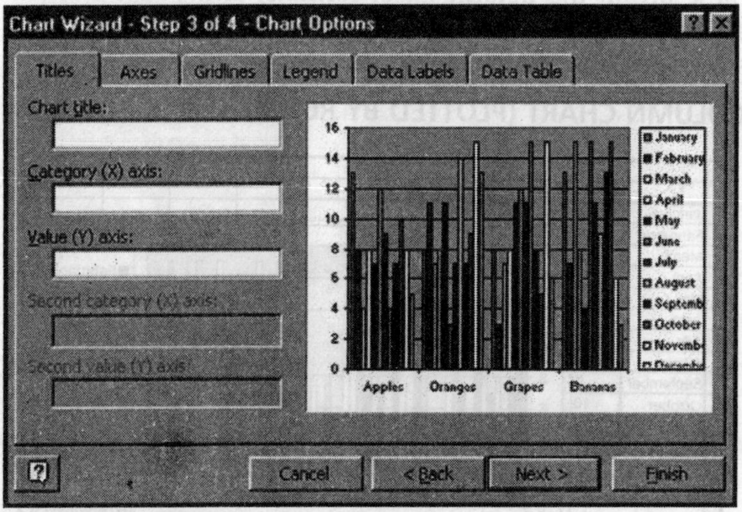

CHART LOCATION

Here you tell Excel where to place the chart. You can put the chart onto its own sheet with a name that you enter in the box (where it says "Chart1").

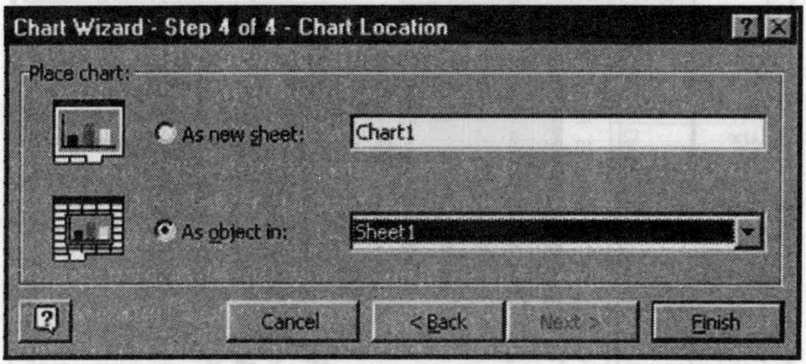

Or you can embed the chart as a chart object in one of

the existing worksheets (or chart sheets), which you select from the drop down list.

CREATING NEW CHART

Here are a few examples of finished charts. Of course, these are in the default Excel formats, and you'll want to adjust the fill colors, marker shapes, background colors, font sizes, and other formats.

COLUMN CHART (PLOTTED BY ROWS)

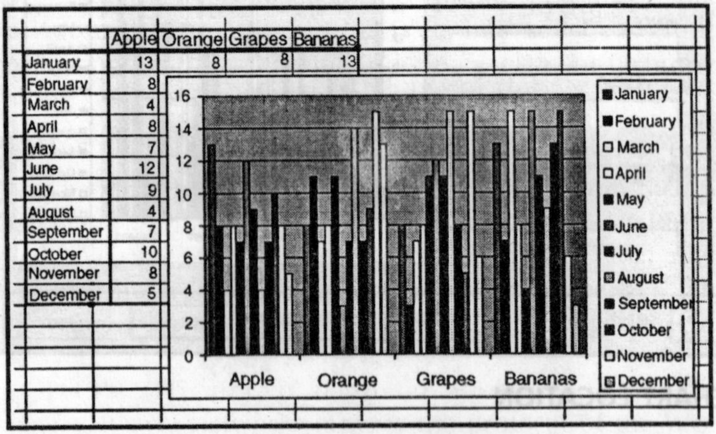

COLUMN CHART (PLOTTED BY COLUMNS)

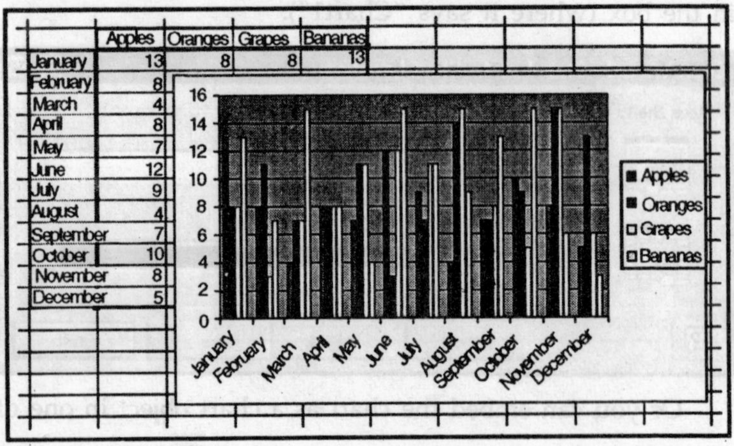

LINE CHART (PLOTTED BY COLUMNS)

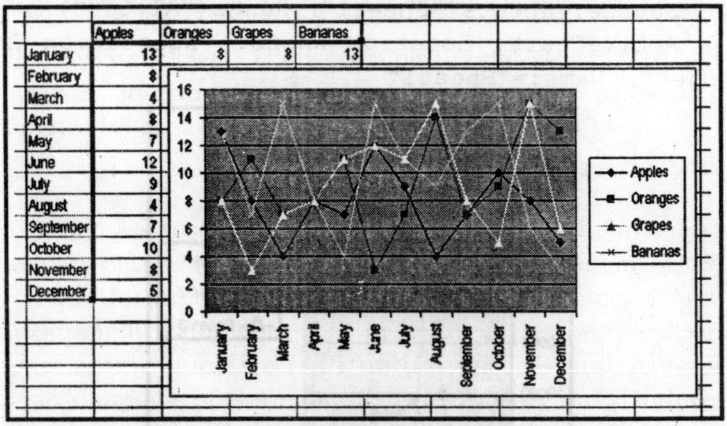

STACKED AREA CHART (PLOTTED BY COLUMNS)

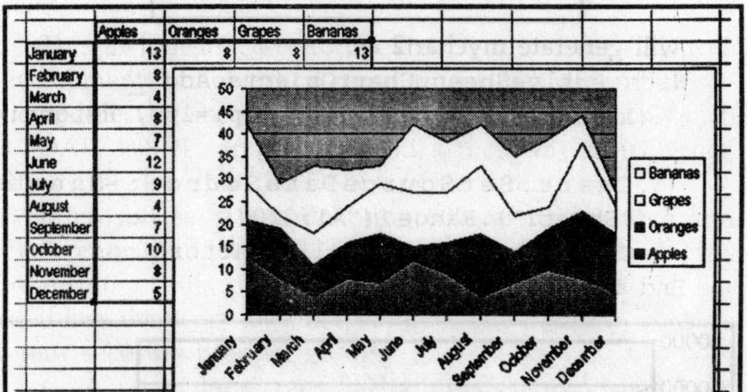

MACRO FOR CREATING AND MANIPULATING CHARTS

MACROS

The complete macro is below and the resulted charts of code portions are given at the end.

```
Sub myCharts()
'will generate mychart1 as:
Charts.Add
ActiveChart.ChartType = xlXYScatterLines
```

```
ActiveChart.SetSourceData
Source:=Sheets("Sheet1").Range("A1:C10")
ActiveChart. Location Where:= xlLocation As
Object, Name:="Sheet1"
```

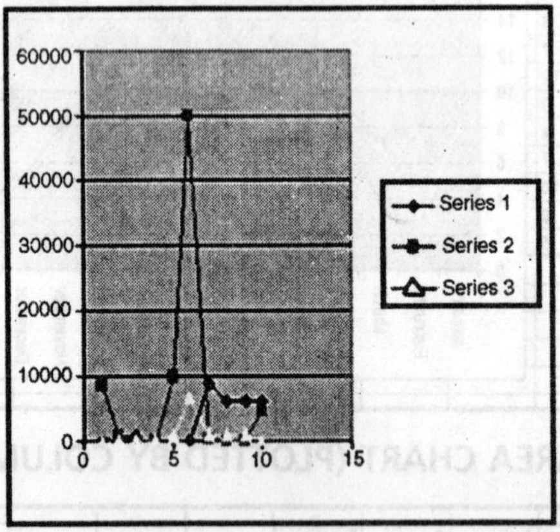

'will generate mychart2 as:

```
With ActiveSheet.ChartObjects.Add _
  (Left:=200, Width:=250, Top:=100, Height:=
  200)
  .Chart.SetSourceDataSource:=Sheets
  ("Sheet1").Range ("A1:C10")
  .Chart.ChartType = xlXYScatterLines
End With
```

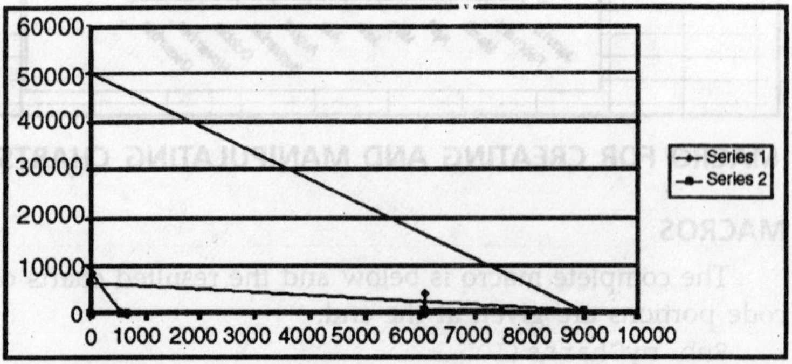

' Remove series will generate mychart3 which is completely blank. ' Remove this code if you want to display all the series

```
With ActiveChart
   'Do Until .SeriesCollection.Count = 0
   '.SeriesCollection(1).Delete
   'Loop
End With
```

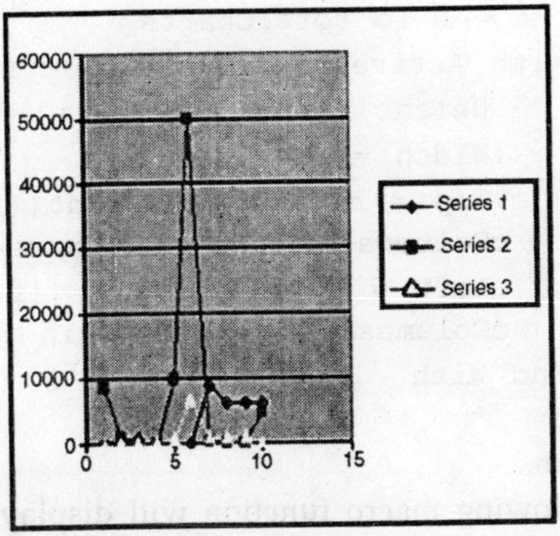

' Reposition the charts statically

```
With ActiveChart.Parent
   .Left = 100
   .Width = 375
   .Top = 75
   .Height = 225
End With
```

' Align all the charts so that all are visible at different positions

' mychart4

```
Dim i As Long
Dim totalCharts As Long
Dim cTopMargin As Double
Dim cLeftMargin As Double
Dim cHeightMargin As Double
Dim cWidthMargin As Double
Dim cColumns As Long
cTopMargin = 75
```

```
        cLeftMargin = 100
        cHeightMargin = 225
        cWidthMargin = 375
        cColumns = 3
        totalCharts= ActiveSheet.ChartObjects.Count
        For i = 1 To totalCharts
           With ActiveSheet.ChartObjects(i)
              .Height = cHeightMargin
              .Width = cWidthMargin
              .Top = cTopMargin + Int((i - 1) /
              cColumns) * cHeightMargin
              .Left = cLeftMargin + ((i - 1) Mod
              cColumns) * cWidthMargin
           End With
        Next
     End Sub
```

The following macro function will display the all the values attached with the graph in the worksheet:

```
     Sub PrintChartValues()
        Dim nrows As Integer
        Dim X As Object
        Counter = 2
        nrows = UBound(ActiveChart.SeriesCollection
        (1).Values)
        Worksheets ("ChartData").Cells(1, 1) = "X
        Values"
        With Worksheets("ChartData")
           .Range(.Cells(2, 1), _
           .Cells(nrows + 1, 1)) = _
           Application.Transpose (ActiveChart
           .Series Collection (1).XValues)
        End With
        For Each X In ActiveChart.SeriesCollection
           Worksheets("ChartData").Cells(1,
           Counter) = X.Name
           With Worksheets("ChartData")
```

```
                .Range(.Cells(2, Counter), _
                .Cells(nrows + 1, Counter)) = _
                Application.Transpose(X.Values)
            End With
            Counter = Counter + 1
        Next
    End Sub
    chart4:
```

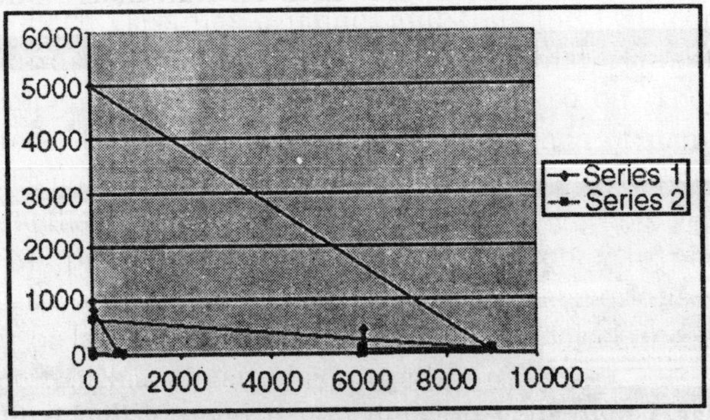

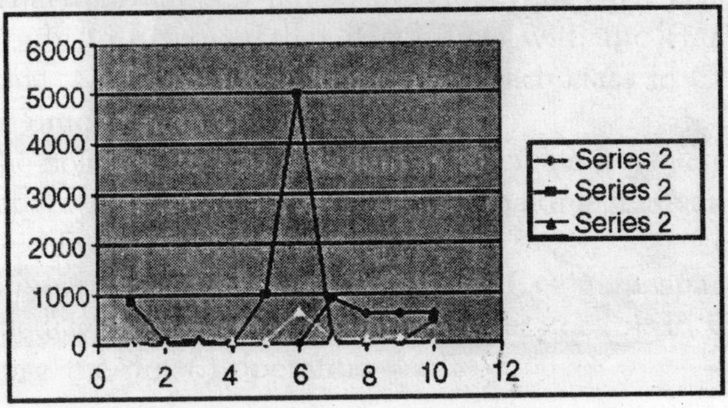

CHART MACRO IN EXCEL MODEL

USING CHART EFFICIENTLY

In the Excel model, you can easily display the figures in the table graphically with a ready-made chart macro. In the chart, figures are readily interpretable, and it may be easier to change the figures, as you can see how your estimate relate graphically to historical quarter figures.

Though, the chart macro is easy to use and you probably need only information how to get started i.e. where to find that macro (1 Running the macro), here are also some other instructions and some hints on how to deal with the graphs.

Running the Chart Macro

Go to the I-divQ sheet and select the Create division chart at the macro menu and click on Run macro button.

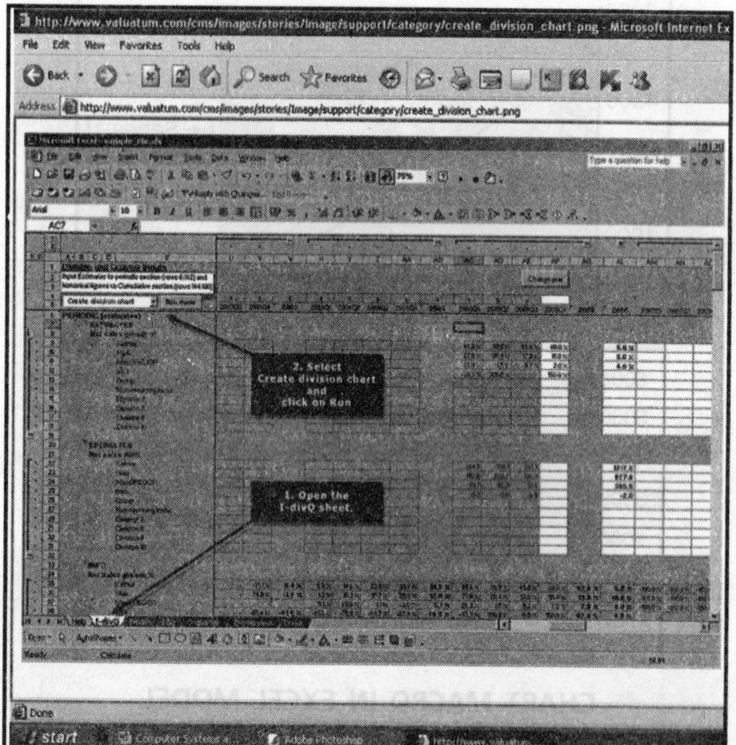

Excluding and Including Years in the Chart

If you want to exclude one or more years from the chart, just click on the minus sign on top of the corresponding year. Including of a year is done similarly, this time just click on the plus sign of the corresponding year.

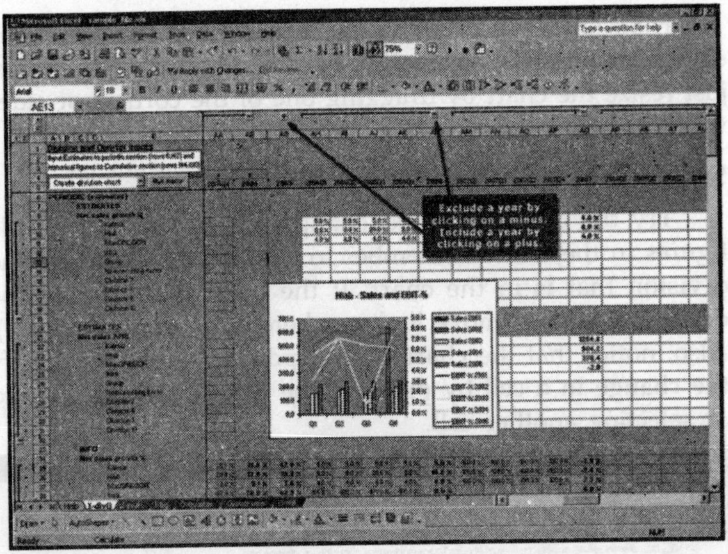

Resizing the Chart

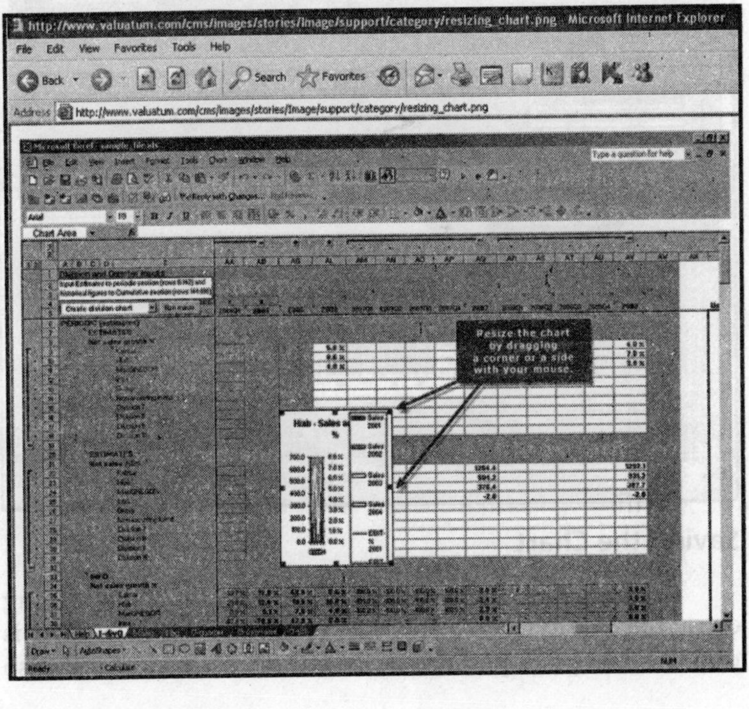

Especially, when excluding a year from the chart, the chart may become too small to be clear anymore. To fix this, just resize the chart by dragging one of the corners or sides with mouse.

Seeing the Figure Changes in the Chart

Try the chart now and change one of the changeable figures in the table. Remember to change the figures of the division that is in the chart! If the chart is on top of the division's figures, move it somewhere else (see the point 3). Also, notice that the chart is not updated before you verify the change in a cell by pressing the Enter on the keyboard or selecting another cell.

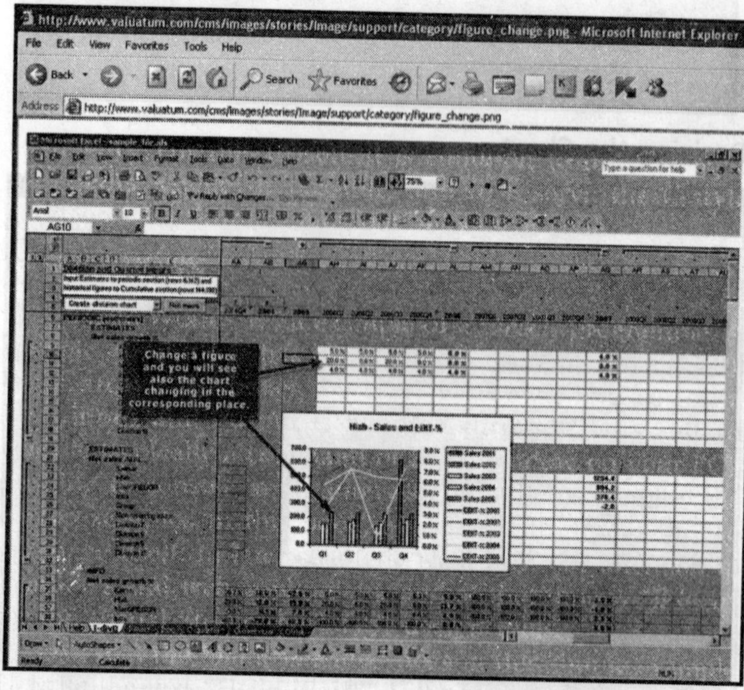

Saving the Chart

To save the chart, you do not have to do anything extra; the chart is saved as you save the excel model, and is usable when you open the file next time. Of course it is also very easy to create the charts again so you can also remove the charts.

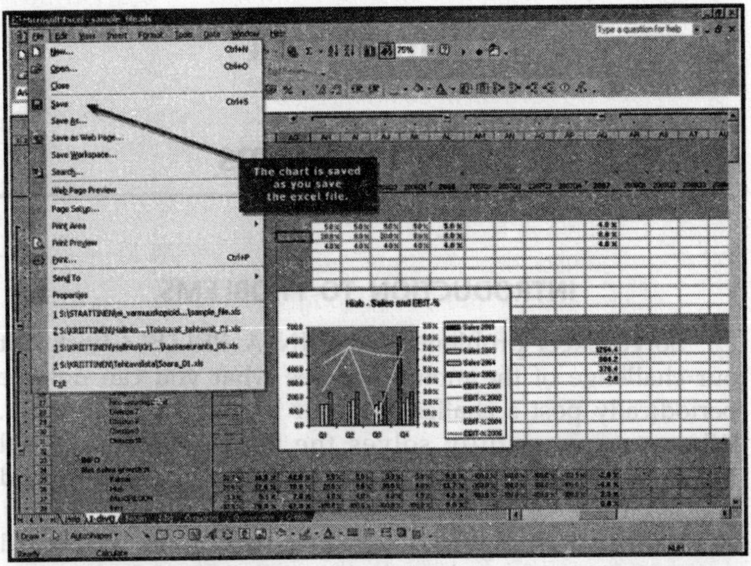

Removing the Chart

You can also remove the chart. Remove the chart by choosing the chart and pressing the Delete button on the keyboard. You can easily create a chart again by following these instructions.

Chapter – 14

Excel Problems

INTRODUCTION TO PROBLEMS

Solve Excel problems and WIN A PRIZE! Check out our challenge of the month and see what you can do! We periodically post a challenge to our Excel user community. Whoever successfully solves the problem wins a cool MrExcel.com prize and bragging rights! What more could you ask for?

Excel Challenge for for June/July 2008: Wildcard VLOOKUP

The VLOOKUP function is one of my most-used tools in Excel. But in this challenge, VLOOKUP won't quite work. The data in column A contains a series of phrases. Every phrase contains one colour in the phrase. The goal of the challenge is to use the lookup table in D2:E10 to assign the phrase to one of the names in column E.

	A	B	C	D	E
1	Phrases	Assigned to		Keyword	Assigned to
2	the ocean is blue			blue	Joe
3	I like his blue shirt			red	Bob
4	blue is my favorite color			yellow	Mary
5	the ocean is red			pink	Fred
6	I like his red shirt			orange	Ralph
7	red is my favorite color			brown	Lora
8	the ocean is yellow			white	Tracy
9	I like his yellow shirt			lavendar	Earl
10	yellow is my favorite color			magenta	Jenny
11	the ocean is pink				
12	I like his pink shirt				

You can use a formula. You can use a User Defined Function. You can use a macro. The solution should be adaptable to any size data in column A and any size table in columns D:E. Yes, someone with Excel 2007 could nest 8 if statements to solve the current problem, but this will not extend to a table with 34 entries, so this is not a valid approach.

Prizes: Include copies of the Live Lessons Power Excel DVD and copies of the Podcast DVD.

Entry: This will be a collaborative challenge. Many people will come up with similar approaches. Post your formula, function, or macro to this thread in the message board. Whoever comes up with a significant improvement to the best solution thus far will win a copy of the podcast DVD. The LiveLessons DVD will be awarded to the best formula, the best user defined function, and to the best macro. While "best" is a subjective measure, the decision of the judges is final.

PROBLEMS AND SOLUTIONS

In order to help you find solutions to your Excel problems that can be solved, we have categorized problems and solutions to help you quickly find a solution.

Sometimes, problems are with Excel. The following are rare problems with Excel that we have seen, and out solutions:

MEMORY PROBLEMS AND OUT OF RESOURCES

What to do if you get an out of memory or not enough resources message

Excel users will sometimes get a message that says their computer is out of memory, enough system resources to display completely, cannot complete this task with available resources or Excel can not open workbook with available resources. These messages are typically rare and they happen inconsistently. Excel 2007 users tend to see them more than Excel 2003 users. Microsoft re-wrote large portions of Excel when they released 2007. This re-write appears to have affected memory usage.

Microsoft Excel, including Excel 2007, can be run in PCs with as little as 512 mg of memory. However, this is probably pushing the Excel memory to the maximum and Excel has little resources to do work. Loading large spreadsheets, spreadsheets with graphics, or running other applications, like Outlook at the same time is very likely to cause Excel to be extremely slow and potentially crash.

Table. Shows Our PC Memory Preferences

Platform and Software	Memory Recommendation
Windows XP and Office 97-2003	1 GB
Windows XP and Office 2007	2 GB
Windows Vista and Office 97-2003	2 GB
Windows Vista and Office 2007	3 GB

Having additional memory appears to make all applications run faster and makes the PCs less prone to crashing. However, it is not always the cure for out of memory or not enough resource problems. We have seen user group postings of people with brand new PCs and lots of memory trying to solve these issues. If you see a lot of disk activity as you are using your PC, you most likely need more memory.

The following shows how much memory is used by Excel 2003 in various situations:

Application	Memory used Excel 2003
Excel with no add-ins installed of any kind	684k
Opening of 12 VBA add-ins (our favourite ones)	+1,800k
Opening of a small workbook (73k in size)	+80k
Closing of the same small workbook - not all memory released.	-50k
Opening a large workbook with data, and several pivot tables (54 meg in size) and very few formulas	+18,800k

Closing of the same large workbook - almost all memory released	-18,400k
Opening of a 2 meg workbook full of formulas	+2700k
Closing of the same workbook (significant amount of memory not released -appears formula related)	-1900k
Opening of a workbook with 100 charts, just a few formulas	-1340k
Clcsing of the same workbook	-1320k

The conclusion we reached from the above testing is that VBA add-ins do not use a significant amount of memory. Workbooks are the major user of memory. And Excel does not release all memory when workbooks are closed. Which supports one approach of closing and restarting Excel after doing a lot of work.

The following are steps one can take that may solve memory problems. It is also possible that none of these steps will solve. Memory problems are often difficult to solve. We have tried to order the steps from easy to do to hard to do. And from inexpensive to expensive (excluding the first step of adding the recommended amount of memory if you have problems).

The easiest way to run out of memory and get the message "Excel can not complete the task with available resources." is to have 1) Multiple Excel sessions open and 2) other applications open. Many Excel users will open new Excel sessions each time a new workbook is opened via double clicking on a workbook link. To see if you have multiple sessions open, press ALT-CTL-DELETE and check how any Excel applications arc running. There should be just one running. Regarding other applications, it depends on what they are and how much memory they need before a problem happens. If a new Excel session opens each time you double click on a workbook, try unchecking the Excel Option "Ignore other applications" if it is checked on the Options General tab.

Some cases of out of memory or resources are caused

by doing a copy and paste that is not valid. Instead of advising that one can not do such an action, Excel says either out of memory or out of resources. It can happen if one is trying to paste a selection containing hidden cells or has merged cells.

EXCEL 2003/ EXCEL 2007

There are many differences between Excel 2003 and Excel 2007. Some of the changes in Excel 2007 are improvements. Some are strongly disliked by users of past releases of Excel. The following are some of our major findings when we compared Excel 2003 to Excel 2007.

We do recommend that if you have Excel 2003, that you do a custom install of Excel 2007 and tell it to keep all prior versions. This will allow you to use your prior version if you need it. The default installation of Excel 2007 automatically removes all prior versions. We think having the prior versions around is a good thing.

Why should you upgrade to 2007? There are a number of good reasons:

- You need more than 65,000 rows on a worksheet. Excel 2007 allows over a million rows.
- You need more than 256 columns. Excel 2007 allows over 16000 columns.
- You do a lot of graphics work and need the new graphics tools and options.
- You do a lot of pivot table work and need the new pivot table features in 2007
- You are receiving workbooks that are Excel 2007 workbooks
- Office XML Formats allow for better data integration between documents and back-end systems. Also, with Excel XML Formats, you can reduce file sizes, improve data recovery, and increase the interoperability of your spreadsheets with other data sources such as line-of-business systems.
- Business dashboards can be easily created from spreadsheets to track key performance indicator.

- You can import external data into a spreadsheet by using pre-configured external sources of business information
- Developers can use the Office Excel 2007 calculation engine in other applications, such as a Web-based mortgage calculator or an options pricing model.

Why should you stay with Excel 2003 (or an earlier version)

- The Excel 2007 interface is harder to use. Yes, more features of Excel are exposed to a user. But compare it to going to a good hardware store versus a mega store like Lowe's or Home Depot. It is easy to find what you want in a hardware store. Finding anything in a mega store can take longer.
- You are used to using Excel 2003. You will find that using Excel 2007 takes longer to do many of the tasks you used to do. This is part experience and part design. The first can be overcome, but it will take time. If you have used Excel 2003 for years, it will take a very long time to catch back up.
- Macro recording of chart macros works very poorly in Excel 2007.

The following table lists a number of key comparison points between Excel 2003 and Excel 2007. It comes from our experiences with Excel and from user postings on news groups. If we mention a problem a problem with Excel 2007, we only mention it if we have experienced it, if there have been many posts of a problem or if a frequent news group poster has verified a problem.

	Excel 2003	Excel 2007 with SP1	Comments
Number of rows	Limited to 65,536	Over 1,000,000	Very few users need large numbers of rows. Excel 2003 workbooks must be converted (saved) in the new Excel format to access the higher number of rows.

Number of Columns	256	16,384	Very few users need large number of columns. See conversion note above.
Calculate speed	FAST	FAST	Worksheet calculations are slightly faster in Excel 2007. However, the speed difference is in almost all cases insignifi- cant. If you have large work books and have to set calcula-tion to manual in 2003, then 2007 may be a big benefit to you.
Macro Speed	FAST	Varies	Some macros run as much as 20X slower in Excel 2007, even after the SP1 release. Charting macros are typically far slower. Macros that do a lot of data manipulation and cell changes are far slower. Small simple macros run as fast.
Lists/Tables	List support was introduced with Excel 2003	Lists were renamed to Tables and Additional features added in 2007 to make them easiser to use.	Support for working with tables of data helps you create and format a table with a rich table styles gallery. Column headings remain in view as you scroll, and auto-fill populates and expands any table automatically
Chart Refresh	Extremely fast, almost instantly	Can be extremely slow.	There have been numerous user group postings of Excel 2007 being very slow when one changes chart data. For example, graphs taking several minutes to refresh when selected. SP1 fixed some problems, but users keep posting problems, so it is still there.

Opening and closing files	Fast	Not as fast	For small workbooks, the time difference is insignificant. For large workbooks, the time difference is very noticeable.
Conditional Formatting	Limited to 3 tests	Many tests are allowed	The improvement is very useful if you need conditional formatting formatting that changes dynamically. However, posts on user forums indicate that using this feature greatly slows down Excel 2007. The alternative is static formatting (I.E., format when you need to) using the Conditional Format Assistant. A bug has been reported in 2007 that results in multiple conditional formats being created when one copies and pastes. Such can then slow down Excel 2007. Look for a patch on this someday. SP1 did not fix.
Customizing toolbars	Very customizable	Limited customization	With Excel 2003 you can remove commands you don't want from the toolbars and add commands you want. And you can create your own buttons for your custom macros. With Excel 2007 you can not modify the ribbons. You can add buttons to the quick access toolbar.
Colour Palette	colors	Limited unlimited colors	Essentially Excel 2003 is easier to use and selection of significant different colors is easy. Excel 2007 gives more choices. We call it a toss up as to the benefit.

Patterns in formatting charts and cells	Many choices	Patterns are no	Microsoft removed a feature that was very useful for those of us who fax or want to print copies from a laser (non colour) printer. There are now some free utilities that add back the patterns to Excel 2007. So, once you get such a utility, you have the same functionality.
Interface	Menus and buttons	Ribbons with buttons and text drop downs	Some will love the 2007 interface, some will hate it. Figure one to four weeks to relearn Excel basics. If you have been using Excel 2003 for years, then expect that it will take a very long time to be as productive. If you want the 2003 interface back, we have added the worksheet menu (File, Edit, ...) back with the Spreadsheet Assistant. (Not all menu items could be added back.)
Macro recording	Fair	Very poor on charting macros	Macro recording is very poor for chart actions such as relocating, resizing, etc. If you retain Excel 2003, you can use it to record chart macros. Then you can copy to 2007 and modify. It does mean learning how to write macros versus relying on the recorder. For books on macros, checkout our downloadable macro books.

Macros and workbook protection	No problems	Major problems	In Excel 2007, if you password protect your workboks and they contain macros, there is no way to enable macros.
Charting - adjusting point values	Easy to do by	Impossible	Microsoft removed the feature that allows one to change the value of data points by dragging the point on a chart.
Customizing Macro buttons	Standard feature	Feature removed	It is possible to customise macro buttons in 2007, but it must be done via a macro and the code is very tricky.
Export/save as DBF file	Standard feature	Not available	Microsoft removed the export/ save as DBF option from Excel 2007.

MICROSOFT EXCEL FREEZING

If you are running one of our add-ins, they normally will complete any task in just a few minutes. Most will complete their tasks in just a few seconds. If your data is extremely long - say a hundred thousand rows, the task can take up to 5-10 minutes to do. While the task is being done there is almost always a status message being updated at the bottom left of the screen.

Sometimes the status message will stop updating. This is a very rare and almost all the time the task is still being done and will be completed in a few minutes. If you hold down the CTL key and press the BREAK key, this will interrupt the code and display a Microsoft Excel visual basic dialog box like the following

When this box appears, click on the Continue button. This will cause the status bar to update.

If Excel is truly frozen, which is extremely rare, you will need to kill Excel via the Task Manager. Press ALT-CTL-DELETE keys, select Excel and click End Task. Any work will be lost.

The primary cause of lockups in Excel are memory related. Some PCs do not have enough memory. Most stores sell PCs with just enough memory to run Windows and the internet and not do anything else. For information on what memory is needed, please see our page on memory problems.

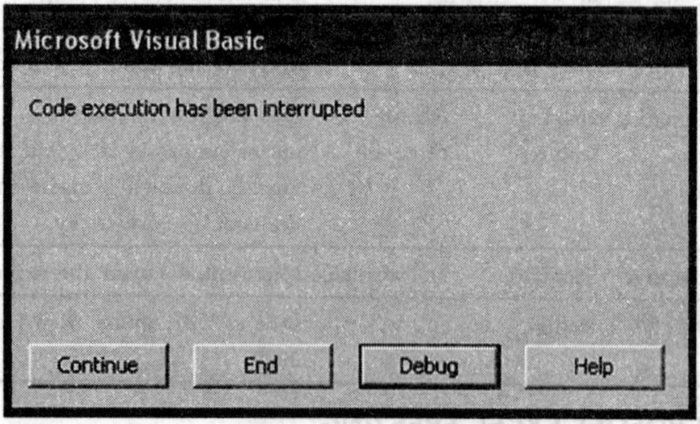

Other than not having enough memory on a PC, the most likely cause of problems are too many add-ins running. Or running any COM add-in. COM add-ins are compiled add-ins, and often have memory conflicts with Excel. COM add-ins from Adobe and other trustworthy companies often get loaded. Unfortunately their COM add-ins often cause memory problems. Having too many VBA add-ins can cause problems. Our page on memory problem gives detailed instructions on how to remove COM and VBA add-ins. Doing so will often solve Excel freeze-ups.

ERROR IN MODULE

If you get a message like "Error in module" (with a number like 1, 2, ... at then end), this means that there is a problem with the installation of Microsoft Office. There is not a problem with the add-ins. Re-installing our add-ins does not solve.

The problem is often caused by un-installing a trial version of Excel 2007, a missing service pack or an Office patch that was automatically run by Windows. It is sometimes caused by getting Office pre-installed on the PC when you purchase the PC.

AUTOMATION ERROR

If you get the message "automation error" when you open Excel after installing or when you click on the icon to open the add-in, the problem is caused by a problem with the installation of Microsoft Office. There is not a problem with the add-ins. Re-installing our add-ins does not solve.

The problem is often caused by un-installing a trial version of Excel 2007, a missing service pack or an Office patch that was automatically run by Windows. It is sometimes caused by getting Office pre-installed on the PC when you purchase the PC.

OBJECT LIBRARY INVALID

If you get the message "object library invalid" when you open Excel or when you close excel after installing the add-ins, the problem is caused by a problem with the installation of Microsoft Office. There is not a problem with the add-ins. Re-installing our add-ins does not solve.

The problem is often caused by un-installing a trial version of Excel 2007, a missing service pack or an Office patch that was automatically run by Windows. It is sometimes caused by getting Office pre-installed on the PC when you purchase the PC.

ADDINS MENUS MISSING OR BUTTONS

If the addin's menus or the sub-menus are missing or the button that activates your addin is not working, there are two very likely causes:

If they had been working and just stopped, then most likely the add-in was partially un-installed. It is simple to re-install:

- If using Excel 97-2003, select Tools, Add-ins.
- If using Excel 2007, select Office Button, Excel Options, Add-ins, Manage Add-ins, Go
- Re-Check the add-in. If not listed, click the Browse

button, go to C:\PROGRAMME FILES\ADD-INS. This is not the default addins folder. Select the add-in and click OK. For the Spreadsheet Assistant, select only "assistnt.xla". For others, the name should be obvious. Do not select an addin with "Main" in the name.

PROBLEM FIXER

If you have installed the Google desktop search software and you are using Excel it is highly likely that you will get a request for an add-in for Microsoft Excel password when you close Excel. And if you do not know the password (which is also highly likely) clicking cancel does not close the dialog. Nor does clicking on the X to close the dialog. It just keeps coming back and back and back.

Some users have been able to close the password request dialog after clicking cancel many many times. If this does not work users have to kill Excel via Alt-Ctl-Delete or even power their PC off and on. None of these are acceptable solutions.

The problem does not affect all users. It does not happen all the time. It is fairly rare (and one must have Google desktop search installed) But to those it happens to it is down right annoying. It happens if the add-in file is protected and especially if the add-in file is opened by another add-in.

Google is aware of the problem. And we (and I suspect others) have told them of the solution. As of Jan 4th 2004 they have not fixed. The response we have gotten from then is that they "may fix it in a future release". Nice to know. They did offer us a free t-shirt. We refused it.

Our recommendation is to un-install the Google desktop search. If you don't need it get rid of it. If you do need a desktop search programme, get one that works with Excel.

Another alternative (other than living with the problem) is to modify the following registry key to a value of 2 (its default value is 3):

HKEY_CURRENT_USER\Software\Microsoft\Office\Excel\Addins\Office.Desktop.Google.com \ LoadBehavior

In our testing, the above change eliminates the password prompt without any problem. Our thanks to Jeff Smith who found this solution and to John Walkenbach for posting it.

If you are not comfortable or do not know how to modify the registry manually then you can download and run the following programme that does the modification for you.

Only run the password prompt fixer after you have installed Google's desktop search. If you run before then the Google installation will overwrite the modification the password prompt fixer makes. If you do not have Google's desktop search installed the password prompt fixer will not benefit you.

"UNSPECIFIED ERROR"

If you get the message "Unspecified Error" when you open Excel or when you close excel after installing the add-ins, the problem is caused by a problem with the installation of Microsoft Office. There is not a problem with the add-ins. Re-installing our add-ins does not solve.

The problem is often caused by un-installing a trial version of Excel 2007, a missing service pack or an Office patch that was automatically run by Windows. It is sometimes caused by getting Office pre-installed on the PC when you purchase the PC.

Chapter – 15

Windows Operating System

INTRODUCTION

An "operating system" is a programme that manages the resources of the computer. An operating system sets up a consistent way for programs to request resources, such as time on the processor, or space in memory, from the computer itself. Operating systems look after all the devices attached to the computer, such as printers, modems, disks, and terminals. Another part of an operating system's job is to maintain a file system; that is, to set up a consistent way for information to be stored and retrieved.

BACKGROUND

The first version of Windows was released in November

of 1985. This programme wasn't very popular as it lacked functionality compared to the Apple operating system. Version 1.0 was not a complete system. Instead, it simply extended on MS-DOS. Version 2.0 was released two years later and achieved slightly more popularity than its predecessor. Version 2.03 was released in January of 2008. This version offered a totally different look that resulted in Apple filing a lawsuit against Microsoft with accusations of infringement.

Windows version 3.0 was released in 1990, the first edition to reach commercial success by selling two million copies within its first six months. This version included numerous improvements to the user interface along with new multitasking capabilities. Version 3.1 offered a facelift and was made available in March, 1992.

The Windows NT operating system was released in July of 1993. This version was based on a new kernel and it was considered to be the first designed for a professional platform. NT was later upgraded to function as a home user operating system with the release of Windows XP.

In August of 1995, Windows 95 was released. This operating system offered a consumer solution with significant changes to the user interface that also utilized preemptive multitasking. Windows 95 was introduced to replace version 3.1 and Windows for Workgroups as well as MS-DOS. The first Microsoft operating system to use the plug and play system, Windows 95 revolutionized the desktop platform and achieved mass popularity.

Next up was Windows 98, released in June of 1998. This operating system was criticized for being slower and less reliable than version 95. Many of those issues were addressed a year later with the unveiling of Windows 98 Second Edition

Microsoft continued their line of professional operating systems with Windows 2000 in February of 2000. The consumer version was released as Windows ME in September of that year. ME integrated several new technologies, most notably the Universal Plug and Play.

Windows XP was released in October 2001. This version was based on the NT kernel and managed to retain the extreme functionality of its home-based predecessors. XP was widely embraced by the public and came in two different editions: Home and Professional.

The Home Edition provided exceptionable multimedia support while the Professional edition offered excellent security and networking capabilities. XP has since been succeeded by Vista but support will continue through April of 2009.

WORKING

When you turn on your computer, it's nice to think that you're in control. There's the trusty computer mouse, which you can move anywhere on the screen, summoning up your music library or Internet browser at the slightest whim. Although it's easy to feel like a director in front of your desktop or laptop, there's a lot going on inside, and the real man behind the curtain handling the necessary tasks is the operating system.

Most desktop or laptop PCs come pre-loaded with Microsoft Windows. Macintosh computers come pre-loaded with Mac OS X. Many corporate servers use the Linux or UNIX operating systems. The operating system (OS) is the first thing loaded onto the computer — without the operating system, a computer is useless.

More recently, operating systems have started to pop up in smaller computers as well. If you like to tinker with electronic devices, you're probably pleased that operating systems can now be found on many of the devices we use every day, from cell phones to wireless access points. The computers used in these little devices have gotten so powerful that they can now actually run an operating system and applications. The computer in a typical modern cell phone is now more powerful than a desktop computer from 20 years ago, so this progression makes sense and is a natural development.

The purpose of an operating system is to organize and

control hardware and software so that the device it lives in behaves in a flexible but predictable way. In this article, we'll tell you what a piece of software must do to be called an operating system, show you how the operating system in your desktop computer works and give you some examples of how to take control of the other operating systems around you.

Not all computers have operating systems. The computer that controls the microwave oven in your kitchen, for example, doesn't need an operating system. It has one set of tasks to perform, very straightforward input to expect (a numbered keypad and a few pre-set buttons) and simple, never-changing hardware to control. For a computer like this, an operating system would be unnecessary baggage, driving up the development and manufacturing costs significantly and adding complexity where none is required. Instead, the computer in a microwave oven simply runs a single hard-wired programme all the time.

For other devices, an operating system creates the ability to:

- Serve a variety of purposes
- Interact with users in more complicated ways
- Keep up with needs that change over time

All desktop computers have operating systems. The most common are the Windows family of operating systems developed by Microsoft, the Macintosh operating systems developed by Apple and the UNIX family of operating systems (which have been developed by a whole history of individuals, corporations and collaborators). There are hundreds of other operating systems available for special-purpose applications, including specializations for mainframes, robotics, manufacturing, real-time control systems and so on.

In any device that has an operating system, there's usually a way to make changes to how the device works. This is far from a happy accident; one of the reasons operating systems are made out of portable code rather than permanent physical circuits is so that they can be changed or modified without having to scrap the whole device.

MICROSOFT WINDOWS AND OTHER USERS

A Windows user can still use the above MS-DOS steps if they wish to create a batch file. If, however, you're more comfortable using Microsoft Windows or your operating system, you can use any text editor, such as Notepad or WordPad, to create your batch files, as long as the file extension ends with .bat. In the below example we use the Windows notepad to create a batch file.

- Click Start
- Click Run
- *Type*: notepad and press enter.
- Once notepad is open, type the below lines in the file or copy and paste the below lines into notepad. @echo off echo Hello this is a test batch file pause dir c:\windows
- Click File and click Save; browse to where you want to save the file. For the file name, type "test.bat", and if your version of Windows has a "Save as type" option, choose "All files", otherwise it will save as a text file. Once all of this has been done click the Save button and exit notepad.
- Now, to run the batch file, simply double-click or run the file like any other programme. Once the batch file has completed running it will close the window automatically.

WINDOWS SYSTEM PROTECTION

INTRODUCTION

From the beginning of electronic computing until 15 years ago, the 'game' of attack and defence was played on a system by system basis, with defenders relying on physical security and ad-hoc operating system protection methods and attackers guessing passwords or exploiting errors and omissions to bypass normal system controls. Over the last 15 years, the computing environment has changed dramatically, with widespread physical distribution of computing power, almost complete loss of physical control over computing hardware, and a dramatic increase in the networking of computers, but defenses have not changed substantially in terms of their reliance on physical security and ad-hoc defenses. As a result, we see new classes of attacks such as computer viruses, which exploit the lack of physical control and fundamental weakness of existing logical controls to spread transitively throughout the computing world. Even the best protection systems available today can quickly and easily be defeated by anyone with physical access and ample knowledge, or by the application of that expertise in a widespread computer virus attack.

One of the major factors in the successful application of information protection techniques is the exploitation of computational advantage. Computational advantage shows up historically in cryptography, where Shannon's theory [Shan49] clearly demonstrates the effect of 'workload' on the complexity of cryptanalysis and introduces the concepts of diffusion and confusion as they relate to statistical attacks on cryptosystems. Most modern cryptosystems exploit this as their primary defence The same basic principle applies in computer virus analysis in which evolutionary viruses drive the complexity of detection and eradication up dramatically and in password protection in which we try to drive the number of guesses required for a successful attack up by limiting the use of obvious passwords. As we will see, one of the major reasons attacks succeed is because of the static nature of defence, and the dynamic nature of attack.

THE ULTIMATE ATTACK

The ultimate attack against any system begins with physical access, and proceeds to disassembly and reverse engineering of whatever programmed defenses are in place. Even with a cryptographic key provided by the user, an attacker can modify the mechanism to examine and exploit the key, given ample physical access. Eventually, the attacker can remove the defenses by finding decision points and altering them to yield altered decisions.

Without physical protection, nobody has ever found a

defence against this attack, and it is unlikely that anyone ever will. The reason is that any protection scheme other than a physical one depends on the operation of a finite state machine, and ultimately, any finite state machine can be examined and modified at will, given enough time and effort. The best we can ever do is delay attack by increasing the complexity of making desired alterations.

THE ULTIMATE DEFENCE

The ultimate defence is to drive the complexity of the ultimate attack up so high that the cost of attack is too high to be worth performing. This is, in effect, security through obscurity, and it is our general conclusion that all technical information protection in computer systems relies at some level either on physical protection, security through obscurity, or combinations thereof.

The goal of security through obscurity is to make the difficulty of attack so great that in practice, it is not worth performing, even though it could eventually be successful. Successful attacks against obscurity defenses depend on the ability to guess some key piece of information. The most obvious example is attacking and defending passwords, and since this problem demonstrates precisely the issues at hand, we will use it as an example. In password protection, there are generally three aspects to making attack difficult. One aspect is making the size of the password space large, so that the potential number of guesses required for an attack is enormous.

In the case of current operating systems, the size of the space is enormous, consisting of all programs that fit in the computer's memory, but the operating system may only have a very small number of versions, all of which are almost identical, yielding a highly coherent subspace consisting of only a few very closely tied points. Thus, only a few guesses are required to determine precisely which version of the operating system is in use, and even that may not be required for many attacks. Operating systems also provide no confusion in that the part of the programme that performs any given operation is immediately apparent to the knowledgeable attacker. For this reason, low-level operating system attack is quite simple.

The problem for defenders is to find a way to increase the difficulty of operating system attack by reducing coherence. The ultimate goal is to obscure defenses so as to make attackers require repeated use of the ultimate attack in order to impact substantial numbers of systems. One solution is to provide each computer with a sound and unique defence.

This would tend to make it infeasible to design an automated attack that could systematically bypass all of the defenses, but then we would have to design a new defence for each system, and the costs of defence would probably become intolerable. We could trade off costs for probability of attack by implementing some fixed number of different defenses, thus requiring a fixed number of ultimate attacks for complete success. This is essentially the situation in the world today, where a wide variety of ad-hoc defenses are on the market. Unfortunately, many of these defenses fall to the same classes of attack, and the number is sufficiently small that defeating most of them requires relatively little effort or expense.

TECHNIQUES FOR PROGRAMME IN WINDOWS

We will consider two programs equivalent if, given identical input sequences, they produce identical output sequences. The equivalence of two programs is undecidable as is the determination of whether one programme can evolve from another. This result would seem to indicate that evolution has the potential for increasing complexity of analysis, and thus difficulty of attack. In a practical operating system design, we may also have very stringent requirements on the space and time used by the protection mechanism, and certain instruction sequences may be highly undesirable because they impact some other aspect of system operation or are incompatible across some similar machines. For this reason, we may not be able to reach the levels of complexity required to eliminate concerted human attack, but we may succeed in increasing the complexity of automated attacks to a level where the time required for attack is sufficient to have noticeable performance impacts, even to a level where no attacker is able to design a strong enough attack to defeat more than a small number of evolutions.

We know that evolution is as general as Turing machine computation, and that an exhaustive set of equivalent programs is easily described mathematically (i.e. the definition of equivalence), but this is not particularly helpful in terms of designing practical evolutionary schemes. We now describe a number of practical techniques we have explored for programme evolution and some results regarding the space, time, and complexity issues introduced by these techniques.

OPERATING SYSTEMS STRUCTURE

SYSTEM COMPONENTS

Even though, not all systems have the same structure many modern operating systems share the same goal of supporting the following types of system components.

Process Management

The operating system manages many kinds of activities ranging from user programs to system programs like printer spooler, name servers, file server etc. Each of these activities is encapsulated in a process. A process includes the complete execution context (code, data, PC, registers, OS resources in use etc.).

It is important to note that a process is not a programme. A process is only ONE instant of a programme in execution. There are many processes can be running the same programme. The five major activities of an operating system in regard to process management are

- Creation and deletion of user and system processes.
- Suspension and resumption of processes.
- A mechanism for process synchronization.

- A mechanism for process communication.
- A mechanism for deadlock handling.

Main-Memory Management

Primary-Memory or Main-Memory is a large array of words or bytes. Each word or byte has its own address. Main-memory provides storage that can be access directly by the CPU. That is to say for a programme to be executed, it must in the main memory.

The major activities of an operating in regard to memory-management are:

- Keep track of which part of memory are currently being used and by whom.
- Decide which processes are loaded into memory when memory space becomes available.
- Allocate and de allocate memory space as needed.

File Management

A file is a collected of related information defined by its creator. Computer can store files on the disk (secondary storage), which provide long term storage. Some examples of storage media are magnetic tape, magnetic disk and optical disk. Each of these media has its own properties like speed, capacity, data transfer rate and access methods.

A file systems normally organized into directories to ease their use. These directories may contain files and other directions.

The five main major activities of an operating system in regard to file management are

- The creation and deletion of files.
- The creation and deletion of directions.
- The support of primitives for manipulating files and directions.
- The mapping of files onto secondary storage.
- The back up of files on stable storage media.

I/O System Management

I/O subsystem hides the peculiarities of specific hardware

devices from the user. Only the device driver knows the peculiarities of the specific device to whom it is assigned.

Secondary-Storage Management

Generally speaking, systems have several levels of storage, including primary storage, secondary storage and cache storage. Instructions and data must be placed in primary storage or cache to be referenced by a running programme. Because main memory is too small to accommodate all data and programs, and its data are lost when power is lost, the computer system must provide secondary storage to back up main memory. Secondary storage consists of tapes, disks, and other media designed to hold information that will eventually be accessed in primary storage (primary, secondary, cache) is ordinarily divided into bytes or words consisting of a fixed number of bytes. Each location in storage has an address; the set of all addresses available to a programme is called an address space.

The three major activities of an operating system in regard to secondary storage management are:

- Managing the free space available on the secondary-storage device.
- Allocation of storage space when new files have to be written.
- Scheduling the requests for memory access.

Networking

A distributed systems is a collection of processors that do not share memory, peripheral devices, or a clock. The processors communicate with one another through communication lines called network. The communication-network design must consider routing and connection strategies, and the problems of contention and security.

Protection System

If a computer systems has multiple users and allows the concurrent execution of multiple processes, then the various processes must be protected from one another's activities.

Protection refers to mechanism for controlling the access of programs, processes, or users to the resources defined by a computer systems.

Command Interpreter System

A command interpreter is an interface of the operating system with the user. The user gives commands with are executed by operating system (usually by turning them into system calls). The main function of a command interpreter is to get and execute the next user specified command. Command-Interpreter is usually not part of the kernel, since multiple command interpreters (shell, in UNIX terminology) may be support by an operating system, and they do not really need to run in kernel mode. There are two main advantages to separating the command interpreter from the kernel.

- If we want to change the way the command interpreter looks, i.e., I want to change the interface of command interpreter, I am able to do that if the command interpreter is separate from the kernel. I cannot change the code of the kernel so I cannot modify the interface.
- If the command interpreter is a part of the kernel it is possible for a malicious process to gain access to certain part of the kernel that it showed not have to avoid this ugly scenario it is advantageous to have the command interpreter separate from kernel

OPERATING SYSTEMS SERVICES

Following are the five services provided by an operating systems to the convenience of the users.

Programme Execution

The purpose of a computer systems is to allow the user to execute programs. So the operating systems provides an environment where the user can conveniently run programs. The user does not have to worry about the memory allocation or multitasking or anything. These things are taken care of by the operating systems. Running a programme involves the allocating and deallocating memory, CPU scheduling in case of multiprocess. These functions cannot be given to the user-level programs. So user-level programs cannot help the user to run programs independently without the help from operating systems.

I/O Operations

Each programme requires an input and produces output. This involves the use of I/O. The operating systems hides the user the details of underlying hardware for the I/O. All the user sees is that the I/O has been performed without any details. So the operating systems by providing I/O makes it convenient for the users to run programs.

For efficiently and protection users cannot control I/O so this service cannot be provided by user-level programs.

File System Manipulation

The output of a programme may need to be written into new files or input taken from some files. The operating systems provides this service. The user does not have to worry about secondary storage management. User gives a command for reading or writing to a file and sees his her task accomplished. Thus operating systems makes it easier for user programs to accomplished their task.

This service involves secondary storage management. The speed of I/O that depends on secondary storage management is critical to the speed of many programs and hence it is best relegated to the operating systems to manage it than giving individual users the control of it. It is not difficult for the user-level programs to provide these services but for above mentioned reasons it is best if this service s left with operating system.

Communications

There are instances where processes need to communicate with each other to exchange information. It may be between processes running on the same computer or running on the different computers. By providing this service the operating system relieves the user of the worry of passing messages between processes. In case where the messages need to be passed to processes on the other computers through a network it can be done by the user programs. The user programme may be customized to the specifics of the hardware through which the message transits and provides the service interface to the operating system.

Error Detection

An error is one part of the system may cause malfunctioning of the complete system. To avoid such a situation the operating system constantly monitors the system for detecting the errors. This relieves the user of the worry of errors propagating to various part of the system and causing malfunctioning.

This service cannot allowed to be handled by user programs because it involves monitoring and in cases altering area of memory or deallocation of memory for a faulty process. Or may be relinquishing the CPU of a process that goes into an infinite loop. These tasks are too critical to be handed over to the user programs. A user programme if given these privileges can interfere with the correct (normal) operation of the operating systems.

SYSTEM CALLS AND SYSTEM PROGRAMS

System calls provide an interface between the process an the operating system. System calls allow user-level processes to request some services from the operating system which process itself is not allowed to do. In handling the trap, the operating system will enter in the kernel mode, where it has access to privileged instructions, and can perform the desired service on the behalf of user-level process. It is because of the critical nature of operations that the operating system itself does them every time they are needed. For example, for I/O a process involves a system call telling the operating system to read or write particular area and this request is satisfied by the operating system.

System programs provide basic functioning to users so that they do not need to write their own environment for programme development (editors, compilers) and programme execution (shells). In some sense, they are bundles of useful system calls.

LAYERED APPROACH DESIGN

In this case the system is easier to debug and modify, because changes affect only limited portions of the code, and programmer does not have to know the details of the other layers. Information is also kept only where it is needed and is accessible only in certain ways, so bugs affecting that data are limited to a specific module or layer.

MECHANISMS AND POLICIES

The policies what is to be done while the mechanism specifies how it is to be done. For instance, the timer construct for ensuring CPU protection is mechanism. On the other hand, the decision of how long the timer is set for a particular user is a policy decision.

The separation of mechanism and policy is important to provide flexibility to a system. If the interface between mechanism and policy is well defined, the change of policy may affect only a few parameters. On the other hand, if interface between these two is vague or not well defined, it might involve much deeper change to the system.

Once the policy has been decided it gives the programmer the choice of using his/her own implementation. Also, the underlying implementation may be changed for a more efficient one without much trouble if the mechanism and policy are well defined.

Chapter – 16

Essential of Word

INTRODUCTION TO MS WORD

While working in MS-WORD you have to work with a mouse. Also one can work, to some extent, through the keyboard. The use of mouse is simpler as it is fully menu driven. In MS-WORD every command is available in the form of 'icons'.

You can go inside MS-WORD by the following way:

- Move into the rectangular area meant for Microsoft word. Click the left mouse button there. The computer will start MS-WORD. You will find the screen as follows.

- Take the mouse pointer to START button on the task bar. Click the left mouse button. The monitor will show like as follows.

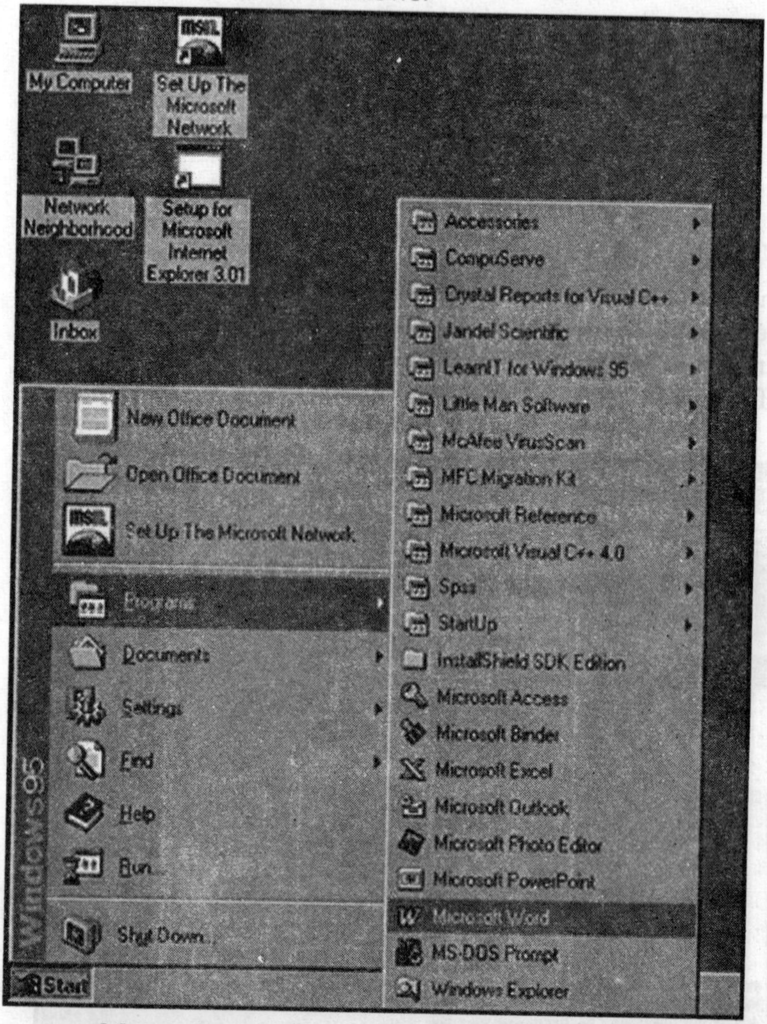

- Move the pointer to programs. You will notice another menu coming up to the right.
- In that menu identify where Microsoft word is

placed. Move the cursor horizontally to come out of programs.

Let us discuss the important components of the screen:

- *Title Bar*: The title bar displays the name of the currently active word document. Like other WINDOWS applications, it can be used to alter the size and location of the word window.
- *Tool Bars*: Word has a number of tool bars that help you perform task faster and with great ease. Two of the most commonly tool bars are the formatting tool bar and the standard tool bar. These two toolbars are displayed just below the title bar. At any point of time any tool bar can be made ON or OFF through the tool bar option of View Menu.
- *Ruler Bar*: The Ruler Bar allows you to format the vertical alignment of text in a document.
- *Status Bar*: The Status Bar displays information about the currently active document. This includes the page number that you are working, the column and line number of the cursor position and so on.
- *Scroll Bar*: The Scroll Bar helps you scroll the content or body of document. You can do so by moving the elevator button along the scroll bar, or by click in on the buttons with the arrow marked on them to move up and down and left and right of a page.
- *Workspace*: The Workspace is the area in the document window were you enter/type the text of your document.
- *Main Menu*: The Word main menu is displayed at the top of the screen as shown in the Fig. 9.1. The main menu further displays a sub menu. Some of the options are highlighted options and some of them appear as faded options. At any time, only highlighted options can be executed,

faded options are not applicable. Infect if the option is faded you will not be able to choose it. You may not that any option faded under present situation may become highlighted under different situations.

FEATURES OF MS WORD

Ms-Word not only supports word processing features but also DTP features. Some of the important features of Ms-Word are listed below:

- Using word you can create the document and edit them later, as and when required, by adding more text, modifying the existing text, deleting/moving some part of it.
- Changing the size of the margins can reformat complete document or part of text.
- Font size and type of fonts can also be changed. Page numbers and Header and Footer can be included.
- Spelling can be checked and correction can be made automatically in the entire document. Word count and other statistics can be generated.
- Text can be formatted in columnar style as we see in the newspaper. Text boxes can be made.
- Tables can be made and included in the text.
- Word also allows the user to mix the graphical pictures with the text. Graphical pictures can either be created in word itself or can be imported from outside like from Clip Art Gallery.
- Word also provides the mail-merge facility.
- Word also has the facility of macros. Macros can be either attached to some function/special keys or to a tool bar or to a menu.
- It also provides online help of any option.

MICROSOFT WORD FOR PREPARATION OF REPORTS

The Insert Caption Figure command only has one bug! If you have text wrap around your figures, then it will not pick it up in the cross referencing. So you must convert the text box to a frame and remove the line.

Here is the procedure for referencing figures.

- Create a Text Box
- Move the figure into the text box
- Select the figure.
- Choose *Insert Caption*
- Type the title of the figure at this time or later
- Select the text box

See the sequence of figures given below:

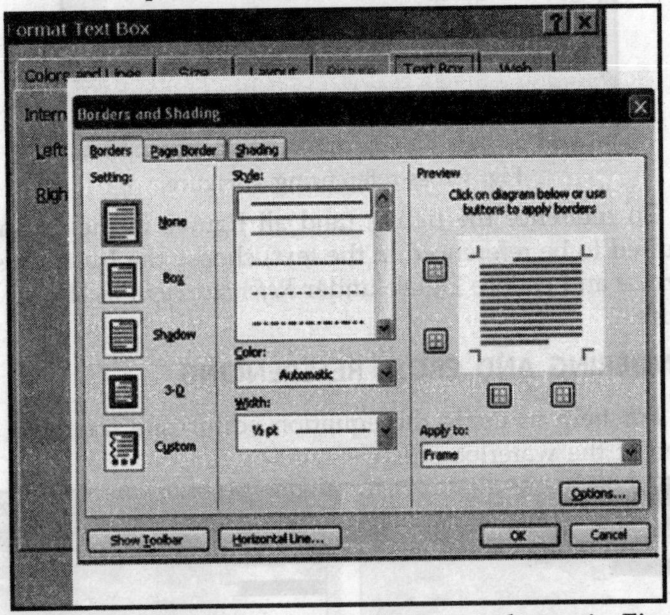

- Then choose Convert to Frame..., shown in Figure, and answer OK to the warning screen shown in Figure.

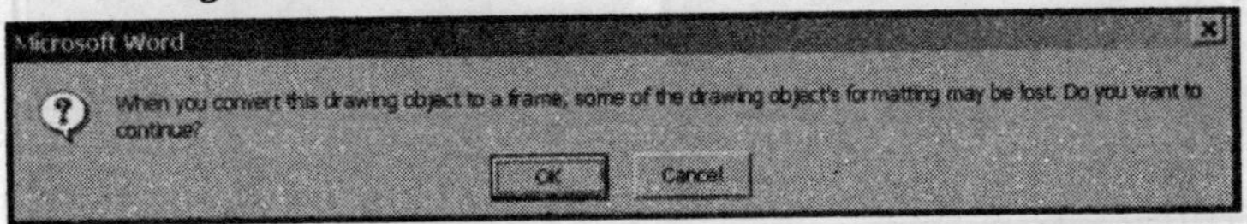

- To remove the line right-click on the frame border and use the *Format, Borders and Shading* command, and select setting = none.

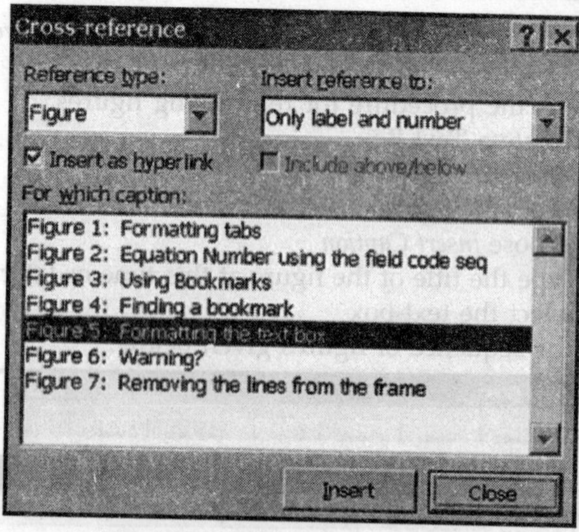

Fig. Cross-referencing a Figure.

To reference the figure, (and all figures in the text are required to be referenced in the text) choose the *Insert Cross-reference* and choose Figure under *Reference type*: as shown in Figure.

NUMBERING AND CROSS REFERENCING

For help in using the equation editor one reference is given at the waterloo site:

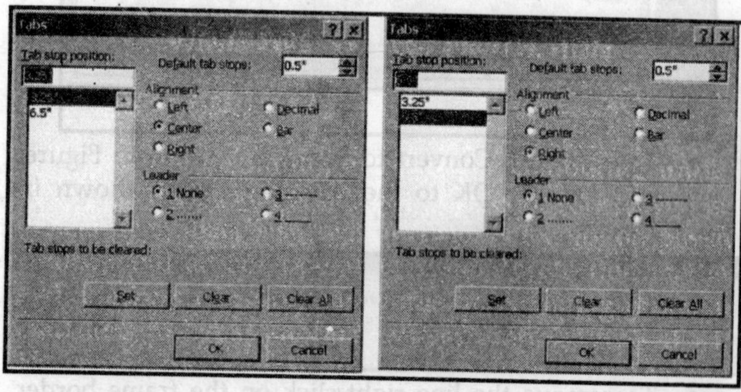

Fig. Formatting Tabs.

At the end of this section I will show you how to create

a macro to automatically number the equations using a macro button.Use the equation editor and put in this equation on the line below. To get the spacing and formatting I use the *Format Tabs* command and create a tab at 3.25 inches that is centered and a tab at 6.5 inches that is right. This is shown in previous Figure.

There is a trick to numbering and cross-referencing equations in a proper format, as shown here:

$$x = y \quad (1)$$

If you use MS word's equation number feature (under Insert Captions) you will not be able to cross reference the equation. Try it and you will see the problems! So you must use the sequence function. To do this choose *Insert Field* Numbering and then Seq. Then give a name to the sequence such as eqn. See Figure for clarification.

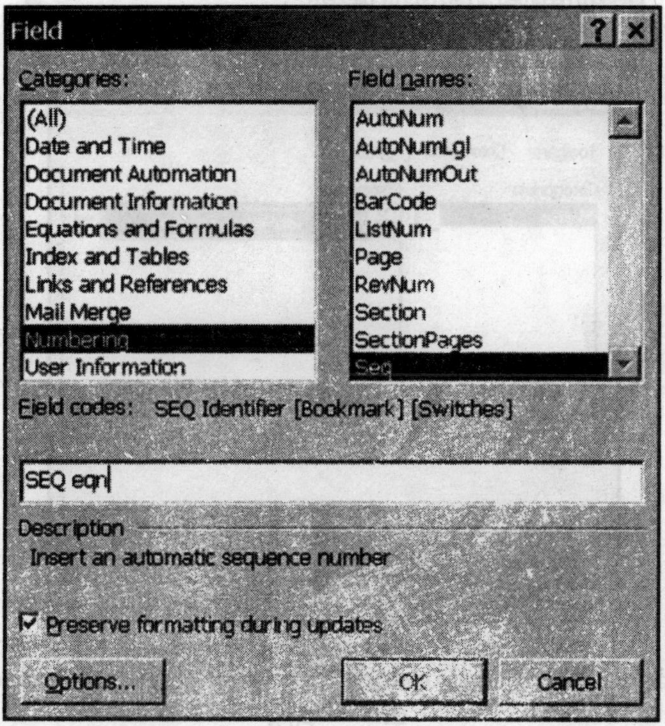

Fig. Equation Number Using the Field Code Seq.

CREATING A MACRO TO NUMBER EQUATIONS AUTOMATICALLY

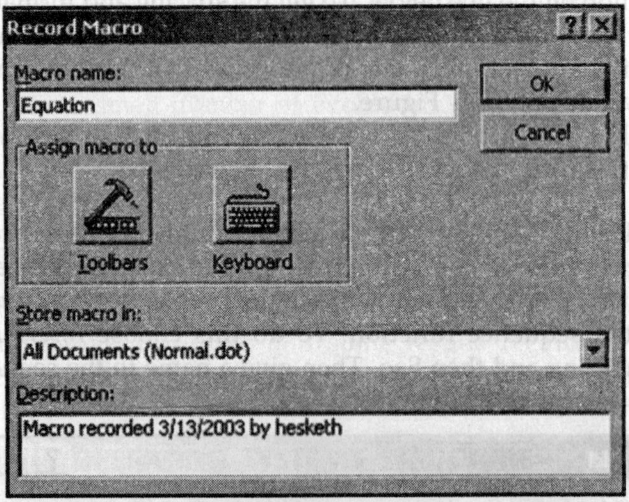

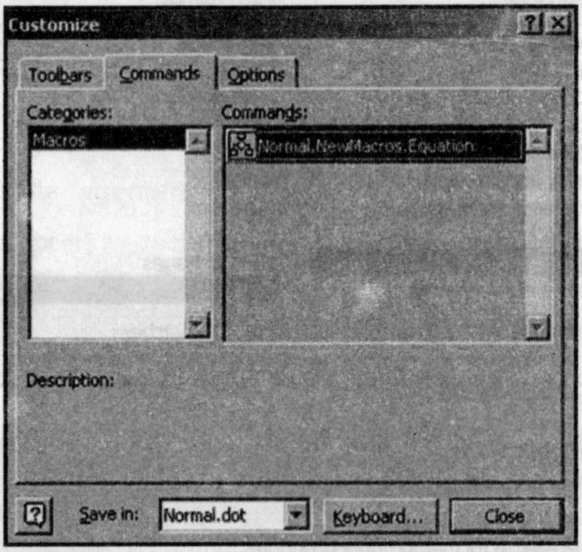

To create a macro you need to repeat the steps above with the macro creation turned on. First create an equation.

$$\frac{dP}{dV} = -\frac{\rho_0}{\rho}\beta_0$$

Then place your cursor at the right hand side of the equation and start the macro: Tools, Macro, Record New Macro

And Assign macro to the Toolbars. Drag the Normal.NewMacros.Equation to the tool bar for future use.

Then do the following:

- *Format Tabs*: Centered tab at 3.25 and a right tab at 6.5 in.
- Press the Home key to move to the left margin
- Type a tab
- Press the End key and type another tab
- Type a parenthesis
- Insert Field Code Numbering, then type eqn as the name of the sequence
- Finally add the closing parenthesis
- Stop recording the macro.

$$\frac{dP}{dV} = -\frac{\rho_0}{\rho}\beta_0$$

- Now you want to edit your button: Normal New Macros Equation because it is ugly and too long! Right click on the macro button and choose customise.
- Now right click again on the Normal New Macros Equation button and choose change button image. I use the 8 ball macro.
- Next chose default style under the options. Now you should have a toolbar with an eight ball in it for automatic number of equations!

Equation Macro Button:

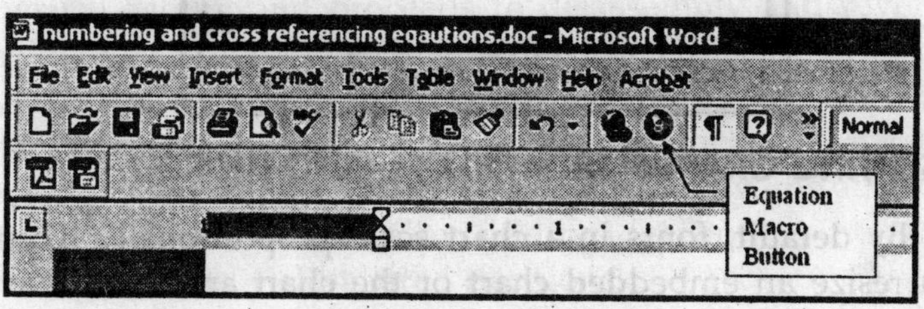

Now test your new macro!

$$\frac{d\overline{H}\overline{N}}{dt} = \sum_{i=1}^{n} H_{i0}F_{i0} - \sum_{i=1}^{n} H_iF_i + \dot{Q} - \dot{W}_s$$

CROSS REFERENCING EQUATIONS

If you have a problem with equations. than you can't cross reference them!.Use the equation and put in this equation on the line below:

x = y

What I really want is to have this equation numbered so I use the handy-dandy Microsoft feature to number the equation as below (Insert Caption Equation)

x2 = y2

The problem with the above is that it puts in the word "equation" You just delete the word that the macro put in and then add to my parenthesis.

x3 = y3

Now refer to equation 2 in the text. So then insert cross reference and choose the option given below x2 = y3. Then to cross reference you had to give a unique name to each equation and call it a book mark.

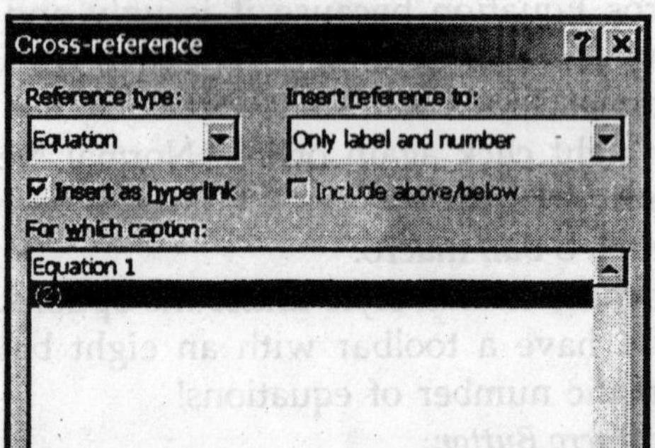

INSERTING GRAPHS FROM EXCEL INTO WORD

By default, fonts in a chart scale proportionally when you resize an embedded chart or the chart area of a chart sheet. If you want the font sizes in a chart to remain constant, select the chart area by clicking the blank area between the border of the chart and the plot area. On the Format menu, click Selected Chart Area, click the Font tab, and then clear the Auto scale check box.

In Excel: Copy

In Word: Paste Special... As Excel Object

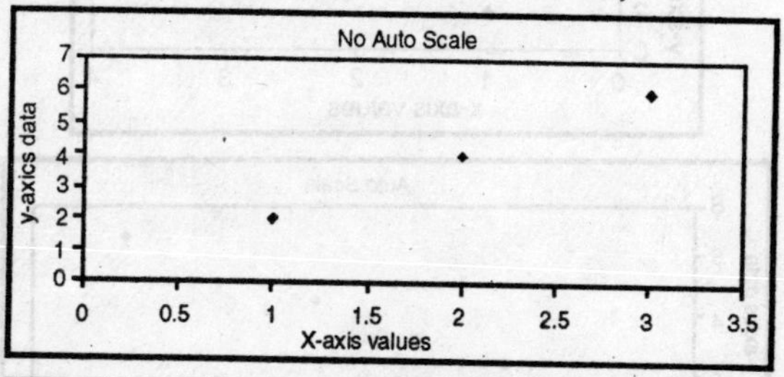

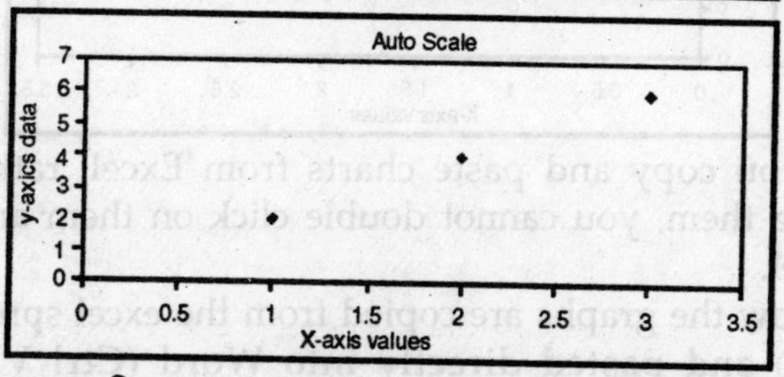

There are 2 ways to resize these. You can do it by single clicking on the box to select it in Word, and then dragging the handles:

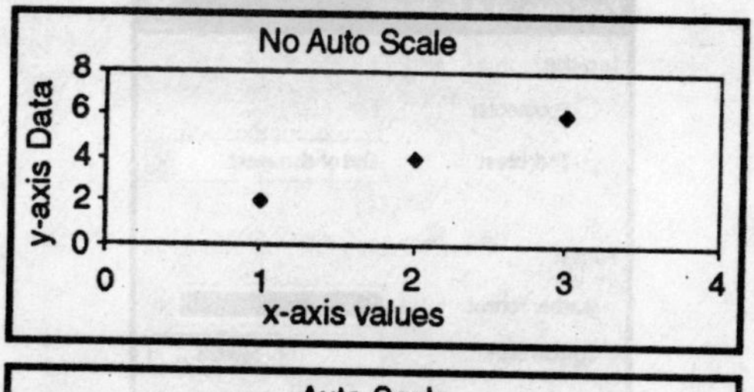

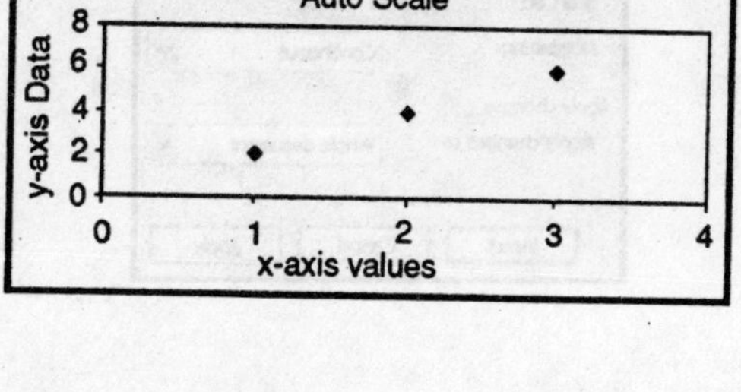

Alternately, you can double-click on the box to open it in Excel. There is still a box around the object, but this time it is a thicker, hatched line. Drag the handles to re-size.

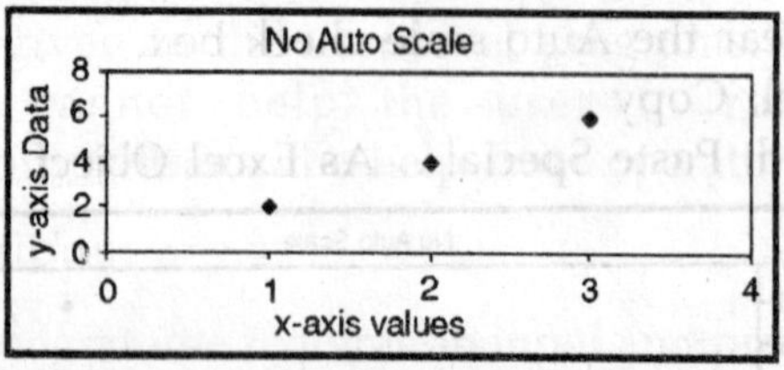

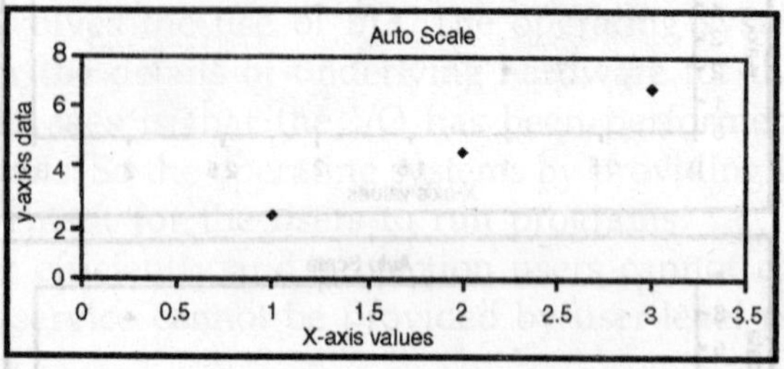

If you copy and paste charts from Excel, rather than inserting them, you cannot double click on them and bring up Excel.

Below the graphs are copied from the excel spreadsheet (Ctrl C) and pasted directly into Word (Ctrl V). Word recognizes them as a picture, and you cannot bring up Excel by double-clicking.

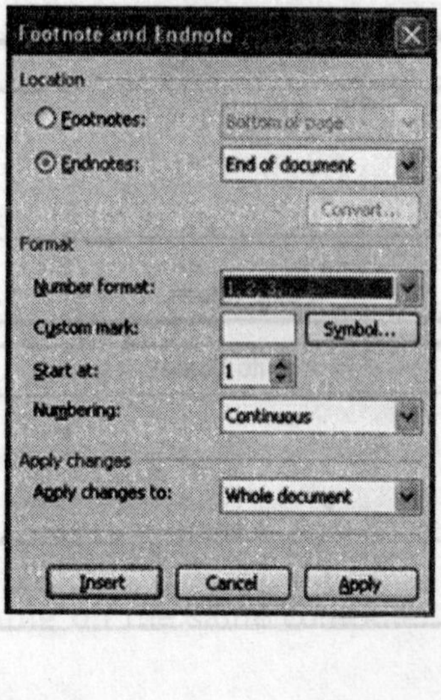

INSERTING AND CROSS-REFERENCING ENDNOTE REFERENCES

To insert an endnote reference that will be numbered automatically:

- Insert → Reference → Footnote
- Choose Endnotes and then change number format to 1,2,3... as shown at right.
- Click Apply[1]

To insert a cross reference to an existing endnote:

- Insert → Reference → Cross Reference...
- Choose Endnote and Endnote number from the drop down boxes as shown at right.

Chapter - 17

Word Techniques

OVERVIEW

Microsoft Word is used to develop various documents. Custom macros can be used to dynamically concatenate multi-file documents. Use a custom template to facilitate new document creation.

Microsoft Visio is used to draw diagrams. Custom styles can be created.

Adobe Acrobat is used to create public versions suitable for distribution and publication.

CHARACTERS

The obvious characters you can type into a document are those on the keyboard. There are additional characters:

Special characters like the em dash (a favourite of mine) are inserted with menu Insert, Symbol then choosing the character on the Special Characters tab.

Unique font-specific characters like ; are inserted with menu Insert, Symbol then choosing the font and character on the Symbols tab.

Unicode characters like the dagger used as a footnote reference mark are inserted by typing the Unicode value then [Alt+X]. For example, the dagger is U+2020, so you type U+2020[Alt+x]: †.

CUSTOMIZING WORD

There are several ways in which you can customise Microsoft Word:

Feature-Functionality	Customization
Toolbar	Change a standard toolbar Create a new toolbar
Menu	Change a standard menu Create a new menu
Shortcut key	Change a standard shortcut key Create a new shortcut key
Macro	Define a series of actions (as a macro) so they can be executed over and over again at will

For a menu item or toolbar item you can:

- Add/change an image,
- Add/change the text,
- Add/change the shortcut key, and
- Assign a hypertext link.

CUSTOMIZATIONS

- Create a custom toolbar with only the commands you use frequently. Note that many standard Word commands do not appear on a menu or toolbar.
- Create a macro to reverse transposed letters, assign a shortcut key to it.
- Create a macro to toggle the case of selected characters, assign a shortcut key to it.
- Create a macro to open a document for use as a template, assign it to a toolbar with a shortcut key.
- Create a macro to define a custom table format, assign it to a toolbar with a shortcut key.
- Create a macro to define a custom bulleted paragraph format, assign it to a toolbar with a shortcut key.
- Create a macro to concatenate several documents and save the new document. Create a macro to toggle a hanging indent, assign it to a toolbar with a shortcut
- *key*: Create a macro to insert a registration mark at the first occurrence of the trademarked

- Word/phrase. Create a macro
- To run automatically when,
  - Word opens,
  - Word closes,
  - New document begun,
  - Existing document opened,
  - Document closed.

SOME WORD TECHNIQUES

HIGHLIGHTING BLOCKS OF TEXT

This one is a little trickier, but not too tricky. To highlight a block of text, do the following:

- Click at the start of the block of text you want to highlight. (For practice purposes, click just before the letter "I" of "It has come ..." on the first line.)
- Hold down the Shift key on your keyboard (The Shift keys are the ones with the block arrows on them, pointing upwards. You hold down a shift key if you want a capital letter.)
- With the Shift key held down, click your left mouse button at the end of the block of text you want to highlight. (Click after the question mark of " ... premature?")
- A block of text will be highlighted

HIGHLIGHT BY DRAGGING

This is another tricky one, when you're starting out. A bit of practice, though, and you'll soon master it.

To highlight some text by dragging, do the following:

- Click with your left mouse button at the start of the text you want to highlight.
- Keep your left mouse button held down.
- Drag your mouse pointer across the screen (Your mouse pointer will change shape. It will be the shape of a capital letter I"".
- You can drag in any direction you like.

- When you've reached the end of the text you want to highlight, let go of the mouse button.
- Your text is highlighted.

HIGHLIGHTING A SINGLE WORD

Highlighting a single word is easy. All you have to do is to double click on the word with your left mouse button. Highlighting with the keyboard (no mouse needed) For more precise highlighting, nothing beats the keyboard.

Line Highlighting

- To highlight a single line, move your cursor to the start of the line you want to highlight. (You can move the cursor about with the arrow keys on your keyboard. Play about with them and see what happens.)
- Hold down a Shift key on your keyboard.
- With the Shift key held down, press the End key on your keyboard
- A single line is highlighted
- To go the other way, from the end of a line to the beginning, move your cursor to the end of the line (or somewhere in the middle will do for. It works just as well.)
- Hold down a Shift key on your keyboard
- With the Shift key held down, press the Home key on your keyboard
- Your text is highlighted

Paragraph Highlighting

To highlight a paragraph with the keyboard alone, do the following:

- Move your cursor to the end of the paragraph you want to highlight.
- Hold down a Shift key AND a Ctrl key (bottom left of your keyboard)
- With the Shift key AND a Ctrl key held down, press the Up arrow.
- A paragraph will be highlighted

If you want to go the other way, from the beginning of a paragraph to the end, press the Down arrow on your keyboard instead of the Up arrow.

Highlighting one Word at a Time

- For practice purposes, move your cursor to the middle of a line of text
- Hold down a Shift key AND a Ctrl key
- With the Shift key AND a Ctrl key held down, press the Left arrow or the Right arrow key on your keyboard

Highlighting one Letter at a Time

- For practice purposes, move your cursor to the middle of a line of text
- Hold down a Shift key
- With the Shift key, press the Left arrow or the Right arrow on your keyboard
- A single letter is highlighted for every tap of an arrow key

And that ends the highlighting section. Practice the techniques outlined above using your library letter. It takes quite a while to master them all, so just pick a couple of highlighting techniques. The ones you find the easiest to do.

RED AND GREEN UNDERLINE IN WORD

One thing you probably will have noticed is the spelling mistakes in the letter. You should have typed the letter exactly as it was, and left any spelling errors in.

More than likely, the spelling mistakes are underlined in red in your document. Anything with a wiggly green line under it is a grammatical error, (or what Microsoft Word insists is a grammatical error). You can turn these off and on if you like. To Turn the wiggly red and green lines on and off, do the following.

From the menu bar, click on Tools. From the drop down menu, click Options:

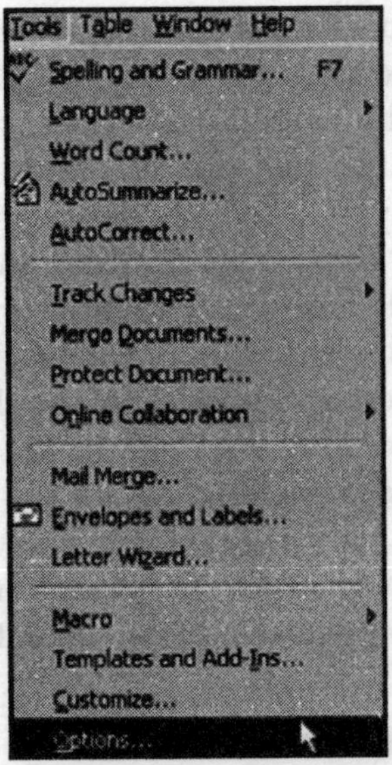

You will get a dialogue box popping up. It looks a very daunting dialogue box. Click on the words "Spelling and Grammar" to get the same screen as the one shown:

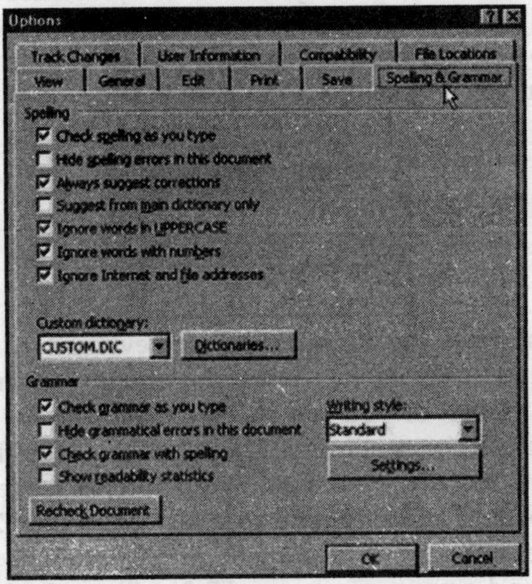

There's a lot to worry about in that dialogue box! But

it is split in to two sections. The top section is for spelling options, and the bottom section is for Grammar.

To get rid of the green wiggly lines, the grammar ones, you need to take the tick out of the box next to "Check grammar as you type". To take a tick out of a box, click inside it. To put it back in, click inside the box again.

The red wiggly lines, the spelling ones, can be quite useful, so we'll leave them in. Set your spelling options to the one above. In other words, you should have 5 ticks in the spelling section, and only one in the grammar section "Check grammar with spelling". We'll see what that does in a moment.

Click OK when you have finished. You should find any green wiggly lines have disappeared, but the red spelling ones are still there.

MICROSOFT WORD SPELLCHECKER

If you have "Check spelling as you type" switched on, you should have red wiggly lines under three of the words in your letter: counsil, libary, and decicion. Microsoft Word has a spell checker that you can use to correct any misspelled words. To launch the spell checker you can either click on Tools, then select Spelling and Grammar

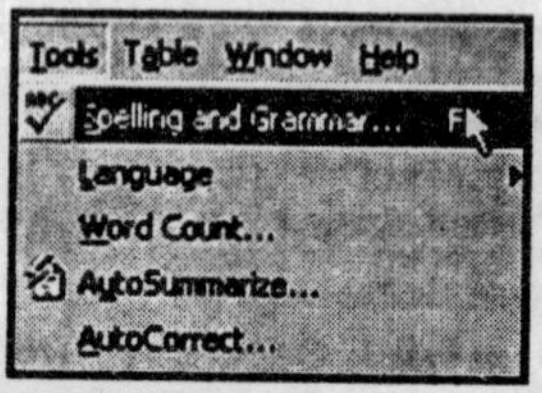

Or just press the F7 key on your keyboard.

You can have Word check the entire document for spelling mistakes, or you can check the spelling for selected areas. To check the spelling of a selected area, you first have to highlight the text you want Word to check. Next, click Tools > Spelling and Grammar. Or just press the F7 key.

To check the entire document, just go straight to Tools > Spelling and grammar, or press F7. You'll get the following dialogue box:

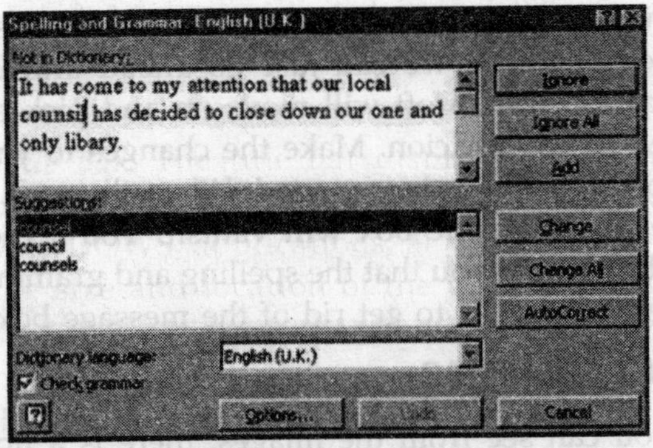

There are two main areas of the dialogue box: Not in dictionary, and Suggestions. The text box below the words "Not in dictionary" shows part of your text, and one spelling mistake at a time. The spelling mistake is in red.

In the text box below the word "Suggestions" are alternatives to the word you got wrong. In the image, you can see that three alternative words are suggested for counsil: counsel, council, and counsels. What we really meant was, of course, council. So we want to change counsil to council.

To make the change, do the following:

- Click on the word "council" in the Suggestions text box
- Click the Change button
- Word moves on to the next word you got wrong

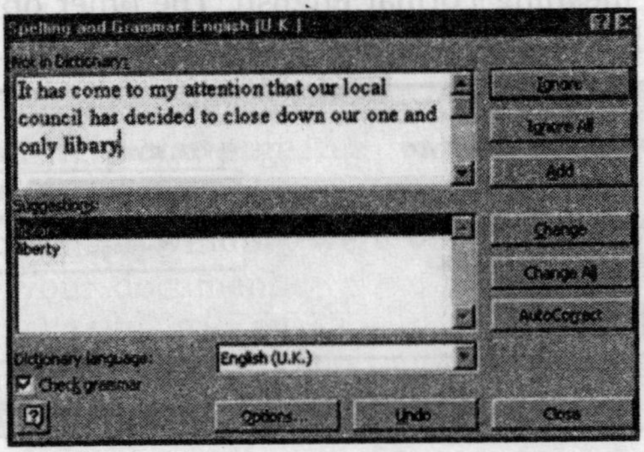

The next word we spelled wrong is now highlighted in red: libary. As you can see, Word is giving us two alternatives in the Suggestions box: library, and liberty. The correct spelling was library, and this is already highlighted in the Suggestions box. So we can just go ahead and click the Change button. Microsoft will move on and pick our third misspelled word: decicion. Make the changes to your letter so that the correct word is inserted. When the spell check is complete, the dialogue box will vanish. You'll then get a message box telling you that the spelling and grammar check is complete. Click OK to get rid of the message box.

CHECKING GRAMMAR

As you can see from the images, there is a tick in the box "Check grammar". Click on the tick to get rid of it, if you don't want Word to check all of your grammatical errors. The grammar checking in Word Processing software can be a little bit intimidating, especially if you have had no training in the finer points of the English language. The grammar checking can also make very strange corrections. Watch what happens when we click the Options button at the bottom, and reset the grammar to Formal.

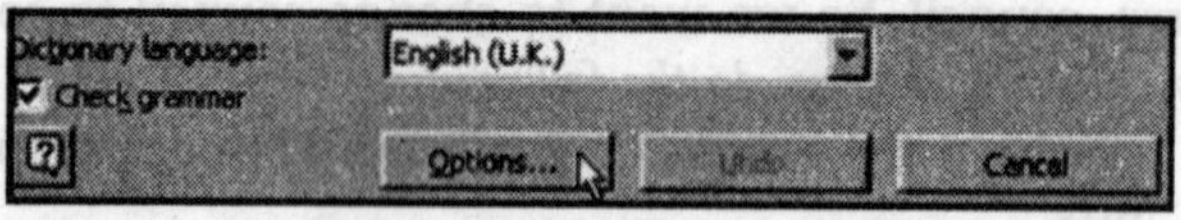

Notice in the image below that "Check grammar with spelling is still ticked, and the Writing style has been reset to Formal, meaning Formal English. The other options here are: Casual, Standard, Technical and Custom.

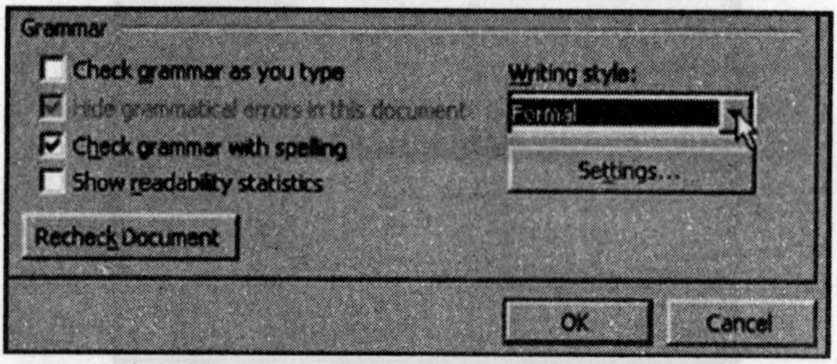

When we click OK we are returned to the Spelling and Grammar dialogue box. Word has now moved on to check the grammar. But notice what it has picked us up on:

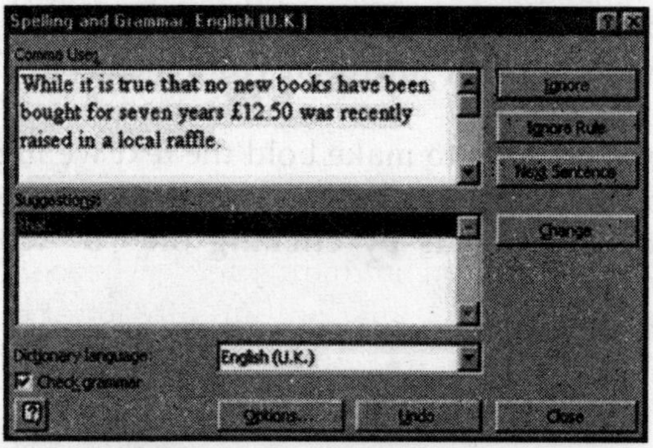

It seems to think we should put a comma after "that". It is suggesting we put this: "While it is true that, no new books have been bought". Which is just plain wrong. The grammar checker also seems to have a bee in its bonnet over the passive voice, and pulls you up about this on every occasion.

BOLD TEXT IN MICROSOFT WORD

To make any part of your text bold in Microsoft Word, you have to highlight the text. So using one of the highlight techniques you learnt in the previous section, highlight the first line of the report. In other words, highlight the words "Constable Tucker's Crime Statistics". Your page should like this one:

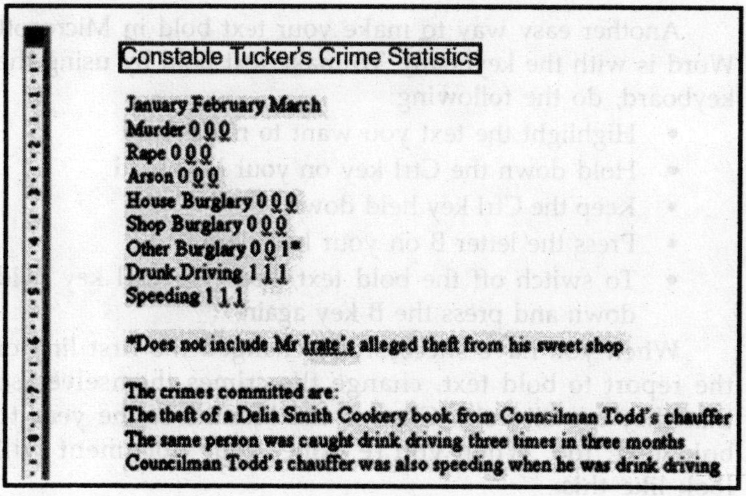

Incidentally, if you haven't got the ruler bar showing, click on View from the Microsoft Word menu bar. Then click Ruler.

But we're going to make bold the text we highlighted. There are two very easy ways to make your highlighted text bold. The first is by clicking the "B" icon on the toolbar.

It looks like this:

With your text highlighted, click the "B" icon. Your text will turn bold. You might not be able to tell because your text will still be highlighted.

Click anywhere on your blank page to get rid of the black highlight.

The "B" icon will change to this:

That indicates that you have Bold text switched on. To turn off Bold text, highlight the text and then click the B icon with the left mouse button.

Use Keyboard

Another easy way to make your text bold in Microsoft Word is with the keyboard. To make text bold by using the keyboard, do the following:

- Highlight the text you want to make bold
- Hold down the Ctrl key on your keyboard
- Keep the Ctrl key held down
- Press the letter B on your keyboard
- To switch off the bold text, keep the Ctrl key held down and press the B key again.

When you have successfully changed the first line of the report to bold text, change the crimes themselves so that they are all bold. Change the Months of the year to bold text, too. When you're done, your document will look like this:

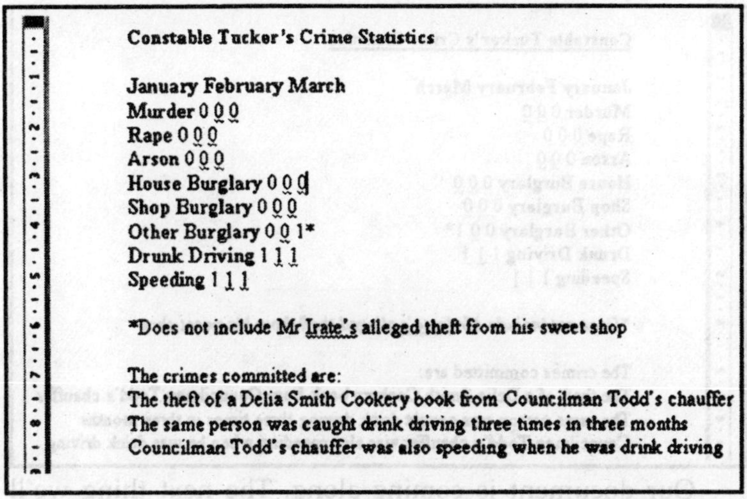
Constable Tucker's Crime Statistics

January February March
Murder 0 0 0
Rape 0 0 0
Arson 0 0 0
House Burglary 0 0 0
Shop Burglary 0 0 0
Other Burglary 0 0 1*
Drunk Driving 1 1 1
Speeding 1 1 1

*Does not include Mr Irate's alleged theft from his sweet shop

The crimes committed are:
The theft of a Delia Smith Cookery book from Councilman Todd's chauffer
The same person was caught drink driving three times in three months
Councilman Todd's chauffer was also speeding when he was drink driving

As you can see, there is a distinct difference between the bold text and the normal text. We'll now use italics and underlining.

ITALICS AND UNDERLINE IN MICROSOFT WORD

Again, we need to highlight the text that we're going to change.

We'll turn part of the text to italics. So highlight the following line. "Does not include Mr Irate's alleged theft from his sweet shop"

When you have highlighted the text, click the italic icon in the tool bar. The icon will look like this after you have clicked the letter "I".

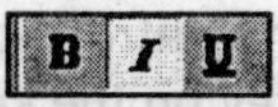

Another way to turn text to italics is to hold down the Ctrl key on your keyboard. With the Ctrl key held down, press the letter "I" on your keyboard.

To underline some text, click the letter "U" of the shown icons. The keyboard shortcut is Ctrl plus the letter "U".

In your report, underline "Constable Tucker's Crime Statistics". When you have finished, the report should now look like this:

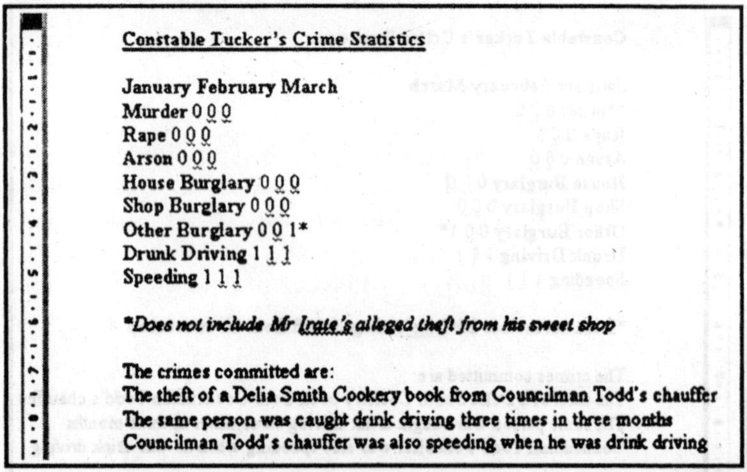

<u>Constable Tucker's Crime Statistics</u>

January February March
Murder 0 0 0
Rape 0 0 0
Arson 0 0 0
House Burglary 0 0 0
Shop Burglary 0 0 0
Other Burglary 0 0 1*
Drunk Driving 1 1 1
Speeding 1 1 1

****Does not include Mr Irate's alleged theft from his sweet shop***

The crimes committed are:
The theft of a Delia Smith Cookery book from Councilman Todd's chauffer
The same person was caught drink driving three times in three months
Councilman Todd's chauffer was also speeding when he was drink driving

Our document is coming along. The next thing we'll do is add some Tabs. The Tabs will help is to push some of the text along.

SETTING UP TABS IN MICROSOFT WORD

A Tab in word processing terms is the jump your cursor makes from one position to another when you press the tab key on your keyboard.

Your tab key looks like this:

Press the tab key on your keyboard and watch what happens. You'll see the cursor jump from left to right in your document. You can control how far the cursor jumps when you press the tab key on the keyboard. But why would you want to?

You typically set tab stop positions for things like indenting the first line of a paragraph, or if you wanted text to start three or four centimetres along the line. We're going to set three tab stops for our line of text with the months of the year.

With your Crime Statistics document open, do the following:

- Move your cursor to the start of the January, February, March line of text in your document
- On the menu bar, click Format
- From the drop down menu select tabs

When you click on Tabs, the following dialogue box will appear:

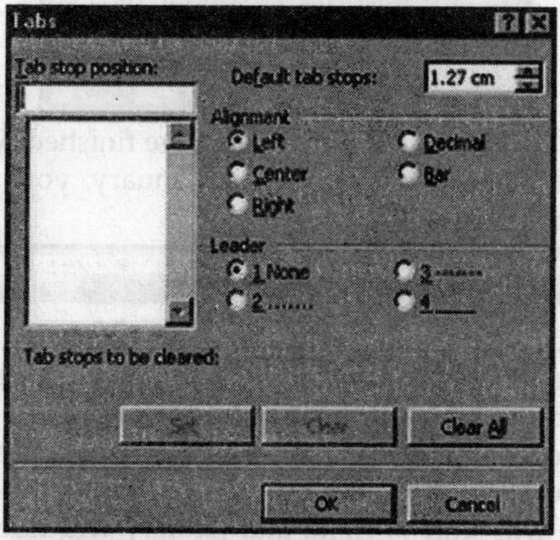

The area to concentrate on is Tab stop position, right at the top. When you want to set a tab stop, you type in a number in the text box below the words "Tab stop position". Then you press the "Set" button.

We are going to set tab stop positions at 3, 5 and 7 centimetres from the left hand side.

- Enter a 3 in the Tab stop position text box
- Click the "Set" button

- Enter a 5 in the Tab stop position text box
- Click the "Set" button
- Enter a 7 in the Tab stop position text box
- Click the "Set" button

When you are finished, your Tab dialogue box should look like this

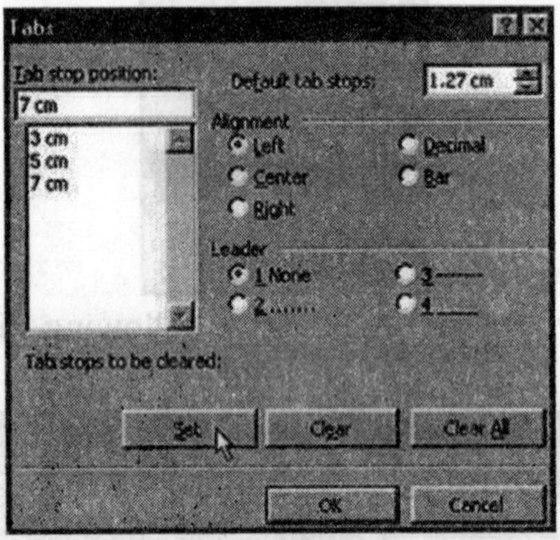

Click the OK button when you have finished. With your cursor still flashing before the J of January, your top ruler bar will look like this:

Notice the three L-shaped lines on your ruler bar. These are your three tab stop positions.

To move your text along, position your cursor before the J of January. Press the tab key on your keyboard. The entire line will shift to right, and January will now be lined up with your first tab stop at position 3. Position your cursor before the letter "F" of February, and then press your tab key again. February will be lined up with your second tab stop at position 5.

Position your cursor before the letter "M" of March, and then press your tab key again. March will be lined up with your third tab stop at position 7. Your document will now look like this:

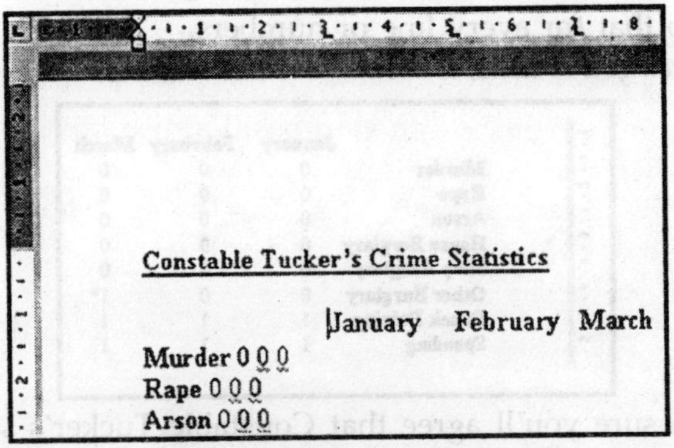

You can see that the three months are line up with the three tab stops in the ruler bar at the top.

Now move your cursor down one line and watch what happens to the ruler bar at the top. The tab stops have vanished!

The tab stops have vanished because we only set them for one line - the months of the year line. To set tab stops for the numbers, highlight the same area of text as in the image below

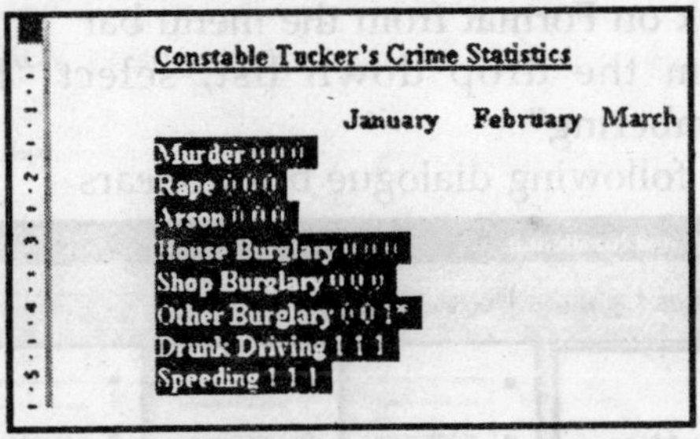

When your text is highlighted, click on Format > Tabs again to bring up the tabs dialogue box. Set three tabs at the following tab stop positions: 3.5, 5.5, 7.5 centimetres.

When you're finished, every line in the highlighted area will have tab stops at those three positions. You now need to shift the numbers across so that one number is underneath one month. So position your cursor before the first number and press your tab key. Position your cursor before the second number and press your tab key. Position your cursor before the third number and press your tab key. Do that for every line of numbers.

When you're done, it should look like this one:

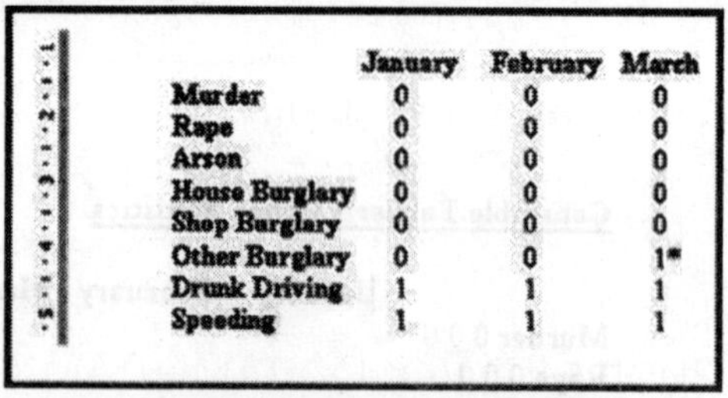

	January	February	March
Murder	0	0	0
Rape	0	0	0
Arson	0	0	0
House Burglary	0	0	0
Shop Burglary	0	0	0
Other Burglary	0	0	1*
Drunk Driving	1	1	1
Speeding	1	1	1

I'm sure you'll agree that Constable Tucker's statistics are looking a lot tidier. We can do something else, though, and that's add some bullets to the list of crimes. After all, what crime list would be complete without bullets!

MICROSOFT WORD AND BULLETS

Bulleted lists have been used throughout this site. To create one of your own, do the following.

- Highlight the last three lines in your Crime Statistics document
- Click on Format from the menu bar
- From the drop down list, select "Bullets and Numbering"
- The following dialogue box appears

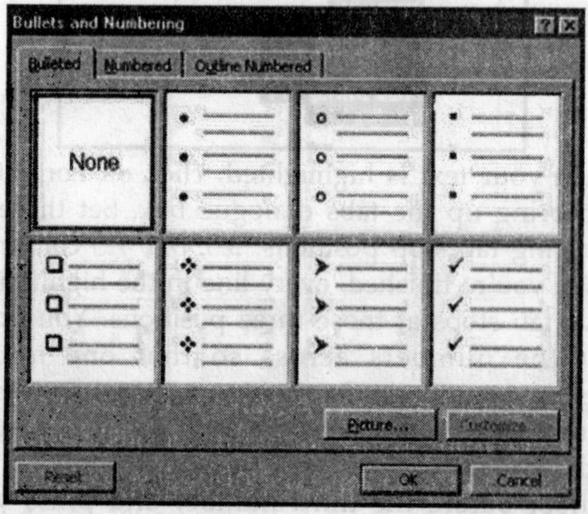

As you can see, there are 7 different bullet styles to choose from. Click on any one of them that takes your fancy. When you click on one, the customise button becomes available.

You don't need to click this customise button. If you prefer, just click OK to see your bulleted list. But the customise options are worth a look.

Click the customise button and take a look at the dialogue box that appears.

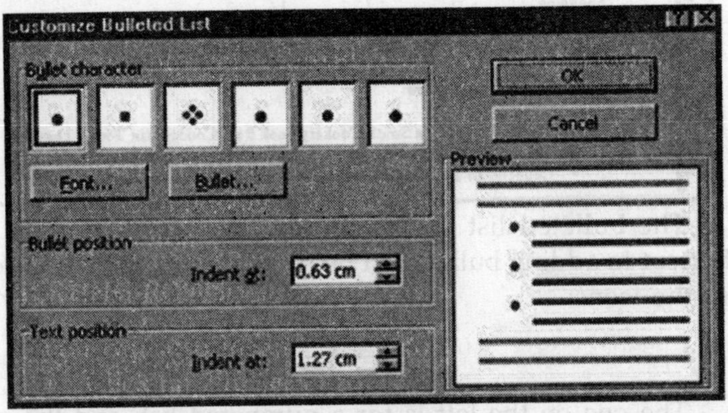

As you can see, there are more options to choose from for your bulleted list. You can click on any of the Bullet characters.

You can change the colour and size with the Font button. The Bullet button gives you more options for the style of bullet you want.

Bullet Position and Bullet text are quite interesting options. The Bullet position lets you specify how far from the left hand side you want your bullets.

At the moment, it is set to 0.63 centimetres from the left of the page. The Bullet text is the text that appears after your bullet. At the moment, the text is set to 1.27 centimetres from the left of the page. You can change these values to anything you want.

But leave them alone for now, and just click the cancel button on the customise option. You will be taken back to the main bullet dialogue box. Once there, choose a bullet style for your highlighted text, and then click the OK button. Your document will now look something like this:

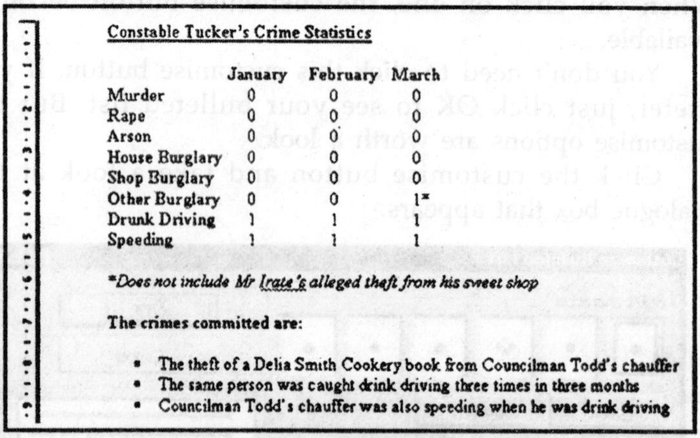

<u>Constable Tucker's Crime Statistics</u>

	January	February	March
Murder	0	0	0
Rape	0	0	0
Arson	0	0	0
House Burglary	0	0	0
Shop Burglary	0	0	0
Other Burglary	0	0	1*
Drunk Driving	1	1	1
Speeding	1	1	1

**Does not include Mr Irate's alleged theft from his sweet shop*

The crimes committed are:

- **The theft of a Delia Smith Cookery book from Councilman Todd's chauffer**
- **The same person was caught drink driving three times in three months**
- **Councilman Todd's chauffer was also speeding when he was drink driving**

The bulleted list makes things a lot easier to read. A shortcut to adding bullets can be found on the toolbar. These are the icons:

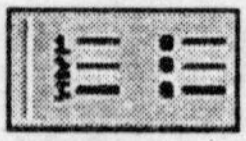

The one on the left is for a numbered list, and the one on the right is the bulleted list. But it will only give you the bullet style you last used. To use them, highlight your text and simply click on one of the icons with your left mouse button.

CHANGING FONTS AND FONT SIZES IN WORD

A font is a style and design of text. Examine this letter:

E

Now examine this one:

E

As you can see, the two style are completely different. Notice how straight and blocky the second one is compared to the first. The first one has little pointy bits on its edges. The pointy bit is called a serif. Fonts are basically split into two types - those that have the pointy edges, and those that don't. The pointy fonts are called serif fonts, and the ones without pointy bits are called sans serif fonts.

The first of the letter e's is the very popular serif font "Times New Roman". The second letter e is the most popular sans serif font "Arial". With Microsoft Word, the font you get if you don't make any changes is Times New Roman. That's because Times is an excellent font to use for your body text. The complementary sans serif font Arial goes well as a heading when Times is used for the body text. Newspapers use this combination a lot - Arial for the heading, Times for the text.

We'll do the same. We'll use Arial for the heading of our report, because the body text is all in Times New Roman.

To change the font heading to Arial, do the following:

- Highlight the heading "Constable Tucker's Crime Statistics"

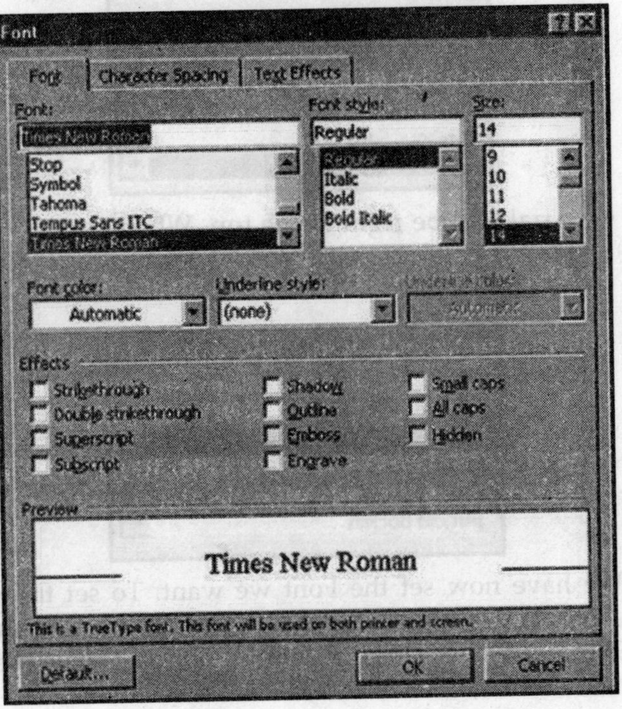

- While the text is highlighted, get rid of the underline by clicking the U icon in the toolbar (The underline looks awful!)
- Click on Format from the menu bar.
- Click the word Font.
- The following dialogue box appears.

There are three main areas to concentrate on: Font, Font style, and Size. The Font that is highlighted is Times New Roman.

This is because it is the font we are currently using. For the same reason, the regular Font style is highlighted and Size 14.

We want to change the Font from Times to Arial.

- Scroll up by clicking the little black arrow in the Font text box.

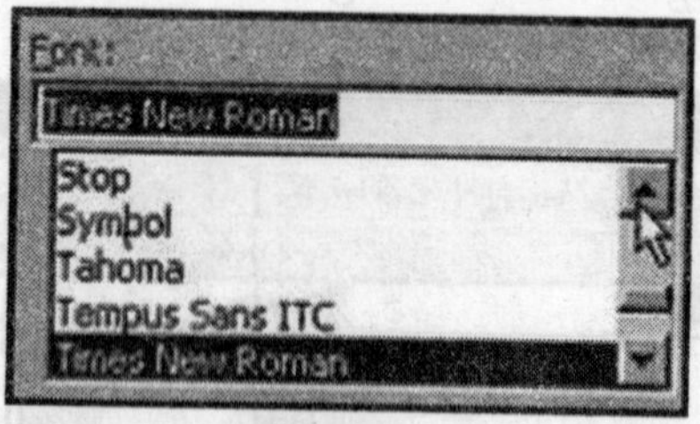

- Arial will be right at the top. When you get there, click on Arial with your left mouse button to select it.

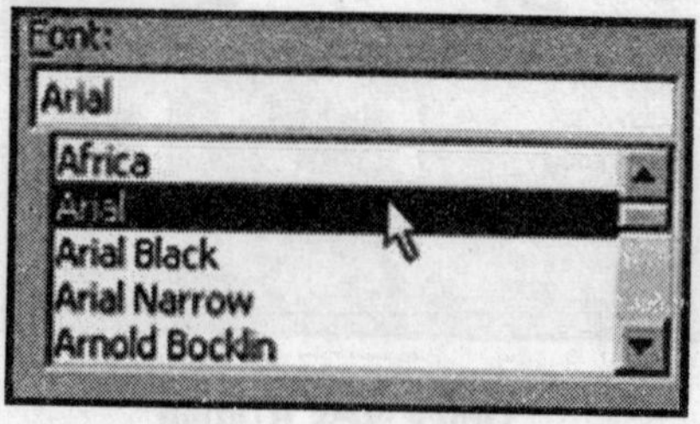

We have now set the Font we want. To set the style, click on bold in the next text box along. Change the size by scrolling down and clicking on 16. Your font dialogue box should now look like this:

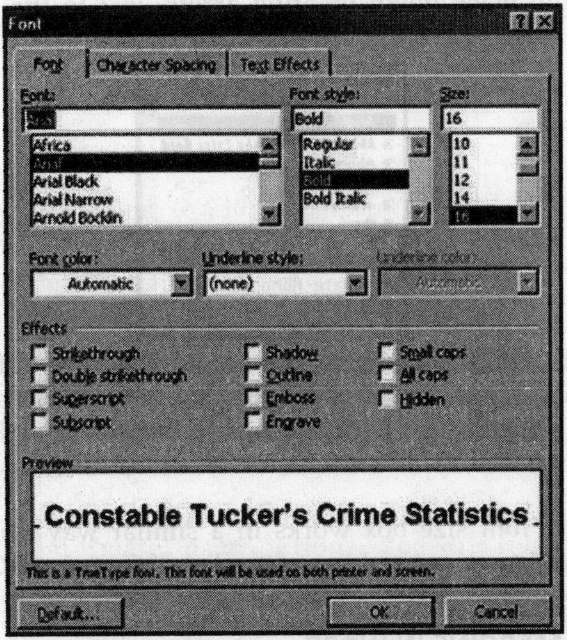

Before you click the OK button, notice the "Font colour" area. As it's name implies, you can set a colour for your Font. To do that, click the black down-pointing arrow just to the right of "Automatic". You'll get the colour box. Click on a colour that takes your fancy. You'll see what it looks like in the Preview box at the bottom.

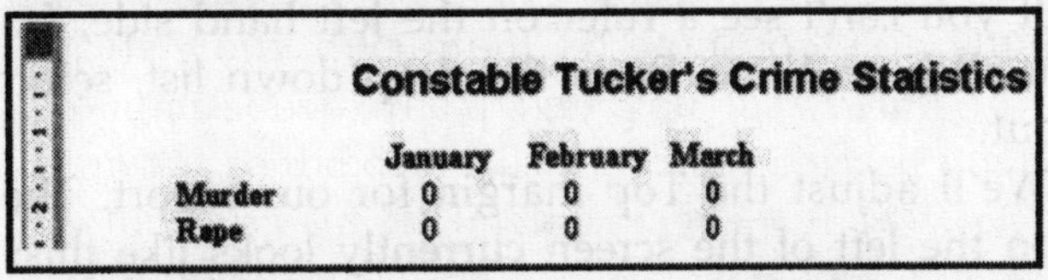

There is another way you can set the font, without opening the font dialogue box.

You have probably noticed this in your toolbar:

This is a shortcut to changing your Font and Font size. Don't worry about the first box "Normal" for now. If you click the black down-pointing arrow, just to the right of "Times New Roman", you'll get a drop down list of fonts:

The Fonts available to you will probably be different to the ones above. To select one, just move your mouse down and click with your left hand mouse button. Click the black arrows to scroll down and see more fonts that you can choose.

The font size box works in a similar way - click the black down arrow and you get a list of font sizes. Click on one to choose it.

PAGE MARGINS IN WORD

If you look at the ruler bar on the left of your screen, you'll see grey areas at the top and bottom of the left ruler, and a white area in the middle. The grey areas are your top and bottom margins. There are a number of ways you can adjust your page margins in Microsoft Word.

If you can't see a ruler on the left hand side, from the menu click on View. From the drop down list, select Print Layout.

We'll adjust the Top margin for our report. The ruler bar on the left of the screen currently looks like this:

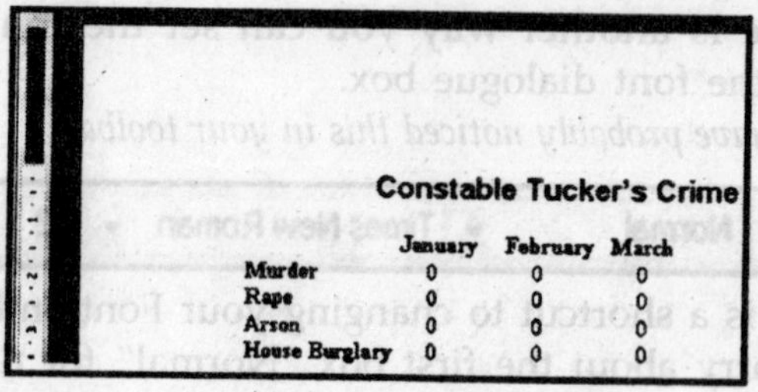

As you can see, there's a grey area to the left, and underneath a white area. The white areas have numbers in them.

If you trace your finger from the bottom of the grey area across and to "Constable Tucker's Crime" you'll find they match up exactly.

This is the top of our page. You can't move your cursor above the white area an into the grey. But you can change the size of the grey area, and therefore your top margin.

There are a couple of ways you can change your margins in Microsoft Word. We'll start with the tricky way!

- Move your mouse pointer half way between the grey area and the white area.
- Your mouse pointer will change to the shape of a double arrow.

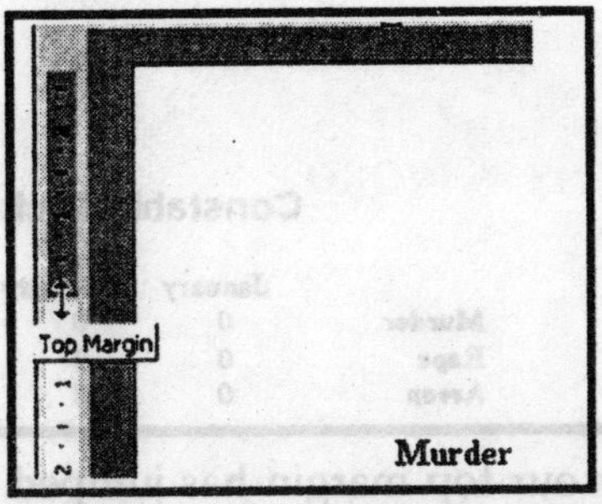

- Next, hold down your left mouse button.
- Your screen should now look like this.

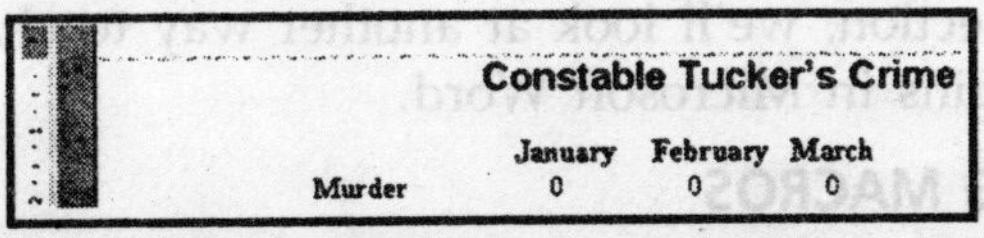

- Notice the thin dashed line running across the page. This is your current top margin.
- With your left mouse still held down drag your mouse downwards.
- The thin dashed line will move with your mouse.
- Let go of your mouse button when you see a 5 at the top of the grey area.

Before you let go of the mouse button:

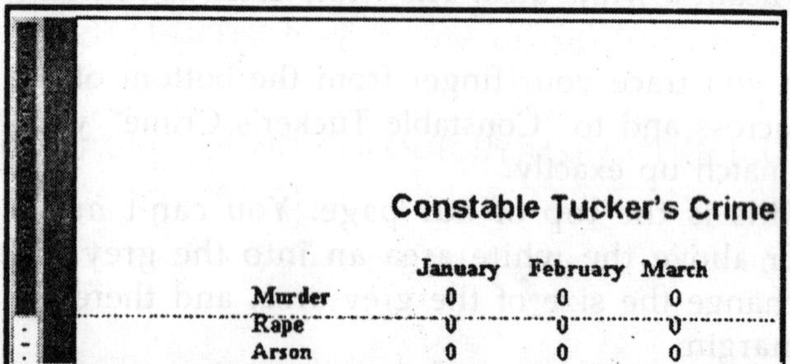

After you let go of the mouse button:

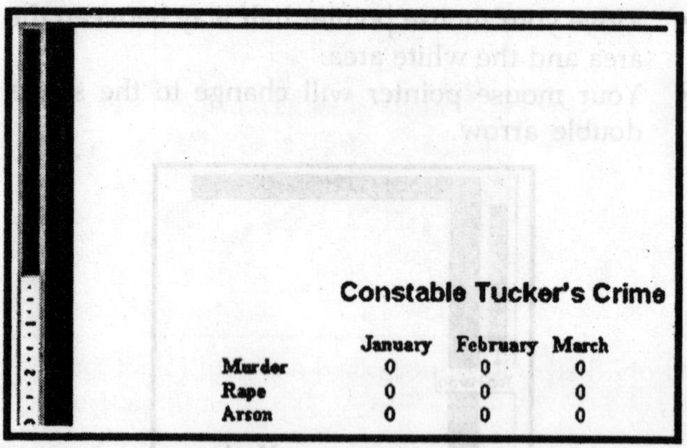

Notice how our top margin has jumped down. We now have a bigger gap at the top, and therefore more space.

OK, that was the tricky way to adjust a top margin. In the next section, we'll look at another way to change your page margins in Microsoft Word.

CREATING MACROS

The easiest way, and one that works for most purposes, is to record it. Use the menu Tools, Macro, Record New Macro. Use the help file for directions.

About Auto Macros

There is a group of macros that run automatically when five different events occur.

These macros are identified by their name:

AutoExec	Word opens
AutoExit	Word closes
AutoNew	New document begins
AutoOpen	Existing document opens
AutoClose	Document closes

The macros can reside in any template, including normal.dot, and in a document file. AutoExec will only run when it is in a global template named in the "Templates and Add-ins" dialog box or in the Startup directory (specified in File Locations).

Either a procedure is named Autoxxxx or there is a module of that name with a procedure named "Main". The latter enables more elaborate processing.

You can prevent an auto macro from running by holding down the [Shift] key until the action is complete. You can block all auto macros by code Word Basic.

Disable Auto Macros:

```
WordBasic.DisableAutoMacros 1   'Disables auto macros
WordBasic.DisableAutoMacros 0   'Enables auto macros
```

Unfortunately these days the innocent helpful macro can be mistaken for a virus. The High security setting (accessed with menu Tools, Macro, Security) disables auto macros that are not digitally signed.

The solution:

- Lower the security setting
- Digitally sign macros.

The second approach is best when you create macros for others to use; it requires you buy a digital certificate from a commercial certification authority like VeriSign.

Shortcut Keys

A shortcut key is a combination of two or more keyboard keys that when pressed simultaneously initiate an action. There are pre-defined shortcut keys. And you can create your own: You can change the pre-defined keys and assign keys to the actions of your choosing, often macros, styles, and menus.

How to Create a Shortcut Key

- Use menu Tools, Customise to open the "Customise" window.
- Select [Keyboard] to open the "Customise Keyboard" window.
- One at a time, select a Category in the left pane, then select a Command from the right pane. Press the desired shortcut key combination, then select [Assign].
- When you are done, close the "Customise Keyboard" window and the "Customise" window. Print Pre-defined Shortcut Keys

You can list Word's pre-defined (built in) shortcut keys with macro "ListCommands." Your own customizations are excluded. Use menu Tools, Macro, Macros to open the "Macros" window. Set Macros in = "Word commands". Select macro ListCommands, then [Run]. The "List Commands" window appears:

In this window select "Current menu and keyboard settings", then [OK]. A new Word document is created containing the settings. Print this document and close it without saving.

These can also be found in the help file.

There is a website with a useful presentation of the built-in shortcut keys:

Print Custom Shortcut Keys

Custom shortcut keys can be listed by a macro. See *Word VBA Techniques* for details.

CUSTOMIZATIONS

Toolbars and macros are stored in a x.dot template file. The default file is *normal.dot*, the default global template. When using customizations, it is best to use a version of normal.dot that is not the standard Word file. As mentioned for toolbars, software upgrades to Word will either restore normal.dot to its original state or change it unpredictably. Either way, your customizations are in danger of disappearing. The only way to protect them is to use a global template file located in a different location, say c:\Data\Template. You can create this file by copying the Word version into your own directory, then configuring Word to use your file: use menu Tools, Options to open the "Options" dialog box. On the File Locations tab, set the location of User templates to your directory (c:\Data\Template).

Be sure to save the template file before leaving Word. This is best done by using menu Tools, Options to open the "Options" window, then select the Save tab, then check the "Prompt to save normal template" box. Then, when you close Word after adding or changing customizations, you will be prompted to save the normal template; be sure to reply OK.

Macros are stored as *procedures* and *functions* within a *module* (these are Visual Basic terms); the Organizer refers to modules as *Macro Project Items*. When copying macros from one file to another, they are copied as an entire module. Your template file can have more than one module; you can use multiple modules to organize your macros.

- The default module is NewMacros. Recorded macros are placed here automatically.
- Add a module in the Visual Basic Editor (menu Tool, Macro, Visual Basic Editor) by using its menu Insert, Module. Then type the code in the code window.
- Rename a module in the Visual Basic Editor by opening the Properties Window with menu View, Properties Window. In the tab section, select the name and then type over it. You can then close the window.
- You can copy procedures from one module to

another by selecting the code text in the code window (open this by double-clicking the module name in the Project Explorer window or with the menu View, Code), copy/cut, then select the other module and paste.

- You can delete a module with menu File, Remove *modulename.*

CUSTOMIZATIONS BETWEEN FILES

Styles, toolbars, and macros can be copied from one file to another by Organizer. Use menu Tools, Macro, Macros to open the "Macros" window, then select [Organizer]. Open both files, then use the [Copy] button to copy one or more objects at a time. Note that Word 2000+ Organizer copies entire modules, not individual macros. This restriction makes the use of multiple modules desirable.

FINDING CUSTOMIZATIONS

- Open the file in Word.
- To look for macros, use menu Tools, Macro, Macro to open the "Macros" window. Change the value of the Macros In text box to reflect the name of your file. The list of macros will then reflect only your file.
- To look for toolbars, use menu View, Toolbars to open a third level menu that is a list of all the toolbars. Custom toolbars are listed after the last standard Word toolbar (WordArt).
- To look for styles, use menu Format, Style to open the "Style" window. Unfortunately, customized styles are not obvious.
- To look for shortcut keys, use menu Tools, Customise to open the "Customise" window. Select the [Keyboard] button to open the "Customise Keyboard" window. Unfortunately, you cannot see a list of all the shortcuts. Instead, you have to look at the individual commands to see if a shortcut exists for it. Even then, you cannot tell if the shortcut is standard with Word or custom.

• Custom shortcut keys can be listed by a macro. See *Word VBA Techniques* for details.

CUSTOM TOOLS

Custom Word global template contains custom menus, toolbars, keyboard shortcut keys, styles, and macros. These are itemized here to inspire you.

Custom Menus

View, Toggle Field Codes: Toggles the display of field codes. Use this to change a field code, especially when starting a new document.

View, Outline 3: Displays the document in outline layout with only heading levels 1–3 visible. Use this to check which headings exist, to rearrange them, and to renumber them.

View, Hide BuiltIn Toolbars: Hides all toolbars except the custom ones. If you use the custom toolbars, this is an easy way to hide unwanted toolbars that appear automatically at certain times, especially when using the custom keyboard shortcut key to change a style to List Bullet.

Format, Para Keep With Next: This is an easy way to toggle a paragraph keep.

Custom Toolbars

Susan: Contains one button linked to the macro to open the *Document Template.doc* file.

*Susan*1: Contains some standard Word commands for viewing and table formatting, and a custom button Hang (runs the macro ToggleHangingIndent).

*Susan*2: Contains some standard Word commands for formatting, and three custom buttons: ListBullet, Box, and ToggleCase which run macros SetListBullet, FigureBox, and ToggleCaseNextLetter respectively.

Custom Shortcut Keys

Alt + *b*: Runs macro SetListBullet.

Alt + *c*: Runs macro ToggleCaseNextLetter.

Alt + *d*: Runs standard Word menu View, Header and

Footer. This is just a way to open the header with one keystroke. Repeating the shortcut key when the header is open causes it to close.

Alt + *h*: Runs macro ToggleHangingIndent.

Alt + *m*: Runs macro FormatTable.

Alt + *x*: Runs macro FigureBox.

Ctrl + *r*: Runs macro ReverseNext2Characters.

Ctrl + *Alt* + *r*: Runs macro ReverseNext2Characters.

Ctrl + *Alt* + *Num5*: Runs macro SelectTable.

Custom Macros

Build data maintenance: Creates concatenated Word document for Data Maintenance section.

Build editors guide: Creates concatenated Word document for Editor's Guide section. [This and the previous macro illustrate the use of macros to build a concatenated document of many other documents. In this case each concatenated document has its corresponding macro.]

Portrait: Changes page setup to portrait. Used by the Build macros.

Change all files in directory: Prompts user for directory name, then for each Word document in the directory, runs the macro SuppressBlankLineAtTopBottom. This macro could be easily cloned to run any other macro against every Word document in a directory.

Figure box: Applies standard border to selected image: double grey lines.

Fix single line paragraph: Acts on selected text to replace the paragraph mark at the end of each line with one space. It puts a paragraph mark at the end of the selected text. It is helpful for reformatting text copied, from sources like TXT files or web pages, that has line breaks instead of automatic word wrapping.

Format table: Applies standard table formatting. The cursor must be in the top row.

Hide toolbars: Hides standard toolbars. Helpful when they are automatically made visible (at odd moments) and are unwanted.

Keep: Sets the paragraph format to keep with next.

Open Template: Opens file Document Template.doc. Used when starting a new document file.

Remove all hyper links: Removes all hyperlinks from the document.

Reset page numbers: Unlinks current section header and footer to previous ones, restarts page numbering at 1. Used by Build macros.

Reverse next 2 characters: Reverses the two characters to the right of the cursor. Invaluable for the sloppy typist.

Select table: Selects the table at the cursor location. There is a custom shortcut key assigned to this, Ctrl+Alt+numeric keypad -, which was standard in Word 98.

Set cell margins: Corrects cell margins for each cell in the table at the cursor location. Necessary after copying cells from an Excel spreadsheet that have zero cell margins. This happens if you choose the wrong paste method.

Set list bllet: Applies the custom ListBullet style to the selected text.

Set notes toItalics: Loops through active document, finds instances of paired square brackets, then sets the text inbetween to italics. This is necessary because Word in all its wisdom removes the italics in an inconsistent and unpredictable manner; re-instating them manually one at a time is a time-consuming nuisance.

Set table column widths: Kept as a sample of setting widths of columns in a table.

Show text boundaries: Toggles the display of text boundaries. The standard Word way of doing this is to use the Tools, Options menu. This macro is assigned to a custom menu button to enable executing it speedily.

Suppress blank line At top bottom: Applies the standard Word feature available with the Tools, Options, Compatibility menu. Run by macro Change All Files In Directory.

Toggle case next letter: Toggles the case of the letter to the right of the cursor. Very helpful for correcting typing errors. Has a custom shortcut key assigned.

Toggle hanging indent: Toggles a hanging indent in the paragraph at the cursor location. The standard Word feature does not work properly. Has a custom shortcut key assigned.

DOCUMENT PROPERTIES

A Document object can have one or more document properties. There are two kinds of document properties: built-in and custom (available in Word 2003). They are accessed from the File, Properties menu. The built-in properties appear on the Summary tab while the custom properties appear on the Custom tab. Version number can be stored as a custom document property. It can be placed in the text of the document by the Doc Property field code.

TEMPLATES

Templates are special files, named x.dot, that can hold text, graphics, and page margins and layout, and also customizations like macros, toolbars, menus, shortcut keys, styles, and auto-text. Every Word document is based on a template. Menu Tools, Templates and Add-ins provides access to the template manager:

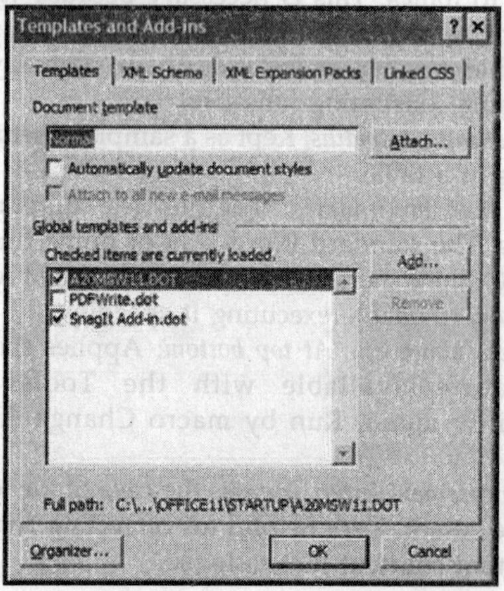

It provides a way to identify global and document templates. Global templates are "loaded" and document templates are "attached." Templates, once added, remain on the list, but must be loaded manually each time you start Word—unless they are located in the Startup directory or you change the file location of the user templates with the "Options" dialog box.

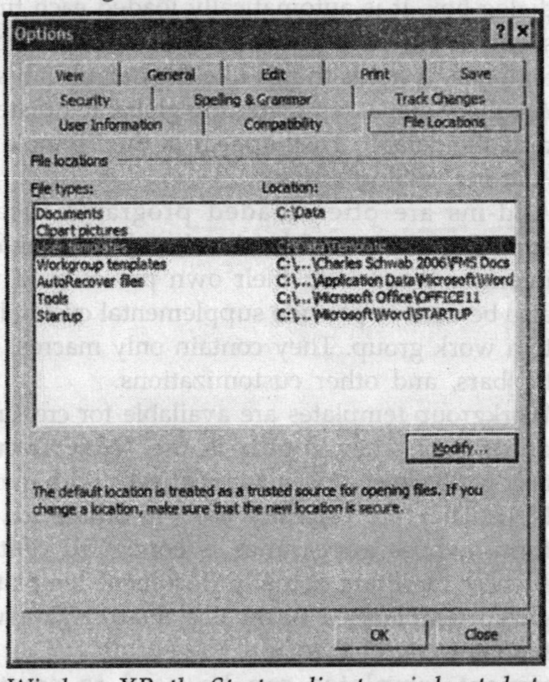

For Windows XP, the Startup directory is located at:

C:\Programme Files\Microsoft Office \ OFFICE11 \ STARTUP.

Word comes with several document templates which are located at:

C:\Programme Files\Microsoft Office\Templates\1033.

Word also stores templates (including normal.dot) in

C:\Documents and Settings\<user name >\ Application Data\Microsoft\Templates.

There are several flavors of global template:

- The default global template, called the Normal template by Microsoft, is normal.dot and is located in a directory indicated on the menu Tools, Options, File Locations dialog box for file type "User template". It does not appear in the "global templates and add-ins" list in the "Templates and Add-ins" dialog box. It is automatically loaded each time you start Word. It is used as the default document template. It holds things like the default tab stop.
- Auxiliary global templates are global templates other than the default. They appear in the "Templates and Add-ins" dialog box.
- Add-ins are often loaded programmatically by applications like Adobe Acrobat that use macros to interface Word with their own processes. They can also be used to provide supplemental customizations to a work group. They contain only macros, menus, toolbars, and other customizations.
- Workgroup templates are available for creating new documents. They appear in the "New Document" task pane which opens automatically with menu File, New. They are typically used in offices for special forms whose appearance is controlled centrally. I suspect these are actually document templates, not global templates. I never use these, and have little familiarity with them.

Document templates can be used to create new documents and ensure a consistency of styles in existing documents. Typically a document template contains page margins and layout, a document outline, boilerplate text and graphics (like logos), page headers and footers, as well as styles. They may omit the outline and boilerplate. Document templates are available only to the documents to which they are attached.

Word comes with a global template file, normal.dot, located in the system directory related to Microsoft Office. You can delete this file, but it will be recreated automatically.

If you have to reinstall Word, any changes you make to this file will be lost. Any changes to a global template (for macros, toolbars, keyboard shortcut keys, and styles) are automatically saved in normal.dot.

The Organizer tool is used to copy, delete, and rename the contents of a template: styles, auto-text, toolbars, (including menus), and macros.

Templates must reside on your C: drive. So when you are working with documents on a file server, copy the global/document template from the server to your own hard drive.

STYLES

All text is styled: all text has a named style linked to it.

There are kinds of styles: paragraph, character, list, and table (new with Word 2003). Paragraph styles include font, paragraph, tabs, border/shading, frame, and bullet/numbering formats. Character styles are limited to font and border/shading formats. Paragraph styles apply to text that ends with a paragraph mark (¶) and includes list items. The formats of a style are considered its definition.

Text formats are applied in descending order of priority:

- Local formats (see definition below),
- The document style definition,
- The document template style definition,
- The global template style definition.

This means that local text-specific formats override those in the document style definition which override style definitions in the document template (when it exists) which, in turn, override style definitions in the global template.

The document template is a DOT file attached to the document with the "Templates and Add-ins" command available on the Tools menu. Setting the "Automatically update document styles" property to Yes causes the format of the document text to automatically change to correspond with the style definitions in the document template. (This is a good practice.) That property is specific to the document and is saved with the document along with the identity of the document template.

The default global template is normal.dot. This is also the default document template for new documents. The default value of the "Automatically update document styles" property is No.

You can set/change local formats (formats for selected text) with commands on the Format menu: Font, Paragraph, Bullets and Numbering, Borders and Shading, Tabs.

You can change formats for all text with a named style by changing the style definition: use the "Style" command available on the Format menu; select the style name and then [Modify]. Optionally, you can have the style definition changes applied to the template, either document template if it exists or global template, when you set the property "Add to template" to Yes.

You can change style definitions in a DOT file directly by first opening it and then using menu Format, Style to make changes. The style changes are saved when you save the file. You can also use the Organizer to copy styles from one file to another.

You can create a document template DOT file based on an existing document:

- Open the base document.
- Save as document template and in the appropriate directory.
- Edit the new template: page formats, text formats, text and graphics.
- Save the template.

You can copy character and paragraph styles from some text to other text with Format Painter:

- Select text having desired format.
- Click Format Painter tool in Standard toolbar.

Document your style sheet:

- How will pages be numbered identified
- How will information sources be d a
- Version numbering scheme an
- Page formats: margins, header, footer
- Typography (e.g., em and en dashes)
- Which named styles are to be used for what tex

TYPOGRAPHY

This has become a favourite subject of mine. *Typography* is the style, arrangement, or appearance of typeset matter—"the visual aspects of written language." Its goal is to transmit a message as clearly as possible. Please consult a writing reference for information on typography. My focus here is to address simple things that can and should be done to improve the quality of your documents.

A possible source of confusion is that Word sometimes uses a vocabulary that differs from that of the writing and typography reference books.

Typographical Elements

The basic element of typography and the starting point for creating a Word document is the typeface of the body text. Typeface is a set of types for an alphabet comprising a single design (a type font is a set of types of the same face design and body size).

Select a body text typeface carefully. Typographers choose typefaces for their legibility, beauty, expressiveness, adaptability, and appropriateness—and so can you. The typeface must be selected in conjunction with body size, line length, and leading (line height) with the goal of achieving the ideal type *colour*. Colour in this context describes the appearance of a mass of type on the page, the precise shade of gray created by the visual mixture of black type and white paper, and the visual texture of the mass. The basic feature of good typesetting is consistent colour.

If you are restricted to the fonts packaged with Word, your choices are few: Palatino Linotype, Slimbach, and Times New Roman. The latter is the built-in font for the Normal style and is way overused. I do not think it particularly attractive.

PAGE MARGINS AND LAYOUT

Do not feel limited to the built-in values for page margins and layout. I've come to accept side margins for portrait pages as 1.25". But I increase top margins to 1.1" and decrease bottom margins to 0.9". For landscape pages I use side margins of 0.5".

Paragraph Margins

Word is a pill when it comes to some paragraph margins. The CSS model is so much better. . .

I'll use the CSS model as a reference. Margins, padding, and line height are the relevant elements. Margins are essentially external to the text block while padding is internal to the text block. When a paragraph has a background colour, it extends to the padding but not the margins. If you want to place text on a thick colored background, then you add top and bottom padding to achieve the desired thickness of the colored background.

Line Height, Aka Line Spacing

Line height is perhaps the worst example of the built-in typography of Word. The built-in value for each style is "Single". In body text especially this makes for lines that are too close together. I prefer to change it to "At least x" where x is 2 points more than the font size. For example, for Adobe Garamond 11 pt, the line spacing is "at least 13 pts".

Unfortunately, as many styles are based on Normal, when you change the line spacing for Normal, it is automatically changed for others. And for some of these "at least 13 pts" is not appropriate: Header, Footer, Footnote Text, all the TOCx styles, all the Heading styles. You will have to change the line spacing for each of these, usually back to "Single."

Indention

The built-in tab stop is 0.5", which I consider too much for indented text lines. I prefer to use 0.3" and 0.6". Be sure to change the default tab stop. And shame on Microsoft for calling indention "indentation."

Insert Characters by Using Character Codes

You do not have to limit the text in your document to

the characters on the keyboard. You can insert other characters like typographical characters (e.g., em dash), letters with dots or accents above or below them (e.g., ü), mathematical characters (e.g., H"), bullets (e.g., and), etc.

Characters can be ANSI or Unicode. The ANSI character set is an 8-bit character set used by Microsoft Windows that allows you to represent up to 256 characters (0 through 255) by using your keyboard. The ASCII character set is a subset of the ANSI set.

The simplest way to insert non-keyboard characters is with menu Insert, Symbol. For characters that cannot be inserted in this way, you must use a more esoteric approach.

Characters must be included in the text font, which means you may have to change the font in order to insert the desired character.

- Insert the Unicode character for the specified Unicode (hexadecimal) character code: type the character code, followed by [ALT+X]. For example, to insert the euro currency symbol (€), type 20AC, and then hold down the ALT key and press X.
- Insert the ANSI character for the specified ANSI (decimal) character code: [ALT+ the character code (on the numeric keypad)]. For example, to insert the euro currency symbol (€), hold down the ALT key and press 0128 on the numeric keypad.

COPY VISIO DIAGRAM TO WORD

All Visio diagrams are created and changed in their own files. Do not edit a Visio diagram from within a Word document; just because you can doesn't mean you should.

After a desired Visio diagram is created/changed, it can be copied to Word. This is a simple matter of selecting the Visio diagram (or a part of one) and copying it to the clipboard, then use Word menu Edit, Paste Special to paste it as a picture. Be careful not to paste it as a Visio object, which makes the file size larger and makes it possible to edit the diagram without doing so in the master Visio file.

Afterwards, apply a border according to the style sheet.

You have three choices for pasting Visio drawings into a Word document, and not surprisingly they affect the Word file size differently. In my test with a drawing that fills one page, I found the following file sizes:

- Visio file 29KB
- Visio drawing in Word as OLE 47KB
- Visio drawing in Word as Picture 28KB
- Visio drawing in Word as Picture Metafile 27KB

USING PICTURES

Word distinguishes between pictures and drawings. *Pictures* are images created outside of Word, including those created by PrintScreen and captured in the clipboard. *Drawings* are images made in Word with the drawing tools. Drawings are also called shapes.

Revision: Graphics can be inline or floating. In your Word document there are multiple layers, including a text layer and a graphics layer (sometimes called a drawing layer). Text and objects that act like text, such as *inline graphics*, reside in the text layer. By contrast, a graphic that resides in the graphics layer can be moved independently of the text. This is a *floating graphic*. You can change a graphic from inline to floating by changing the text-wrapping style; any wrapping style other than "In line with text" will create a floating graphic.

Floating graphics have an anchor symbol and a green rotation handle at the top.

The default layout (wrapping style) for inserted pictures is specified on the Edit tab of the "Options" window accessed by the menu Tools, Options; it is labeled "Insert/paste picture as". The value is chosen from a list box. If the layout you want for a particular picture is not the default, you will have to change it for the individual picture after insertion.

Commonly pictures are inserted between paragraphs without word wrap. When the picture is the only content of the paragraph it is logically "inline". Caution when controlling the paragraph line spacing: if it is set to "exactly" some number of points, the graphic will only show that many points—in other words it will be truncated. If you specify a paragraph style with line spacing as "exactly", change it to "at least" so the graphic will show in its entirety.

Floating graphics, i.e., images in the graphic layer, are not visible in Normal View. Switch to Print View to see and access floating graphics.

A floating graphic can be repositioned, resized, cropped, rotated, given a border, and its text wrapping property changed. First you must select it. To reformat a floating graphic, first make it visible by setting Print View, then open the Drawing Toolbar (with menu View, Toolbars). The Drawing Toolbar is placed near the bottom of the Word window. In the toolbar click the button to activate the Select Object tool, the pointer icon will change to a 4-headed arrow. Click the graphic/image to select it. When a graphic is selected, its appearance changes: an anchor icon appears as well as small circles at each corner and edge midpoint, and a green rotation handle. In addition the Picture Toolbar automatically opens.

USE TAB STOPS

A tab stop is a horizontal position on a line where a tab character can align the text that follows it. Tab stops are relative to the left page margin. A tab stop also has a text alignment (as left, centre, right, and decimal) and an optional leader (as periods, dashes, or underscores).

Tab stops and tabs are used to align text by pressing the [Tab] keyboard key. Tab stops are paragraph-specific properties, i.e., they apply only to the paragraph in which they are defined.

New documents have default tab stops, typically for every half inch. These tab stops are used until a tab stop is set explicitly in a paragraph. The default tab stops can be removed.

You can set a tab stop in several ways:

- For the paragraph with menu Format, Tabs. Use the "Tabs" dialog box to set a tab stop.
- For the style with menu Format, Styles and

Formatting, which opens the eponymous pane, then use dropdown menu Modify to open the "Modify Style" dialog box, and set the tab stops in the "Tabs" dialog box.

- With the Horizontal Ruler (visible with menu View, Ruler). There is a tab stop button in the left corner of the ruler. When you click it, its appearance changes to reflect text alignment. A tool tip will appear (if you wait long enough) to explain the setting when the pointer is hovered over the button. First position the insertion point cursor just in front of the text to be tabbed. Then set the ruler tab stop button to the desired alignment. Then click at the position in the ruler—an icon will appear at that position that matches the tab stop button.

You can remove (clear) a tab stop in several ways:

- For the paragraph with menu Format, Tabs. Use the "Tabs" dialog box to clear one or more tab stops.
- For the style with menu Format, Styles and Formatting, which opens the eponymous pane, then use dropdown menu Modify to open the "Modify Style" dialog box, and clear the tab stops in the "Tabs" dialog box.
- With the Horizontal Ruler (visible with menu View, Ruler). Click the tab stop character in the ruler and drag it off the ruler—down into the document.

LAYOUT TEXT IN A GRID

Perhaps the simplest way to layout text in a grid is with a table. Use column dimensions, inside margins, and text alignment to create the desired layout. Use borders or not; the default is borders on, but they are easily turned off (with dialog box "Borders and Shading" accessed from menu Format, then set Borders Setting = None).

For me the downside of using a table this way is that the grid lines are visible in Print View, even when there are no borders. (The grid lines can be made invisible in Normal View only.) There areother challenges in using tables this way, principally page breaks, spacing between paragraphs, and the inability to set keeps (keep with next).

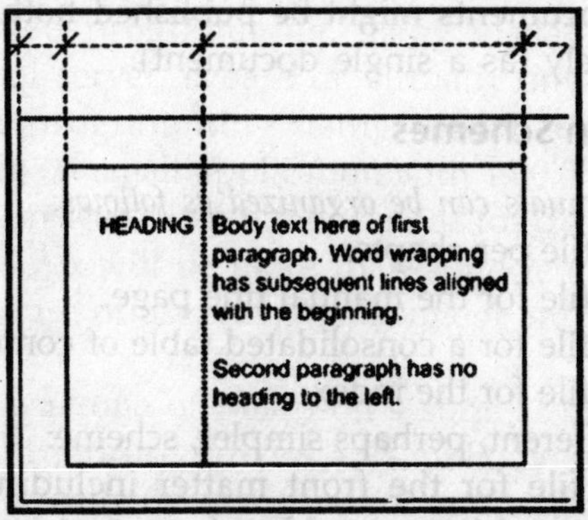

This layout can be achieved with an hanging indent and tabs. Given the preceding diagram as an example of margins and alignments, make the following format settings:

- Left page margin = 1"
- Right page margin = 1"
- Style Normal left indent = 2"
- New paragraph style FirstPara based on Normal, left indent = 0", hanging indent = 2", tab stops: right at 1.7", left at 2"

new character style HeadText font size = smaller than Normal. Then in the text apply the style FirstPara to text and enter tab characters:

[Tab]HEADING[Tab]Body text here of first paragraph. Word wrapping After which apply the style HeadText to HEADING. Apply style Normal to the second and following paragraphs. The limitation of this approach is that if the HEADING requires two lines, then the first line of the body text will align vertically at the baseline of the second heading line.

ORGANIZE DOCUMENTS

A large, complex document needs more organization than a short, simple document. These days the phrase *document set* is often used to refer to a group of several-to-many documents that together address a particular subject for a particular audience. Within a document set the individual documents might be published both individually and collectively (as a single document).

Organization Schemes

Large manuals can be organized as follows:

- One file per chapter.
- One file for the manual title page.
- One file for a consolidated table of contents.
- One file for the index.
- A different, perhaps simpler, scheme:
- One file for the front matter including title page, revision history, table of contents, and table of figures.
- One file per chapter.
- One file for the back matter including index.

DESIGNING PAGE HEADERS AND FOOTERS

Use the page header to identify the manual title, section title (if appropriate), and chapter title. Use the page footer to identify revision date, page number, and perhaps filename and/or confidentiality statement. If there are separate files for each chapter, assign each a chapter number and include it in the heading (e.g., 4.2 or B.2) and page number (e.g., 4-5 or C-4).

If you find a need for sections, consider making them separate manuals. If that is undesirable, then refer to *Using Section Title Pages* on page 36 for details on how to handle them.

CONCATENATE MULTIPLE FILES INTO ONE

Use a macro to concatenate the various files into one. See Assembling Multi-File Document in *Word VBA Techniques* for details.

This approach can be hazardous:

- Page number formats and numbering can be problematic; Word has idiosyncrasies and deficiencies in this area, especially when more than one section has roman numerals.

- Watermarks must be placed in every primary header of every section. A document with many sections requires care in placing the watermark.
- If the same style sheet is not used for all the individual files, then the combined document may have problems related to styles, margins, headers, and footers.

INSERT CHAPTER NUMBER AND/OR TITLE IN PAGE HEADER/FOOTER

There are three variations:

- Use field code StyleRef;
- Use Seq field code;
- Use cross-reference to styled text.

Using field code style ref to insert text:

- Does not require a special section.
- Insert field code with appropriate switches.

Example: { StyleRef "Heading 2"} causes the topmost heading2-styled text on the current page to appear in the header/footer; as you scroll through the document, the header text changes automatically.

The inserted text will not include any Seq field result. Neither will it include any numbering defined in the style. The only way it will include numbering is if that numbering is typed text and a part of the styled text.

You can place both the StyleRef and Seq field codes in a page header/footer.

Using field code seq to insert number:

- Does not require a special section.
- Assign chapter number in document text with Seq field code; e.g., {SEQ chapter \n}.
- In header/footer insert Seq field code with appropriate switches, e.g., {SEQ chapter \c * arabic }

Using cross-Reference:

- Each chapter must be its section.
- Type chapter title with built-in heading style.
- In Header-Footer View, be sure header/footer is not linked to the previous one.

Chapter – 18

FoxPro Concepts

DEFINITION

FoxPro is very powerful Database Management System. Its integrate development Environment allows programmer's language. It is both an interpreter and true compiler. As interpreted language, it translates each command into computer instructions, as it is executes the translation time, most possibly during loops.

A compiler improves performance by translating command to machine instructions just once. It replaces commands such as PRINT or LIST with blocks of machine code. This compiled programs run faster than interpreted codes.

FoxPro supports arithmetic functions such as addition, subtraction, multiplication, and division. It also provides many special mathematical and financial functions. The main screen combines a menu bar across the top line with a command prompt environment based on the command window. FoxPro opens the command window at the beginning of each session. Commands entered into it execute immediately.

FOXPRO DATABASE

It is a collection of related and relevant information. It could be check register, accounting ledger, payroll, client list or inventory. Or it could be any of thousands of applications in business, education, engineering, and the professions, the sciences and other fields.In general, a database consists of number of RECORDS .In FoxPro, a record may consist a number of items such as employee code number, employees name, address, date of joining, salary, designation etc. A number of such items in FoxPro's record are known as FIELDS. Number of fields make up a single record of single person, and number of such record made up an entire DATABASE.

Employee Registry

Field 1	Field 2	Field 3	Field 4	Field 5	Field 6
Code	Name	Address	Date of Joining	Salary	Designation
R001	Raman	A/3 Andheri	01-01-1967	12,500	Accountant
Goo5	Gauri	154/ Andheri	03-06-1988	6,000	Personal Secretary

Set commands: Fox Pro environment functions. Set talk on/off : Determines whether or FoxPro display command result.

Set Bell on/off: Turns the computer bell on or off and set the bell attributes.

Set status on/off: Set the status bar on or off.

Set safety on/off: Specifies the format for date expresses DD-MM-YY

VARIABLE TYPES

Character type Date type Numeric type Logical type:

- Store space (35) time.
- Store {99/99/99} birthdate
- Store 0 to Salary,
- Store.1. pass fail ('.Y.', '.N.') OR ('.T.', '.F.')

DATE FUCTIONS

- DATE (): Return the current system date. ?TIME () : Return the current system time.
- Day (date()) : Return the numerical day of the month or the given date expression.

Example:

- Store {03/10/75) birthDate. The birthday along with other command.

- Month (date()): Return the numeric month for the given date.
- Year (date()): Returns the numeric year of the given date.
- Dow (date()): Return the numeric day of the week for given
- Date. ?Cdow (date()): Return the character day of the week for given date.
- Dtoc 0: Will convert Date type variable to character type. We cannot find day, month of variable which is of character type.
- CtoD (): Converts a character expression or variable to a date related function to Cow, month on when a character expression is converted to date expression. Eg. Store CtoD to vdate.

DATABASE FUCTION

Create: Creates a new database file create Employees.dbf. Use Emplyoees.Dbf: Use command opened the database file and it's associated in.

Close all: Closes all open databases, index file etc. Append - use for adding records in a database. First open database with USE command then appends records in it.

Modify structure: Allows adding new or deleting of in database field.

Display structure: Display the structure of database.

Rename <filel> to<file2>: Renames the name of <filel>to<file2>

Edit: Allows the user to edit or modify record.

Replace: Replace command replaces the field with mentioned text or values.

Syntax: Replace all bonus with 7500 for Designation "officer"

You can also use. And.. or. clause for applying two or more condition for query record.

LIST AND DISPLAY FUCTION

- *List*: Display the entire record list.
- *List all*: Same as list command.

- *List off*: Will list the records without displaying the record numbers.
- List for name="s"
  Example: List for salary>2500 .and. salary<4750
- List Code, Surname, Firstname, Salary, Doj for Doj>={01/04/1998}
- List to printer
- You can use. And., Or. Clauses with list for applying two or more conditions.

MOVING TO RECORDS

Go/Goto<recordno>: Positions the record pointer on the specified record number in dbf.

Eg: Goto 16

Go top: Position the record pointer on the first record of the database. Go bottom: Position the record pointer on the last record of the database.

Skip: Positions the record pointer on the next record from the present record. Try Skip+5 and also Skip -3 while status is on. A database should be used or open, and observe which record becomes your present record.

BROWSING THE RECORDS

Browse: Browse for NAME="s" Browse fields NAME, SALARY, DESIGNATION Browse nomodify, nodelete, noappend: Browse the records but you can not modify them or delete them or add more records to your database.

DELETING RECORDS

Delete: delete the record on which your record pointer is positioned.

Delete for: Used for deleting records which match the conditions specified, e.g. Delete for dateofjoin>{01/01/1969}

Recall: Unmarks the records, which is marked for deletion. Only unmark the record if the record pointer is positioned on the deleted record.

Pack: Peımanently removes the record marked for

deletion. Once records are packed they cannot be Recalled.

Zap: The use of this single command permanently deletes all the records of the entire database.

Deleted (): this command along with list command will display only records, which are marked for deleted.

Syntax: list for deleted().

SPECIAL FUCTIONS

Note: A database has to be opened for working with the following commands.

Fcount ()- Returns the number of fields in an open database.

Recsize Q-Display the size of the records.

RecnoQ- Displays the current record number.

Reccount()-Counts the number of records in a database file.

Count- can be used for counting records, which match a criteria.

E.g. Count for Salary>4500

Int (<expN>)- Returns a Integer portion of a numeric expression. ? Len (<expN>) - Returns the number of characters in a character expression.

Abs(<expN>)-Retum the absolute value of the specified numeric expression.?

Right (Vname2): Returns the specified number of rightmost characters from a character string.

Left (<expN>)- Return a specified numeric of character expression starting with the leftmost character.

Replicate ("*", 35) -Returns a character string that contains a specified character expression repeated a specified number of times.

CurDir()- Returns the currents MS-DOS directory.

Dikspace()- Returns the number of bytes available on the default disk drive.

Lower () Returns a specified character expression in lower case letters.

Upper (): - Returns the specified character expression in upper case letters.

TRIM FUCTIONS

"xname=Abraham Lincoln" Ltrim():-Returns the specified character expression with leading baink removed.

It rim(xname) will remove blank from name.

RtrimQ:- Return the specified character expression with trailing blank remove rtrim(xname): will remove blank from name.

SubstrQ:- Return a specified number o character from the given expression or mem field.

Zname="Anthony"

Substr(zname,l,3) will display only 'ant'

Substr(zname,5,2) will display from character and 2 more characters of the variable Only 'on' will be displayed.

ARRANGING RECORDS IN ASCENDING /DESCENDING ORDRER

Records entered in the database need not be in ordered form. But while printing displaying reports, we need to show them in a ordered form so as to give meaning to the reports. Sometimes reports may be needed on alphabetically listing of the Salesman name or on the Data wise bill entries.

From one data to another may be required for reporting and extracting information from them. Hence it is of utmost importance that records entered should be arranged so as it arrive to decision-making. FoxPro provides two simple and most efficient ways to arrange the record entered and not only to view them in that form but also to query them so as to quickly search to the user mentioned criteria.

Methods

1) Sort
2) Index.

1) *Sort*: is a mentioned in which the user mentions the field on which he wants the performs the sort and the output is generated and stored in a different target database file contain the sorted output on the fields mentioned in the sort command. You have to

open the target database file to view the sorted records. /D is use to sort in a descending order, otherwise it will sort in ascending order.]

Syntax:

```
Use <filename>
Sort on <field> /D to xfile -/D is used for
Sorting in a descending order.
Use xfile
Browse
To sort on more than one field:
Use SALES DBF
Sort on STATE, CITY to STATE
Use STCT.dbf
Browse
```

2) *Index*: Index command arrange the record in ascending or descending order but the fundamental different between sort and index is that, with Index command a number of the database which are indexed in Ascending or Descending order. In the sample given below, in the friends' database the field has three names, which are not in alphabetical order. If we index it and store it in the index file name.idx only the record numbers will exist but arranged in such a way that the corresponding names are in alphabetical order.

OTHER COMMAND

Clear all: Clear all the memory variables and activate Windows, menus, popup etc from the memory.

Clear: Clear the screen or Active window.

Quit: To exit from FoxPro. Be sure to close all open database and other files before

Quitting: Run or ! (Exclamation marks) - is used or running a MS-DOS command without quitting it. IV) File deleting commands

Delete File <Filename>: Deletes a file from the disk.

Erase <File name>: Erases the file from the disk.

REPORT AND LABEL

Report: This command produces reports using report layouts that have been designed earlier. If CONSOL has not been SET OFF, the report is displayed on the screen. They can also be sent to the printer or a text file.

Before this command is used, the report form must have been created a saved in a file. The command CREATE REPORT lets you design these report form using the report Layout Window. The default extension for these files FRX.

Label: This command produces mailing labels for the database file that is open in the currently selected work area if CONSOLE has not been SET OFF, the label at displayed on the screen. They can also be sent to the printer or to a text file.

Create a one .dbf file with the help of following field and solve the questions answer.

Field Name	Type	Width
Name	Character	20
DOJ	Date	8
Eng	Numeric	3
Hindi	Numeric	3
marathi	numeric	3

DEFINITIONS

Read/write pointer <—> An invisible record pointer that floats through a database file.

Current record <———> The record pointed to by the read/write pointer

SAMPLE STRUCTURE

Let us assume the Client.dbf for the following illustrations. The structure/layout is as follows:

Name	Character	26
Address	Character	30
City	Character	16

State	Character	2	
Zip	Character	8	
Phone	Character	12	
Male	Logical	1	
No	Numeric	4	0
Notes	Memo	4	

USE - OPEN/CLOSE DATABASE

Use FileName <— close any database open in the current work area and opens the specified database. The database must have a .dbf extension. The read/write record pointer is positioned at the first record when file is opened/re-opened.

Use <— close any database open in the current work area.

Use Client <— close the current database, if any, and open database file Client.dbf in the current work area.

or

Use Client.dbf <— same as above. Specifying the extension is optional.

The FoxPro database programme has multiple work areas. Only one database may be opened in each work area.

MOVING THE READ/WRITE POINTER

GoTo Top <— move read/write pointer to first record.

GoTo 1 <— move read/write pointer to first record.

GoTo 5 <— move read/write pointer to record 5.

GoTo Bottom <— move read/write pointer to the last record.

5 <— move read/write pointer to record 5.
1 <— move read/write pointer to first record.

GoTo RecCount()<— move read/write pointer to the last record.

Skip 1 <— move read/write pointer forward 1 to the next record.

Skip 2 <— move read/write pointer forward 2 records.

Skip -1 <— move read/write pointer backward 1 to the next record.

Skip -2 <— move read/write pointer backward 2 records.

LIST- LIST INFORMATION FROM ALL RECORDS

List [fields] <— an uninterrupted display of database information. The list command will always move the read/write pointer to first logical record and display all of the fields of all records. Upon completion, the read/write pointer will always reside at the end of the file. Since the display is uninterrupted, there will be no pause when the screen is full.

List <— uninterrupted display of specified fields of all records.

List Name, State, Phone<— uninterrupted display of the Name field, the State field, and the Phone of all records.

List Phone, Name, State<— uninterrupted Phone field, the Name field, and the State field of all records.

List Name, State For State = "TX" <— uninterrupted Name field & the State field of all of the Texas records all records.

List Name, State For State = "TX" .And. Male <— uninterrupted Name field & the State field of all male Texas records.

List Name, State For State = "TX" And Male <— uninterrupted Name field & the State field of all male Texas records.

List Name, State For State = "TX" .Or. State = "CA" <— uninterrupted display the Name field & the State field of all Texas and all California records.

List Name, State For State = "TX" Or State = "CA" <— uninterrupted display the Name field & the State field of all Texas and all California records.

CONTINUATION LINES

It is important to keep lines reasonable in length; lines more than 80 characters will not necessarily print in their entirety. When a semicolon is placed at the end of a line, it can be broken and extended to the next line. See below.

List Name, State For State = "TX" ; <— uninterrupted Name field & the State field of all male Texas records And. Male

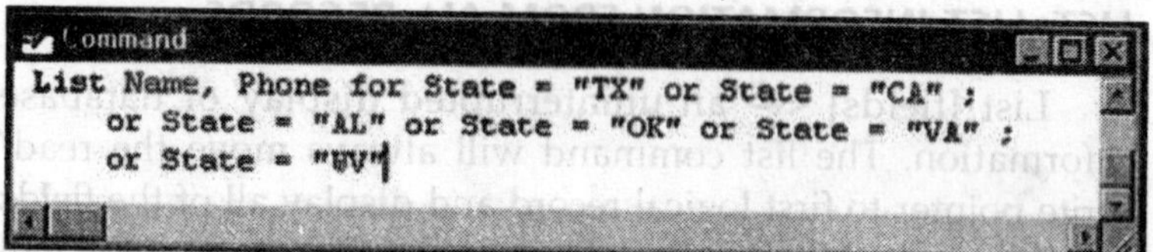

Since the command window will allow you to enter very long lines (255 characters), most database programmers do not frequently use the continuation (;) within that window. You may use the continuation within the command window if you use the down arrow key to get to the next line.

Display- Display Information From Current Record With Pause H]

Display <— an interrupted display of database information. The display command will display all of the fields of the current record. Upon completion, the read/write pointer remains unchanged. There will be a pause when the screen is full.

Display [Fields] <— interrupted display specified fields of the fields in the current record.

Display Name, State, Phone <— interrupted display the info stored in the Name field, the State field, and the Phone of the current record.

DISPLAY ALL- DISPLAY INFORMATION FROM ALL RECORDS

Display all <— an interrupted display of database information. The display all command will always move the read/write pointer to first logical record and display all of the fields of all records. Upon completion, the read/write pointer will always reside at the end of the file. Since the display is interrupted, there will be a pause when the screen is full. With the exception of the pause, the display all command is identical to the list command.

Display All Name, State For State = "TX" And Male <—

interrupted display the Name field & the State field of all male Texas records.

Display All Name, State For State = "TX" .Or. State = "CA" <— interrupted display the Name field & the State field of all Texas and all California records.

MODIFY STRUCTURE - ALTER THE DATABASE LAYOUT

Modify Structure<— alter the database layout/structure. The modify structure command returns you to the file/ creation programme. You will have the opportunity to change the name of the fields, change the field datatypes, change field sizes, add fields, delete fields, and/or reorder fields. copy structure to - Create A New Database With The Same Structure

Copy Structure To FileName <— create a database file, called FileName, that contains the same structure/layout as the current database. The new file has 0 records.

Copy Structure To A:\New<— create a database file, called New.dbf, that contains the same structure/layout as the current database. File New.dbf contains no records.

TO PRINT- ROUTE A COPY TO PRINTER

Adding To Print to the end of any Display command or any List command sends a copy of the output to the printer, as well as the current user defined window. List is more often used with to print.

List Name, State For State = "TX" To Print <— display on the monitor and print the Name field & the State field of all of the Texas records.

Display all Name, State For State = "TX" To Print <— display on the monitor and print the Name field & the State field of all of the Texas records.

There display will be interruped by a pause when the screen is full.

Display Name, State To Print <— display on the monitor and print the Name field & the State field of the current record.

List Structure To Print<— display on the monitor and print a copy of the current database layout/structure (no pause).

EDIT - EDIT FIELDS OF ONE RECORD

Edit <— edit the current record with a very crude data entry editor. (See Above)

Edit Record 4 <— move the read/write pointer to record 4 and edit this record with a very crude data entry editor.

Edit 4 <— move the read/write pointer to record 4 and edit this record with a very crude data entry editor.

Edit Fields Name, State<— edit only fields Name and State of the current record with a very crude data entry editor. (See Above)

Edit Fields Name, StateRecord 4<— move the read/write pointer to record 4 and edit only fields Name and State of this record with a very crude data entry editor.

CHANGE- EDIT FIELDS OF ONE RECORD

Change <— change the current record with a very crude data entry editor. The Change command is identical to the Edit command.

Change Record 4 <— move the read/write pointer to

record 4 and edit this record with a very crude data entry editor.

Change 4 <— move the read/write pointer to record 4 and edit this record with a very crude data entry editor.

Change Fields Name, State<— change only fields Name and State of the current record with a very crude data entry editor.

Change Fields Name, StateRecord 4<— move the read/write pointer to record 4 and edit only fields Name and State of this record with a very crude data entry editor.

CLEAR - CLEAR WINDOW

Clear <— clear the current user-defined window (desktop if none).

Clear All <— close all databases, erase all memory variables, erase all user-defined menu bars, pop ups, windows, etc.

Clear Memory <— clear all public and private memory.

clear windows<— release all user defined window definitions.

BROWSE - SPREADSHEET LIKE BROWSE WINDOW

Browse [fields] <— the browser is a tabular editor in which each record is manipulated on a single line. The browser opens a resizable, movable, slide-bar window which contains the field names across the top.

The simple browser allows any fields to be edited/ changed. New Records may be appended at the end of the browser.

Browse <— all fields of all records are opened in the browser.

Browse Fields Name, State, Phone <— the Name field, the State field, and the Phone of all records are opened in the browser.

Browse Fields Phone, Name, State <— the Phone field, the Name field, and the State field of all records are opened in the browser.

Browse Fields Name, State For State = "TX" <— the

Name field & the State field of all of the Texas records all records are opened in the browser.

SET DELETED ON/OFF - SET THE DELETED FILTER TOGGLE

Set Deleted On<— turns on the deleted filter. Deleted records fail to pass through.

Set Deleted Off <— turns off the deleted filter. Deleted records shall be included.

? Deleted( ) <— displays .T. if the current record has been tagged for deletion, else .F.

List For Deleted( )<— display on the monitor all of the information about all of the records tagged for deletion.

List For Deleted() = .T. <— display on the monitor all of the information about all of the records tagged for deletion.

List For Not Deleted( )<— display on the monitor all of the information about all of the records not tagged for deletion.

List For Deleted() = .F. <— display on the monitor all of the information about all of the records not tagged for deletion.

RECALL - REMOVE RECORD DELETION TAGS

Recall <— removes the deletion tag from the current record.

Recall Record 4 <— removes the deletion tag from the record 4.

Recall All <— removes the deletion tag from all records.

Recall All For State = "CA"<— removes the deletion tag from all California records.

Recall offers an opportunity to undelete records. This is an important database un-do opportunity.

Pack - Physically Delete Records Tagged For Deletion

Pack <— permanently removes all records tagged for deletion.

Zap - Delete All Records From Database

Zap <— permanently removes all records.

POSSIBLE ERRORS IN THE COMAND WINDOW

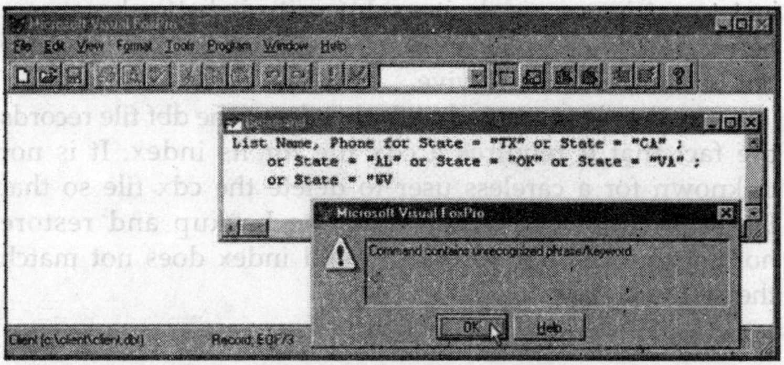

Eventually, you will make an error entering something in the command window. (See Above) The right quote is missing from WV. Most of the time, a little research and the help system will enable you to correct the error. There will be times that you don't understand why your code did not work; when this happens, print the contents of the command window and seek help. (See Below)

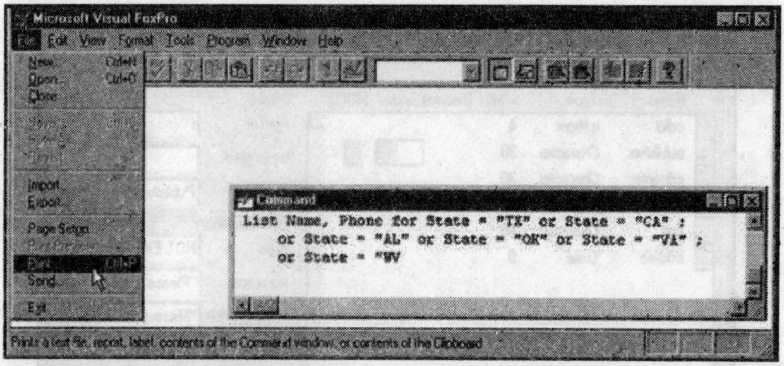

File—>Print [Using the mouse, hold down the File Menu and Select Print to print all of the commands entered into the command window during this FoxPro session.]

TABLE FILES

FoxPro stores its data as a collection of individual files which improves performance on small databases. Performance is better than Access because the programme does not need to bring all the data from all the tables across the network just to retrieve a single item. Integrity is better because a network error or a power failure might corrupt a single table but all the rest will survive.

The disadvantage is that the header of the dbf file records the fact that it requires a cdx file for its index. It is not unknown for a careless user to delete the cdx file so that FoxPro cannot open the dbf; or to backup and restore nothing but the dbf so that the old index does not match the restored data.

DATABASE

The first versions of FoxPro used flat tables but Visual FoxPro added features which organised these tables into a relational database. The information about the links between tables, the relational integrity and the stored procedures are stored in a Database Container file with a .dbc extension. When a table is part of a database the Table Designer is extended with new fields:

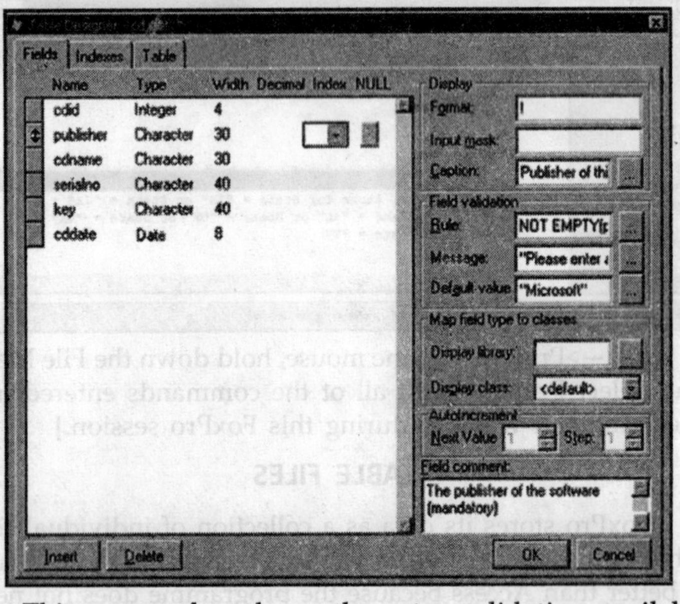

This screen shot shows the extra validation available

for each field on the Fields page of the Table Designer. The Table page includes validation for the record as a whole and triggers which run stored procedures when a record is added, altered or deleted.

COMPATIBILITY

The FoxPro data format changed when the database features were added because every dbf had to have an entry in its header holding the name of the database file. There are now two dbf formats, one for databases up to FoxPro version 2.6, the other for Visual FoxPro 3 onwards. Earlier versions of FoxPro do not recognise the new format but Visual FoxPro can use and create tables in the old format. Compatibility is complete. A Visual FoxPro system can run in parallel with an older system and share the same data files and respect the same record-locking strategies.

You can use ODBC or OLE to connect to any database with a suitable driver. You can also call the ADO and DAO libraries from within FoxPro programs for tasks such as the maintenance of an Access database.

DEVELOPMENT ENVIRONMENT

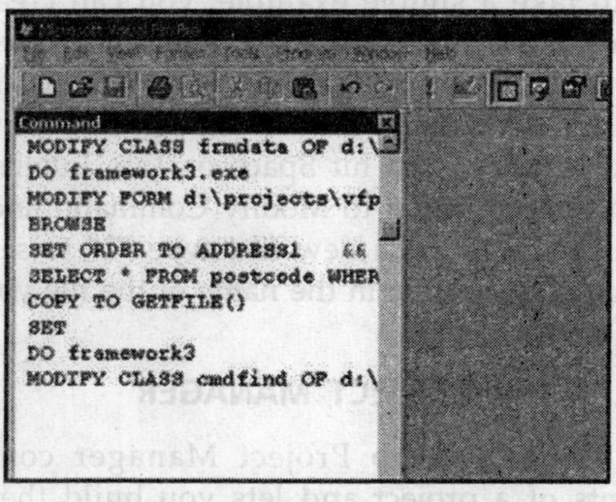

Visual FoxPro is unusual amongst the current generation of Microsoft development tools in that it still retains a command-line interface. It has a toolbar across the top of the window with all the familiar buttons that you would expect but you are also faced with a command window where you can enter FoxPro commands.

INTELLISENSE

The keywords of the FoxPro language appear as upper case in blue because this is the default setting of Visual FoxPro's Intelligence feature. As soon as Fox recognises the word that you are typing it displays the rest of that word in blue. If you press the Space or Tab keys then Fox will complete the word for you and follow it with a list of parameters and options that can apply to that command. Unlike other Microsoft languages, the Visual FoxPro IntelliSense is open and documented - it is actually a lookup into a FoxPro table - and you can add your own entries to the list.

USING THE FOXPRO COMMAND WINDOW

When you first start to learn Visual FoxPro you might be tempted to close the Command Window because it looks so old-fashioned and drive FoxPro in the same point-and-click style as you would do with Access. This is possible but it is a slow and restricted way of working.

Just to take a simple example, you can create a new programme file (code module) by selecting New from the Filemenu and specifying that you want a new file of type Code. It is so very much quicker though to type mc in the Command Window and hit Space or Tab. Intellisense will expand this abbreviation to Modify Command and you can either hit Return to get a new file, type "?" to see a list of programme files, or type in the name of the file you want to open.

PROJECT MANAGER

The Visual FoxPro Project Manager controls the components of a project and lets you build then into an executable or DLL. It also provides an easy way for you to create and modify files for programs, forms, reports and classes. Rather than having to use the menu or the Command

Window to open a file you can just double-click on it it the Project Manager. This applies to all types of file. If you have added a file of type bmp to the project then FoxPro will open Paint when you double-click.

Although the Project Manager looks very like the Database Window from an older version of Access it does not hold the programme code or the design of the project components. It is in fact just a table of project information with details of the files required, where they are stored, and any comments you want to associate with them. This means that many database projects can share the same files of common procedures or class libraries.

Create a new project by typing CREATE PROJ in the Command Window:

This shows an empty project. As files are added to the project the nodes on the TreeView will expand. As an example, the Data node will expand to show 'Databases', 'Free Tables' and 'Queries'. Each of the main nodes of the tree has its own tab and if you wanted to concentrate forms and reports then you could see them on the 'Documents' tab.

USING THE PROJECT MANAGER

The first thing to do with the Project Manager is to get it out of the way. If you click on the title bar then you can drag it into the main menu and dock it clear of the main desktop area. Click on a tab to drop down a list when you need one of the files.

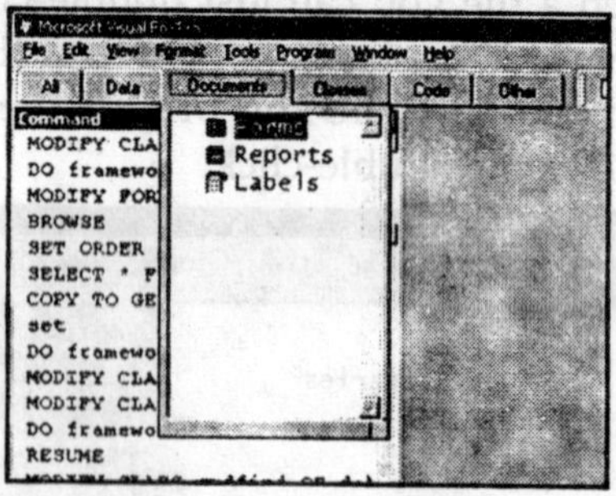

DATA TABLES

TABLE FILES

Unlike Access or SQL Server, FoxPro stores all the tables of its database as separate files. Fields of fixed-length data are held in a file with an extension of .dbf (database file); the variable-length data, graphics and OLE objects have an extension of .fpt (foxpro text and the indexes are .cdx (compound index. This separation has good and bad points but is proved reliable over many years.

DESIGNING A TABLE

We will skip the first and most important phase of this process and assume that the structure of the table has already been considered. This project has a single table named CD with the following structure:

Field	Type	Size	Description
CDID	I		Unique sequential number to identify each CD
Publisher	C	30	Publisher of this CD - eg 'Microsoft'
CDName	C	30	Name of this CD - eg 'Visual FoxPro 8'
SerialNo	C	40	Manufacturer's serial number
Key	C	40	Security Key
CDDate	D		Date received

CREATING A TABLE

Click on the Data tab of the Project Manager then right-click on Free Tables

Select New File then New Table from the dialog that appears. This dialog allows you to start the Table Wizard which can be useful if your application matches one of the templates provided.

An explorer dialog will appear offering to create a table named 'Table1.dbf'. Change the name to 'CD.dbf' and save it in the same folder as the project manager file. A real life project typically has its files in a directory tree structure but we'll put all the files in the same folder here for simplicity.

The Table Designer will appear. Add the six fields from the list above and click OK when you have finished. Note that no size has been given for the Integer and Date fields, these are fixed by FoxPro.

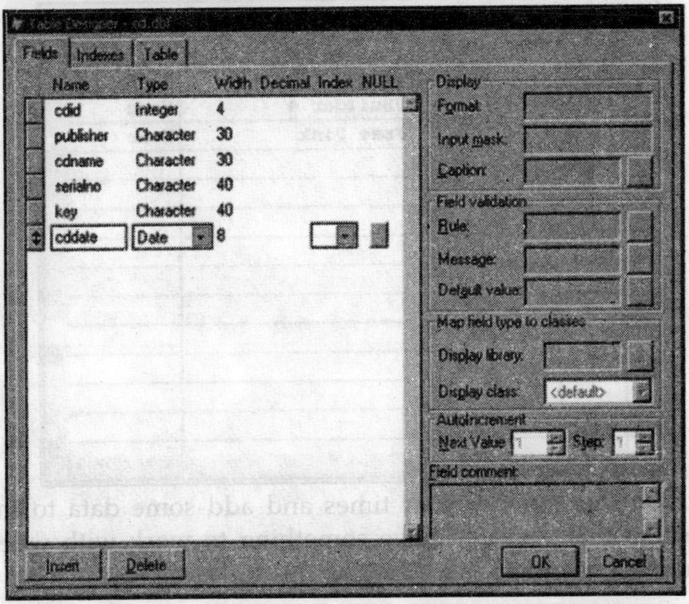

The greyed-out fields on the right of the designer are only available for tables which are part of a database. You can leave the main route through the tutorial and go to this page to learn about Visual FoxPro databases.

VIEWING THE TABLE

When you have closed the Table Designer you should see an entry like this in the status bar at the base of the screen:

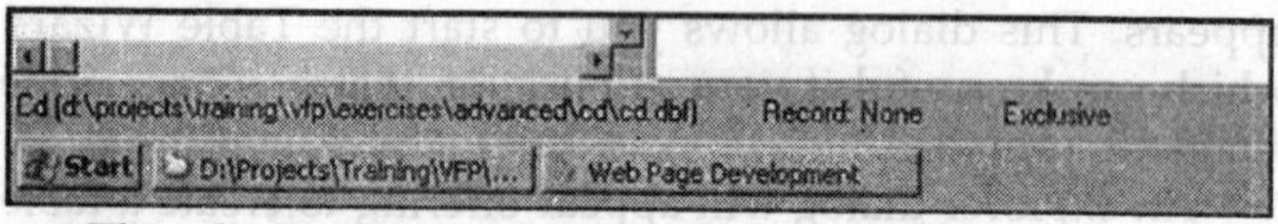

This shows that the table named 'CD' is open, it's open for your exclusive use, and it holds no records.

ADDING SOME RECORDS

Unlike Access, you cannot just create a new record by typing on a blank line in the grid. You have to selectAppend New Record from the Table menu. This menu pad appears whenever a Browse window is open on the desktop.

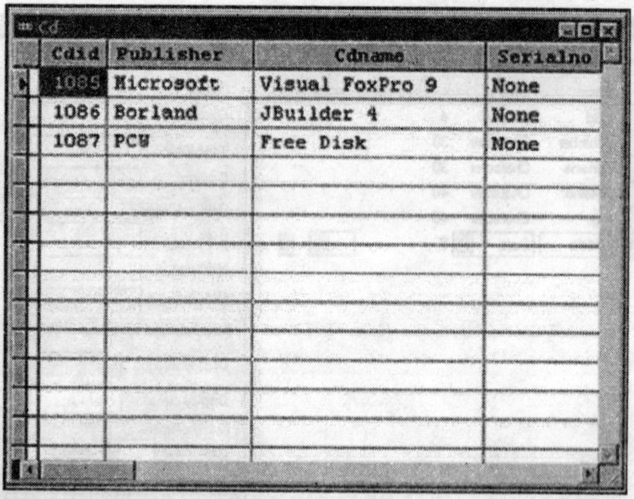

Do this three or four times and add some data to the table so that you will have something to work with when you design a form.

FORM DESIGNER

As with any other Windows development tool, the form is the basic interface for the user in Visual FoxPro.

FoxPro has a Form Wizard which will produce a good-looking form very quickly but the design relies on a number of complex class libraries and is difficult to understand or modify. We will build a straightforward form by hand.

CREATE A FORM

Click on the Documents tab of the Project Manager then right-click on Forms. Select New File then New Formfrom the dialog.

The Form Designer will appear:

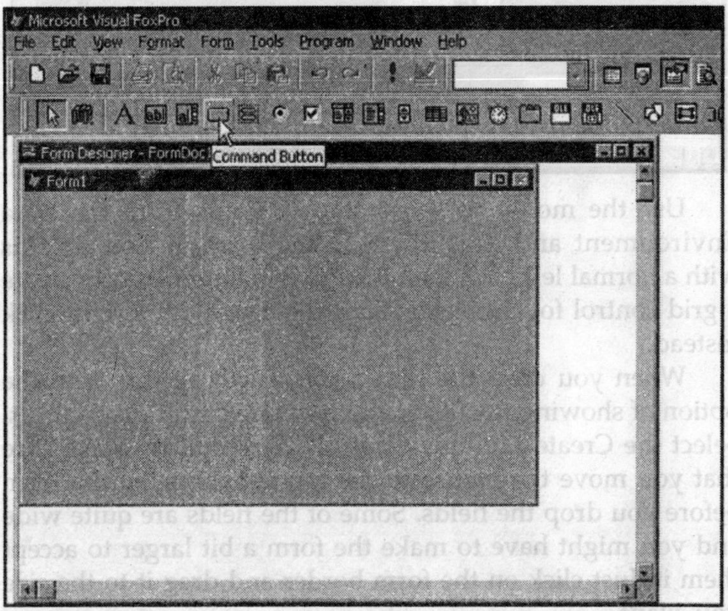

The screen shot shows the Form Designer and the Form Controls toolbar with the mouse positioned above the Button control.

ADD DATA

The form has to be connected to a data table. Right-click on the form and select Data Environment .... A directory tree will open so that you can select a table. Click on CD.dbf then close the Add Table dialog. This should leave you with the form and the Data Environment windows visible:

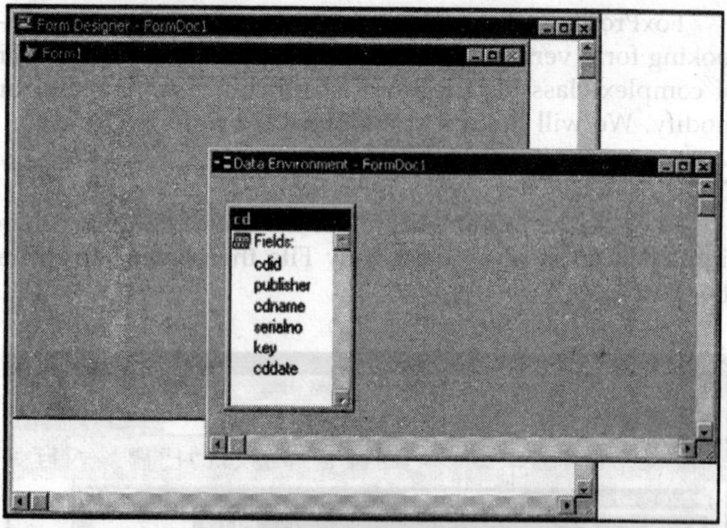

Use the mouse to select the six fields from the Data Environment and drag them to the form. If you do this with a normal left-click then FoxPro will automatically create a grid control for the fields. Start the drag with a right-click instead.

When you drop the files a menu will appear with the option of showing the fields as a grid or as multiple controls. Select the Create Multiple Controls Here option. Make sure that you move the mouse to the top-left corner of the form before you drop the fields. Some of the fields are quite wide and you might have to make the form a bit larger to accept them it. Just click on the form border and drag it to the size you want.

Close the Data Environment and leave the Form Designer on screen.

RUN THE FORM

There are three ways of running the form.
You can:

- Click the red exclamation mark on the toolbar
- SelectRun Form from theForm menu
- Use the keyboard shortcutCTRL+E

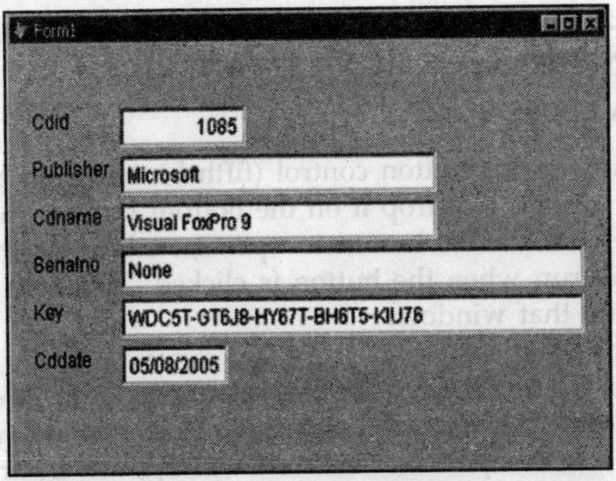

MOVING AND ADJUSTING THE SIZE OF CONTROLS

The obvious way to do this is to drag with the mouse and this is the fastest technique for making crude adjustments. Use the cursor keys for fine adjustments. Each key will nudge the control one pixel in the appropriate direction. Hold down shift and use the cursor keys to stretch or shrink the control by one pixel at a time.

The Format menu has options to align and size groups of controls. You can select multiple controls by shift-clicking on the controls one-by-one or by dragging a selection marquee around the group of controls. The selection marquee does not have to surround a control, it will select any control that it touches.

NAVIGATION

All the basic controls are available on the Form Controls toolbar. This is shown docked above the Form Designer but can be dragged or docked anywhere on the desktop.

The FoxPro toolbar looks familiar but there are subtle differences between it and the equivalent toolbars in Access and Visual Basic. To add a control to the form you click once on the toolbar then once on the form. This will add the control to the form at its default size. You can click on the toolbar then click on the form and drag the control to a new size but it's easier to get the control onto the form in one operation and adjust the size later.

ADD A CLOSE BUTTON

Click on the button control (fifth button from the left) on the toolbar and drop it on the bottom right of the form. Double-click on the button to open an editor on the code that will run when the button is clicked. Type this line of code into that window:

```
ThisForm.Release
```

ThisForm is the FoxPro equivalent of Me in Access and refers to the form which holds this object. As you type the period a list of possible methods will appear. By the time that you have typed 'rel' Fox will have identified that you want the Release method and will pop up a tooltip to identify it. Press Enter to confirm.

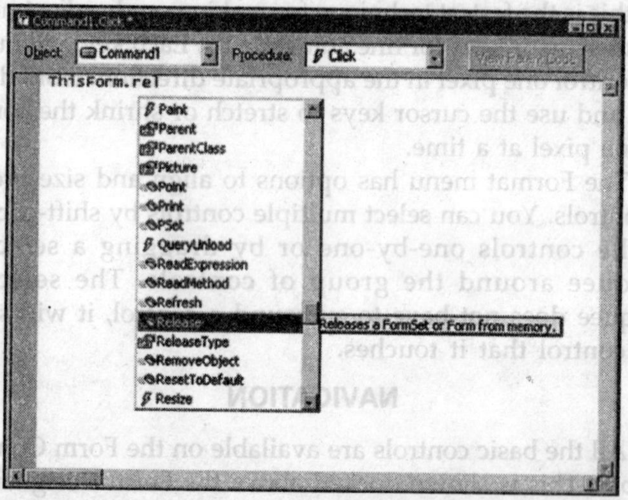

Close and save the code window by pressing CTRL+W or by clicking the Save button on the toolbar. Then pressCTRL+E or the exclamation mark on the toolbar to run the form.

Click the button and the form will close and return you to the Form Designer. The caption on the button is not quite right and we will correct this by changing the Caption property of the button. Right-click on the button and select Properties... from the menu.

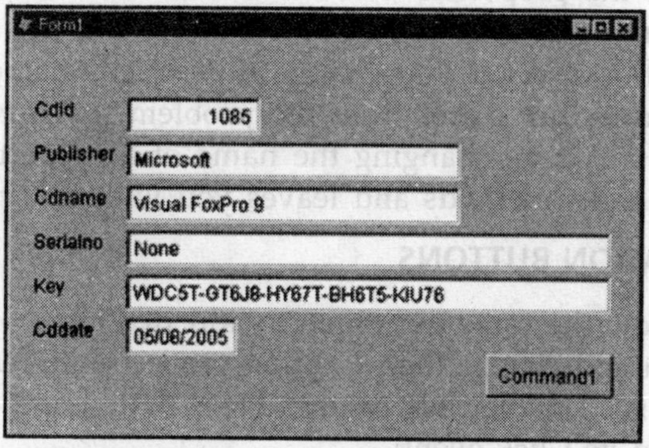

CONTROL PROPERTIES

FoxPro is a flexible object-oriented system with a wide range of properties. You can reduce the number displayed so that you only see those which have been changed from their default values. Right-click on the name 'Command1' at the top of the Properties Window and select Non-Default Properties Only from the menu. This will filter the list to just the seven properties shown.

Click on the Caption property and type Close as a new value. Note that you cannot type where the value is shown in the list, you have to type the new value of the property into the textbox above.

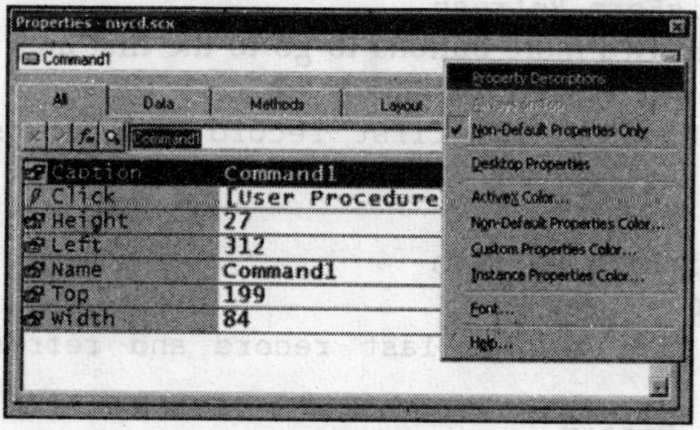

Whilst you are in the Properties Window you can also change the name of the control from its default value of

"Command1" to something more informative. You can see amongst the properties that the Click event holds a 'User Procedure'. This code is part of the object and will still be a part of the object if you change the object's name. Visual FoxPro does not suffer from the problem that Access and Basic have where changing the name of a property breaks the link to its methods and leaves you with an orphan.

NAVIGATION BUTTONS

Follow the same technique to add two more buttons to the form and change their Caption properties to read 'Prev' and 'Next'. Double-click on the 'Prev' button and type this code into its Click event:

```
* Move to the previous record and refresh the form
Skip -1
ThisForm.Refresh
```

The code in green is a comment. If a line starts with an asterisk then everything on that line becomes a comment and is ignored by the compiler.

Close the edit window, double-click on the 'Next' button and type this very similar code into its Click event:

```
* Move to the next record and refresh the form
Skip 1
ThisForm.Refresh
```

Add two more buttons to go to the first and the last record. The FoxPro commands are:

```
* Move to the first record and refresh the form
Go Top
ThisForm.Refresh
```

and

```
* Move to the last record and refresh the form
Go Bottom
ThisForm.Refresh
```

These four buttons are so similar that we would be

thinking about subclassing them all from the same source in a real system.

RUN THE FORM

Click the red exclamation mark on the toolbar or select Run Form from the Form menu.

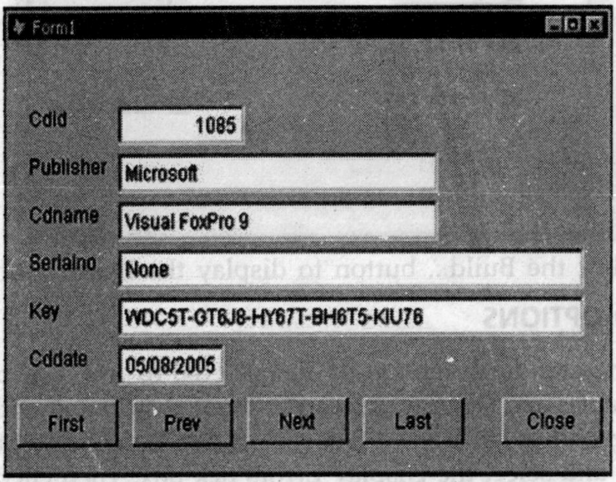

IMPROVE THE NAVIGATION

These navigation buttons are too simple to be useful in real life. They need extra code to prevent you trying to move to a position before the first record or after the last record. Go to this page to learn more about FoxPro programme.

BUILD AN EXECUTABLE

The last stage in the tutorial is to build an executable. For this step we need the FoxPro Project Manager back on the screen. If you are very careful with the mouse then you can drag the Manager off the toolbar but it is very easy to drag a single tab instead of the whole manager. Being able to drag a tab off the toolbar is a useful feature during form design but it's not what we want to do at this stage. The easiest way to undock the Project Manager is to right-click on the docked manager and select Undock from the menu that appears.

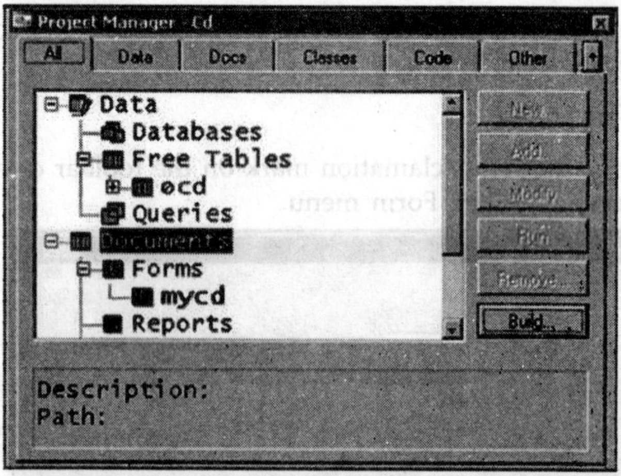

Click the Build... button to display the Build options.

BUILD OPTIONS

The standard version of Visual FoxPro lets you build executables and DLLs which can be freely distributed without paying additional licence fees. Select the Win32 Executable option and select the Display Errors tick box. Then click OK to build the executable.

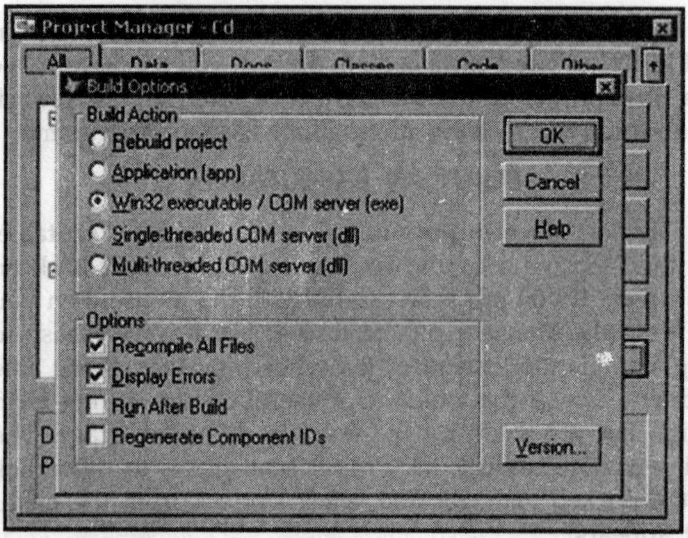

You will be asked for the name of the executable. The default is for the executable to have the same name as the project and to be in the same directory but you can override both these options.

If you have Set Safety On and the project has been built before then you will be asked whether you want to overwrite the existing file.

The FoxPro development environment is not a verbose one. The cursor will change to an hourglass when the build starts and you may see progress messages flickering in the Status Bar as the build proceeds but that is all that will happen. There will be no message to say that the build has succeeded. If the cursor returns to normal without there having been any error messages then the build will have succeeded.

Chapter 19

Intermediate FoxPro

INTRODUCTION

Beyond the basics of Visual FoxPro's use of connections and views to make remote and local computing very similar, there are a number of things you can do with client-server beyond the basic model of reading and writing data. In this session, we'll look at techniques for taking advantage of the capabilities of back-end servers and look more closely at the native VFP capabilities of working with server databases.

VISUAL FOXPRO

This short paper is not meant to be a comprehensive reference for all things client-server. Rather, it is intended to serve as a short introduction to the concepts and the techniques used to do client-server applications in Visual FoxPro. Attendees should have a familiarity with Visual FoxPro and the use of FoxPro's Database Container and Views in working with local data.

We'll start out with some simple definitions of the terms, examine why you would want to do client server, and then dig into the commands and functions that make it possible. We conclude with some discussions about some of the more advanced techniques and how you might consider integrating client server into your framework.

CLIENT-SERVER

There are a number of definitions, more or less scholarly, more or less robust, about what exactly is client-server. One vendor, a few years ago, quipped "Client-server? Well, that's whatever it is I have to sell right now." Typically, for our purposes, the key element of client-server is that two separate processes are going to be running, one Visual FoxPro, the other the process that provides data to Visual FoxPro. These two programs can be running on either the same machine or separate ones, with some form of connection between them (network, serial, or Internet) to allow them to communicate.

Many clients seem to be interested in client-server for reasons that go beyond the technical merits. This is certainly as valid, but be aware of the pitfalls of creating a client-server solution if it is not done primarily for a technical reason. There are three primary reasons for considering client-server:

WHY NOT CLIENT-SERVER

As mentioned above, clients may be disappointed if they have selected a client-server architecture only to find the resulting product less than satisfactory. There are several reasons to consider other solutions other than client-server:

Resource constraints: Client-server is fundamentally more complex than a single-tier, monolithic application. A new application needs to be learned, with its foreign terminology, syntax and language. Connectivity, ODBC and network issues will need to be addressed. New APIs may need to be mastered. Anomalies, infelicities, and plan old bugs in the vendor's interface and drivers need to be resolved. If your team is already maxxed out and behind schedule, don't think that client-server will be a silver bullet.

Ongoing maintenance: While vendors are trying to make their applications more "set it and forget it" installations, there are no "hands-free" installations. A Data Base Administrator (DBA) has to be available, at least part-time, to check logs, ensure backups are working, ensure disk space is adequate, etc. Realistically, this is a requirement for any computer installation, but servers typically need a little additional attention.

CLIENT SERVER WORKING

The primary difference between working with local (native VFP data) and client-server data is that you need to establish a *connection* to the server. After the connection is established, a view can be used to read and write data. In addition, the equivalent of FoxPro's native SQL statements can be used to provide more direct control than is usually available via views. Finally, like nearly everything else in Visual FoxPro, there is even another layer of fine control available to developers who require it.

Connections

A connection uses portions of Microsoft's Open DataBase Connectivity (ODBC) to establish a two-way communication channel between Visual FoxPro and the target server. This means that each client machine must have installed on it specific drivers for the target server. Each vendor has their own mechanism for providing, installing, configuring and supporting these drivers. Once established, the connection from FoxPro can be configured.

There is some confusion in the terminology VFP uses regarding connections. When you CREATE or MODIFY a CONNECTION using the syntax below, you are modifying the definition of a connection, and not actually affecting an existing connection. The connections stored within the DBCs are definitions of connections to be used when called upon.

FoxPro's connection can be defined visually within the DataBase Container (DBC) or directly from the Command Window with CREATE CONNECTION. Similar visual and command-based equivalents exist to DELETE, MODIFY, RENAME and DISPLAY CONNECTIONs.

Connections can refer to an ODBC Data Source Name (DSN), defined with the ODBC Control Panel Applet, or they can specify the equivalent parameters directly.

In code, the connection settings might look like:

```
* The first connection depends on a pre-
established
*DSN defined using the Control Panel
```

```
DEFINE Connection cnTest;
  DATASOURCE dsnAccessNWind; && a pre-
  existing ODBC DSN
  DATABASE C:\Access\NWind.MDB && point
  directly to the data
*The second connection, a DSN-less connection
DEFINE Connection cnVFPFile;
  CONNSTRING "DRIVER={Microsoft Visual
  FoxPro};" +;
              "SOURCETYPE=DBF;" +;
              "SOURCEDB=C:\VS98\VFP98\"
```

To find out what parameters are required by your ODBC driver, check out the documentation by calling it up in the Control Panel's ODBC Applet, and selecting Help.

Finally, connections do not need to be maintained at all within a DBC. If the remainder of the system is using SQL Pass Through, connections can be created on the fly as well, using the SQLConnect() and SQLStringConnect() functions:

```
* Open a connection using a DSN, User ID and
password
lnHandle = SQLConnect("mySQLServerDSN", "SA",
"")
* Connect to a VFP table via the ODBC driver
without a DSN:
lnHandle = SQLStringConnect
          ("DRIVER={Microsoft Visual
          FoxPro};" +;
          "SOURCETYPE=DBF;" +;
          "SOURCEDB=C:\VS98\VFP98\")
```

VIEWS AND CONNECTIONS

The reason you need to be concerned about how many connections you establish with the server is because each connection consumes resources, resources that tend to be precious to the server and tend to limit the scalability of the entire system. Also, some vendors license their servers by connection, rather than by user, so this could become a licensing issue.

SQL PASS-THROUGH (SPT)

As mentioned in the previous sections, all of the functionality that can be achieved using the Database Container and the visual tools is available programmatically within the language as well. Always one of the hallmarks of Visual FoxPro, it is particularly well implemented here.

Function	Purpose
SQLTables()	Returns a list of tables or view for a specified connection. Handy for black-box utilities.
SQLColumns()	Returns field specifications in one of several formats, useful for matching VFP's capabilities to that of a foreign database.
SQLConnect(), SQLStringConnect()	Described above, used to establish a connection with the server.
SQLExec()	Passes commands to the server, via ODBC, to be executed.
SQLCommit(), SQLRollback()	Provides the means to complete or abort a transaction. The transaction must be started in a manual mode, with a SQLSetProp(), described below.
SQLSetProp(), SQLGetProp()	Reads and sets properties for an existing connection.
DBSetProp(), DBGetProp()	Reads and sets properties within the DataBase Container on views, connections, tables, etc. These are the only settings persistent between sessions.
CursorSetProp(), CursorGetProp()	Set or read properties on open cursors, including buffering.

ADVANCED CLIENT-SERVER

While the details of these topics are way beyond what is appropriate to cover in an introductory session, exposure to these concepts may give you some ideas on where you can consider taking these products in more advanced applications:

Batch SQL: Multiple SQL statements can be sent to the back end, with processing continuing on the front end, and occasional check son the status of the back end processing.

SUGGESTIONS FOR LEARNING CLIENT-SERVER

Client-server applications can seem like a lot to take on, but they are not too difficult if learned one piece at a time. I recommend learning to use the basic ODBC functionality within Visual FoxPro by experimenting directly with another table or database on your machine, using the VFP ODBC driver. As you gain experience, try DSN-less connections, direct connection using SPT, and attempt to rollback and commit various changes to the data. After you have gotten familiar with the basic commands and functions within Visual FoxPro, take a look at the server software. Learn how to install and configure it, if necessary, and what components are required to be installed on the client machines for connectivity and ODBC driver interfaces.

FRAMEWORK SUPPORT

All FoxPro developers should be using a consistent framework for developing their applications. Rather than starting from scratch and re-inventing the wheel, a framework can provide a good starting point for development, and an ever-growing level of sophistication in the services provided. One of the key features a framework should provide is the routine services of retrieving and saving data.

Visual FoxPro is ideal for providing framework support for data services because there are several consistent and rich models of working with data. Selecting one of these models and using it consistently within your framework will provide a robust data mechanism.

Chapter – 20

FoxPro Functions

OVERVIEW

Function is something in programming that gives us an answer, in other words, returns a value. Functions always have brackets (). Below are common foxpro functions.

DATE & TIME FUNCTIONS

```
Date() Give you today's date. E.g. 11/30/01
Day(), Month(), Year() To get Day, Month or
Year separately. E.g. Day(Date()) returns 30
CDow(),CMonth Give name of the day/month.
E.g. cdow(date()) to Friday
Time() Give Current's Time E.g. 20:19:27
DateTime() Give both date and time E.g. 11/
30/01 08:19:49
Sec(),Min(), Hour() Get Seconds, Minutes,
Hours separately. E.g. Sec(DateTime()) to 49
```

TEXT FUNCTIONS

```
Upper() Convert the text to capital. E.g.
Upper("Computer") Result: COMPUTER
Lower() Convert the text to lower cases.
E.g. Lower("CoMpUTER") Result: computer
Proper() Convert the text to Proper case
E.g. Proper("coMPutEr") Result: Computer
Alltrim() Take out all spaces in betweens.
E.g. Alltrim(" computer ") Result: "computer"
Str() Convert Number into Character E.g.
```

Str(12) Result: "12"

Val() Convert Character into Number E.g. Val("12") Result: 12

Left(), Right() Get a starting letters on the left/end letters on the right in specific no. of letters. E.g.Left("Computer",4) to "Comp", Right("Computer",3) Result: "ter"

SubStr([String], [Starting Index], [No. of letters]) More effective than left() or Right() Get a specific no. of letters of specific starting position. E.g. SubStr("Computer",2,4) Result: "mput"

IsAlpha(),IsDigit() Check that it is a Number or Character. E.g. IsAlpha(23441) Result:.f.

IsBlank() Check that the data/text is blank or not E.g. IsBlank("IT") Result:.f.

Those functions should be used in the project at all times. Please note those functions carefully.

IMPORTANCE

Many functions allow you to have consistent expectations and set standards both for your programme and the database. Fox an example, case functions such as Lower, Upper, and Proper allows the programme to set the case to store in the database to make sure they are consistent. This will help when you want to search for the data for that field, since searching by default is case-sensitive.

In the case you keep everything standard in the previous example, like lower cases, when user enters the data, you convert it to lower case, so new record stores as lower cases. When user searches, you convert the user search's word into lower cases, so it matches the database's standard.

OTHER USEFUL FUNCTIONS

Pi()	Give out the Pi value
Tan()	Calculate Tan E.g. Tan(PI()/4) = 1.00
Rand()	Random the number (From 0 to 1)

Chr()	Give out the character from the ASCII code
Asc()	Give out the ASCII code from the character
RecNo()	Give out the current record no. selected E.g. ? RecNo()
RecCount	Give out the total no. of records in the table. E.g. ? Reccount()
FCount	Give out the total no. of fields in the table
BOF()/EOF()	This will explain under *Database programming with* FoxPro topic
LastKey()	Return ASCII no. of the key last pressed

THIRD-PARTY CUSTOM FUNCTIONS

InWords()	Converts numbers into English words. E.g. ? InWords(130) Result: One Hunred Thirty Dollars Only

EXTENDED: MESSAGEBOX() FUNCTION

This function let you create a message box. (Like the one pops up when you are closing the document asking you to click Yes | No | Cancel, when you didn't save your work yet)

Messagebox ([message as string], [Options as numbers],[Title as string])

E.g.

- Messagebox ("Hello World!") This will pops up the message saying Hello World!
- Messagebox ("Hello World!","Welcome") Same as above, but its title is Welcome

You want it to be like having different buttons, like Yes & No. You want it to have Question mark sign or Exclamation sign, and you want to know how you can get the user's choice. Here will explain how to do all those things.

Now, How can you get user Input? Messagebox() function returns user's input as a number. (From 1-7) E.g. No. 6 is "Yes" and No. 7 is "No". You can use If..Else…EndIf statement to help you. Below is the example:

Answer = 0 To Store the user's input

Answer = MessageBox("Are you sure that you want to exit?",4+32,"Confirm Exit")

Get the user's input form Message Box

```
Do case
   case Answer = 6 then    If User answer Yes
                           then
     @ 5,5 say "You have chosen to Exit the
     programme"
   case Answer = 7 then    If User answer No
                           then
     @ 5,5 say "You have chosen NOT to Exit
     the programme"
endcase
```

Messagebox() function references

Value	Dialog box buttons	Value	Icon
0	OK button only	16	Stop sign
1	OK Cancel buttons	32	Question mark
2	Abort Retry Ignore buttons	48	Exclamation point
3	Yes No Cancel buttons	64	Information icon
4	Yes No buttons		
5	Retry Cancel buttons		

Return value	Button
1	OK
2	Cancel
3	Abort
4	Retry

5	Ignore
6	Yes
7	No

USE MESSAGEBOX() AS A MODULE

If your programme is going to use a lot of this function then, you might want to use it as a module. This section will tell you how to use Messagebox () Function in a proper way.

Below is the example: (Using the previous example)

```
Answer = 0      To Store the user's input
Message = "Are you sure that you want to
Exit?"          To store the message
Title = "Confirm Exit"
                To Store the title
Options = 4 + 32
                To Store the Options
Answer = MessageBox(Message, Options, Title)
```

You can even extend this idea further by preparing generic Message boxes in a module that you either pass in a name or number and that module will show up that particular message box. For example, you may want to say information saved, there can be a generic message box for that.

Chapter – 21

FoxPro Programming

VISUAL FOXPRO PROGRAMMING LANGUAGE

Visual FoxPro is a data-centric object-oriented programming language by Microsoft. It is derived from FoxPro which was developed by Fox Software beginning in 1984; FoxPro merged with Microsoft in 1992 and the software acquired further features and the prefix "Visual".

Foxpro is a member of the class of languages commenly refered to as "xBase" languages, which have syntax based on the dBase programming language. Other members of the xBase language family include Clipper, dBase, and Recital.

Visual FoxPro, also known as VFP, runs under Microsoft Windows and is mainly used to write desktop database applications running on Windows; it can be used to write fat client, middleware, and web applications.

In late 2002, it was demonstrated that Visual FoxPro can run on Linux under the Windows emulator Wine. In 2003, this led to complaints by Microsoft: it was claimed that the deployment of FoxPro code on non-Windows machines violates the End User License Agreement.

Rumors suggesting that Microsoft intends to end support for Foxpro have been common since Microsoft's aqquisition of the product. As of 2004, Foxpro remains in active development by Microsoft with version nine (Europa) planned for release sometime during 2004. The volume of new programs written in Foxpro has decreased recently, matching the increase in popularity of.net applications.

Technology is a perfect destination to get the top quality

service as we have expertise in FoxPro programming language. Our team comprises of specialists of FoxPro programming language enabling our clients to take maximum benefit in FoxPro. We have here by offered you a brief account about the technologies letting you know about there use.

FoxPro is a text-based procedurally-oriented programming language and DBMS, originally published by Fox Software and later by Microsoft, for MS-DOS, MS Windows, Apple Macintosh, and UNIX. Although FoxPro is a Database Management System (DBMS) and it does support relationships between tables, it is not considered a Relational Database Management System (RDBMS) as it lacks transactional processing. The final published release of FoxPro was 2.6, after which the name was changed to Visual FoxPro. Although no longer sold or supported by Microsoft, there is still an active worldwide community of FoxPro users and programmers.

FEATURES OF VISUAL FOXPRO

- Highly customizable forms: Toolbars, docking, page tabs, grids - change colour
- Developer tools - OO, debugger, profiler powerful event driven forms
- Supports for XML and web services to interact with.Net and SQL Server
- OLEDB for support for web application that need to access FoxPro data via SQL queries
- COM programming to interact with Microsoft Office applications - Word, Access, Excel
- There are a wide variety of add-on components that extend beyond the supplied functionality of Visual FoxPro.
- Runtime royalty free.

FOXPRO A PROGRAMMING LANGUAGE

Foxpro is a very powerful database management system(dbms) language. foxpro comes on dos as well as windows. and visual foxpro is a very powerful gui with object oriented programming. using visual foxpro u can connect to sql server, sybase or virtually any rdbms. u can also do net programming using visual foxpro. if u are concentrating on small application with 1,00,000 records and not using it on web, then either foxpor for dos 2.6 or foxpro for windows 2.6 will be more than suffecient. maintenance of the code, ease of use, easy deployment are the features of foxpro.

Foxpro was one of Microsoft's stars at one time. They told everybody to use Foxpro and millions did. It is based on Xbase and really the last survivor of the Xbase languages. A sort of programing language and database combined designed for small business.

No it is not used much any more. Microsoft dumped on it when Visual basic became it's new star in the 90s. Not sure if there has been a Foxpro release in 5 years or more. In general learning a Microsoft language is a lesson in futility as they will dump support for it. Then all your code and experience in that language is worthless.

COMMANDS

WAIT COMMAND

Wait command uses to wait for use to press any key. Wait [Message] Timeout [seconds] E.g.

```
Wait Wait for user to press any key, then
continue
Wait Timeout 2
     Wait for user to press any key for 2
     seconds, then auto continue
Wait "Press any key to go back to Main menu..."
Timeout 10
     Wait for 10 secs before auto continue,
     and also display the specific message.
```

**Timeout* is how long it will wait for in seconds. If Timeout is 10, then it will wait for 10 seconds. If you don't put Time out, it will wait forever until a key is press.

ADVANCE: GET USER FEEDBACK ON WHAT KEY WAS PRESSED

You can also get what key user pressed, with that you can create a choice for user to enter, like Yes or no by using Decision Making statements to check. Wait [Message as string] (Timeout [Duration in seconds]) to [Variable as string] E.g.

```
UserKey = ""        Set Variables to store user's
                    key press
Wait "Press a key" to userkey
                    Use wait command, set UserKey
                    to store key press
? "You press " + userkey + " key."
                    Display message showing user's
                    key press
```

Below is the example of when combined Decision making:

```
UserKey = ""        Set Variables to store user's
                    key press
                    Use Wait command to ask user
                    to enter Y or N and store key
                    into UserKey:
  Wait "Are you sure that you want to Exit?
(Y/N)" to UserKey
Do case
  case upper(Userkey) = "Y" then
                    If user chooses Y, then do
                    the following
     @ 5,5 say "You have chosen Yes"
  case upper(UserKey) = "N" then
                    If user chooses N, then do
                    the following
     @ 5,5 say "You have chosen No"
 en0dcase
endif
```

This should give an idea, however, if user enters any other keys, it doesn't do anything. So we can use loop command to help.

```
UserKey = ""  While key press is not "Y" or
              not "N" then:
do while (upper(UserKey) <> "Y") and
(upper(UserKey) <> "N")
  clear
  wait "Are you sure that you want to
  continue? (Y/N)" timeout 2 to UserKey
  do case
  case upper(UserKey) = "Y"
     @ 5,5 say "You have chosen Yes"
  case upper(UserKey) = "N"
     @ 5,5 say "You have chosen No"
  endcase
enddo
```

SET CURSOR COMMAND

Set cursor [ON/OFF] Most uses when you use WAIT(), GET() functions.

SET DATE COMMAND

Set date [Country's format] E.g.

```
Set date USA        MM/DD/YY format (Default)
Set date British    DD/MM/Y Y format
Set date Italian    DD-MM-YY format
```

Below is the table of other possible date formats available:

Setting	Format
AMERICAN	mm/dd/yy
ANSI	yy.mm.dd
BRITISH/FRENCH	dd/mm/yy
GERMAN	dd.mm.yy
ITALIAN	dd-mm-yy
JAPAN	yy/mm/dd
TAIWAN	yy/mm/dd
USA	mm-dd-yy
MDY	mm/dd/yy

DMY	dd/mm/yy
YMD	yy/mm/dd
SHORT	Short date format determined by the Windows Control Panel short date setting.
LONG	Long date format determined by the Windows Control Panel long date setting.

SET DEFAULT COMMAND

This uses to set the default location path. Set default to [Path as string]. E.g. Set Default to "P:\FoxPro"

So every time you call a module or use the database, you can just type the name of the file.

SET DEVICE/PRINTER COMMANDS

Use with Printing functionalities. See Printing section for more information.

Quit command -Let you quit FoxPro completely!

Quit

All MS FoxPro exits and returns to desktop. Simple as that!

Also note: If you are going to put this into your project, I recommend you to put in at a very last stage when you finalize your programme.

Chapter 22

Programming Examples

BOF AND EOF FUNCTIONS

Brettell uses E.O.F. function in common, so this section will only mention about EOF() function. This function usually uses with Do-While statement. E.g.

```
Set default to "P:\FoxPro"
Use Emplist.dbf
Do While not EOF()   While it's not the end
                     of file then (not at last
                     record)
? Emplist.Fname      Display First name in
the database
Skip                 Move to the next record
                     Enddo
Use
```

Another main use will be to check that the record is end of file or not. E.g.

```
If EOF() then        EOF() function will
                     return value as True or
                     False (Boolean)
  ? "End of File"
endIf
```

OPEN & CLOSE THE DATABASE

USING COMMANDS

Use [filename] [Options]

E.g.

```
Use "P:\Foxpro\Emplist.dbf"
                          Open as normal
Use "P:\Foxpro\Emplist.dbf" exclusive
                          Open as exclusive
```

OR (Recommended Option to use with Set Default)

```
Set default to "P:\FoxPro"
Use Emplist.dbf
```

Reminder: You only need *Set default to* command once in your main module.

USE COMMAND TO CLOSE THE DATABASE

E.g. Use

It is important to close the database once you opened it by calling use command

ADD THE RECORD INTO THE DATABASE

Use Replace command

Replace [Table.Fieldname] with [value]

E.g.

```
FirstName          =          space(20)
Set default to "P:\Foxpro"
Use Emplist.dbf          Open the database
Get FirstName            Get user input
Read                     Read in
Append blank             Add new blank record
Replace Emplist.Fname with FirstName
                         Replace name in Fname
                         field
Use                      Close the database
```

This means that you replace the Name [Variable that you set to get user's input, with the field name on the table (Emplist.Fname – [Table's name].[Fieldname])

EDIT THE RECORD

There are 3 main ways you can apply replace command into your project.

1. Edit the record using Replace command. The programme itself edit the data by replacing new data

2. Edit the record through the Textbox user edit the data through the Textbox contains existing data
3. Edit the record manually The user manually edit the data in the table

Using Replace command

Replace [Table fieldname]* with [value] (See above section for more info.)

NOT FINISH

BROWSE BETWEEN RECORDS

Go command

E.g.

```
Go Top    Select Top record
Go Bottom
Go 5      Select fifth record
Skip command
E.g.
Skip      Select the next record
Skip 4    Move to next 4 record from current
          one
Skip -2   Move back 2 records from current
          record
```

SEARCH THE TABLE

Using Locate command

Locate for [Field name] = [Search Value]

Locate for [statement]

E.g.

```
Locate for TestTable.Fname = "Jutiphan"
```

This will search the database, but not going to display on the screen. To display:

```
Do While Found()       If found,
  ? Fname              Print the result
  continue Continue    searching
enddo
```

SORT THE TABLE

Using Sort command

Sort to [New table's name] on [fieldname1] (, [fieldname2]) [ASCENDING/DESCENDING])

If you use sort command, it doesn't actually sort the table, but instead it creates a new table with sorted records. Below is the example using Emplist database

```
Set default to "P:\FoxPro"
Use emplist.dbf         Open the table you wanted
                        to sort
Sort to SortedEmplist.dbf on Emplist.Fname
                        Sorted by Fname, in
                        SortedEmplist database
Use                     Close the Emplist
                        database
```

The above example will create a new table named SortedEmplist.dfb with Fname sorted and it will be in P:\FoxPro (where you set default to.)

EXTENDED: USING SORT COMMAND

You can also use Sort command to sort in different fields, and in different order (Ascending or descending). E.g.

```
Sort to SortedEmplist.dbf on emplist.fname,
emplist.lname descending.
```

This will sort fname in descending order and follows by lname order

```
Sort to SortedEmplist.dbf on emplist.fname/
a, emplist.lname/d
```

USING INDEXES

You can also use Index to sort the table. This method is much better than using Sort command. Soon the information will be available. For now, Use Helpfile or ask Mr. Brettell directly.

Delete the record Delete record [Record no.], Delete for [Statement] E.g.

```
Delete all          Delete the whole table records
Delete              Delete current selected record.
                    (Best with Browse between
                    recordscommands)
```

```
Delete record 3 Delete record 3
Delete for Fname = "Jack"
                Delete the record where Fname
                = Jack
```

Delete command doesnot actually delete the record, it just appears to be deleted by marking it as deleted. Using *Pack*command will permanently delete the marked records. Becareful: The record will be deleted permanently and the table has to be opened as exclusive. Here is how you can delete the data permanently in one go:

```
Set default to "P:\FoxPro"
Use Emplist.dbf
Delete for Fname = "Jack"Mark the record as
                         deleted
Pack  Permanently delete all records makred
      as deleted
Use   Close the database
```

RESTORE THE RECORD (UNDO DELETION)

Use Recall command. (Same structure as Delete command) This is possible only for records that aren't yet permanently deleted by Pack command. You can use the same statements as shown in *Delete the record* section. E.g. Recall All (Undo delete all records)

DISPLAY THE RECORDS/FIELDS BY USING COMMANDS

Using List command

- List Specific field: List fields [field's name] E.g.
  - List field Fname
  - List fields Fname, Lname
- List Specfic record: List record [record no] E.g.
  - List record 1
- List all records: List

Using Display command

This will only display the selected record.

Display [Field's name] E.g.

```
Goto 3  Move to third record
```

`Display Fname, Lname`	`Display Fname and Lname of that record`

PROGRAMMING BY EXAMPLE

Programming by Example encompasses a number of approaches to creating programs by giving examples of their behaviour or effect. All approaches emphasize working on concrete examples rather than describing a procedure in the abstract.

The earliest approach, historically called Automatic Programming but now often referred to as Programming by Input/Output Examples, relies on the system's ability to generalize from examples. The programmer presents examples of data before and after processing; the computer must find a method of transforming the input to the output.

A more recent approach that has proven quite successful is Programming by Demonstration: the programmer (often the end-user) demonstrates actions on example data, and the computer records and possibly generalizes these actions.

Another recent approach is Programming by Teaching (sometimes called Instructible Systems or Agents), which extends the demonstrational approach by enabling users to give verbal or gestural hints. These focus the system's attention on relevant generalizations.

SOME PROJECTS ON PROGRAMMING BY EXAMPLE

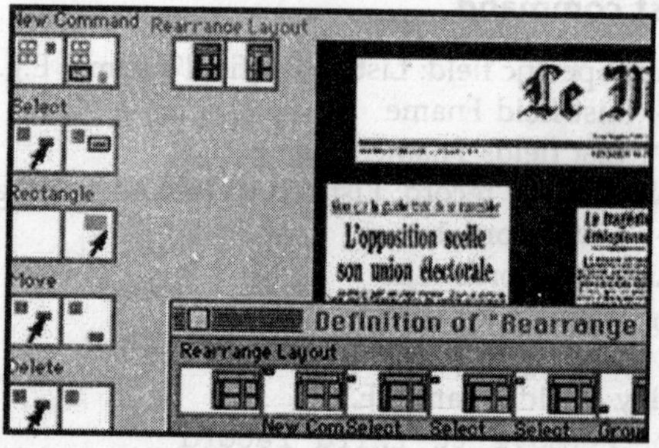

Programming by Example projects at the MIT Media Lab:

- Mondrian, a graphical editor programmable by example.
- Tinker, a PBE system for Lisp with conditionals and recursion.

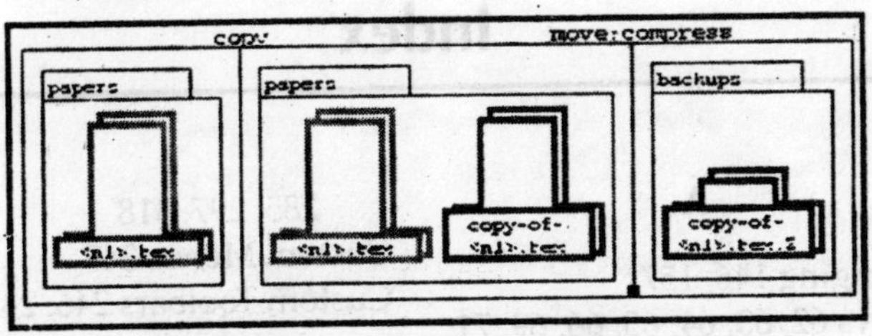

Projects at StageCast Software:

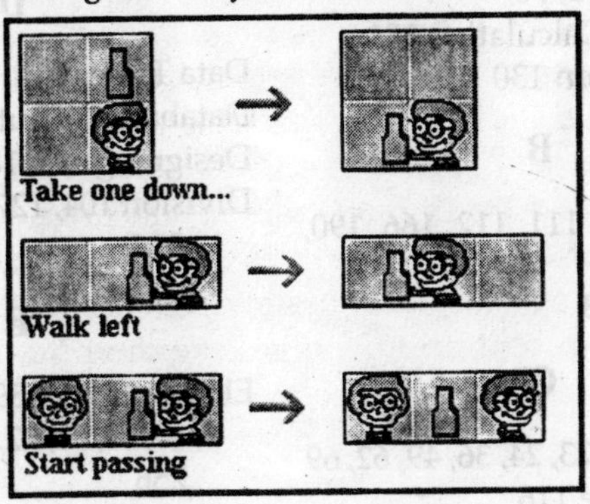

Index